Somerset Maugham
and the Cinema

WISCONSIN FILM STUDIES

Patrick McGilligan, series editor

Somerset Maugham and the Cinema

Robert Calder

THE UNIVERSITY OF WISCONSIN PRESS

The University of Wisconsin Press
728 State Street, Suite 443
Madison, Wisconsin 53706
uwpress.wisc.edu

Gray's Inn House, 127 Clerkenwell Road
London EC1R 5DB, United Kingdom
eurospanbookstore.com

Printed in the United States of America
This book may be available in a digital edition.

Library of Congress Cataloging-in-Publication Data

Names: Calder, Robert, 1941– author.
Title: Somerset Maugham and the cinema / Robert Calder.
Other titles: Wisconsin film studies.
Description: Madison, Wisconsin : The University of Wisconsin Press, 2024. |
Series: Wisconsin film studies | Includes bibliographical references and index.
Identifiers: LCCN 2023019867 | ISBN 9780299346201 (hardcover)
Subjects: LCSH: Maugham, W. Somerset (William Somerset), 1874–1965—
Film adaptations. | Film adaptations. | Motion pictures and literature.
Classification: LCC PR6025.A86 Z5588 2024 | DDC 823/.912—dc23/eng/20230816
LC record available at https://lccn.loc.gov/2023019867

To DENNIS WILLS
with gratitude

Contents

Acknowledgments   ix

Introduction: Maugham, Hollywood, and Screenwriting   3

1 A New Industry Finds Gold in Somerset: The Silent Era   17

2 Swanson, Crawford, and Hayworth: *Rain*   40

3 Eagels and Davis: Evil behind the Smile   60

4 Rebellious Wives, Secret Agents, and Beach Bums:
  Early Sound and the 1930s   83

5 Bette Davis's Corrosive Mildred: *Of Human Bondage*   131

6 Garbo Speaks Maugham: *The Painted Veil*   147

7 Fascism, Bigamy, and the Creative Spirit: The 1940s   160

8 The Greatest Generation's Quest: *The Razor's Edge*   187

9 Life in Short, Sharp Strokes: The Omnibus Films   200

10 Twenty-First-Century Perspectives: *Up at the Villa* and
   Being Julia   215

Conclusion: Looking Back and Looking Forward   229

Appendix: Film Productions of Maugham Works   237

Notes   261

Bibliography   277

Index   283

Acknowledgments

This book might not have been written had it not been for Dennis Wills, a friend of more than forty years. In addition to being an antiquarian bookseller extraordinaire, he has a vast knowledge of Somerset Maugham's life and writing as well as a love of, and knowledge of, movie history. After suggesting, nudging, and prodding me into undertaking a book on the film adaptations of Maugham's works, he offered endless good advice about sources of information and tireless help in the publication process.

A number of people have generously offered their varying expertise, notably Dr. Jerry White, Dr. Wendy Roy, Dr. William Bartley, and Dr. Allison Muri. Stephen Michael Shearer, Deborah Ritchken, Noah Isenberg, and Patrick McGilligan were instrumental in this book finding its home at the University of Wisconsin Press. At the press, its production was guided by the expertise of Dennis Lloyd, Jacqueline Nora Krass, and Jennifer Conn; and the careful readings of Mary Magray and Sheila McMahon greatly improved the text.

Despite the frustrations of living with an obsessive writer, my wife, Holly, has remained supportive and encouraging of my work, shouldering more of the household burdens than she deserves. Just as importantly, I have frequently relied on her own wide-ranging expertise as a graphic artist specializing in vintage movie posters. Her knowledge of the early twentieth-century movie industry was invaluable.

Somerset Maugham
and the Cinema

Introduction

Maugham, Hollywood, and Screenwriting

For more than half of the twentieth century, William Somerset Maugham was one of the most famous and most widely read authors in the world. Born in 1874, he qualified as a medical doctor in London in 1897, but the publication of a moderately successful novel, *Liza of Lambeth*, in the same year persuaded him to abandon medicine in favor of a career as an author. Over the next fifty-one years he wrote nineteen more novels, most notably *Of Human Bondage*, *The Moon and Sixpence*, *Cakes and Ale*, and *The Razor's Edge*. He was also a dramatist who struggled to get his plays produced until 1908, when he suddenly scored a stunning success by having four plays running simultaneously in London. From then until 1933, when he wrote the last of his thirty-two dramas, he was one of the most acclaimed playwrights on either side of the Atlantic. Very few authors have been able to achieve such success in both genres, but Maugham completed an even rarer trifecta by writing around 120 short stories, some of which—notably "The Letter" and "Rain"—are among the most memorable in the English language. In his later career he turned to nonfiction, producing the highly regarded autobiography *The Summing Up* and books of essays and literary criticism. By then he had become a Grand Old Man of English Literature, and the public sought his opinions on both writing and the world in general. And while carving out such a varied and prolific career, Maugham became one of the richest authors of the twentieth century.

Maugham's writing, stretching from the 1890s to the 1950s, reveals various recurrent themes and preoccupations, at the heart of which is a concern for freedom: physical, emotional, and intellectual. At the end of his life, he told an interviewer that "the main thing I've always asked from life is freedom. Outer and inner freedom, both in my way of living and my way of writing."[1] This concern with freedom manifests itself in many variations of human bondage and independence in his fiction and drama. Although the situations may differ and the forms may vary, the essential theme that runs throughout his writing is that of autonomy and enslavement. It is most profoundly explored in *Of Human Bondage*, but the titles of many of his other works—*The Narrow Corner, The Razor's Edge, The Painted Veil, The Merry-Go-Round*—carry the connotation that humans are faced with narrowness and restrictions on all sides. He wrote of people trapped by poverty or the class system, people restricted by a role—colonial administrator or humble verger—and people imprisoned by their emotions. He even wrote of the enslavement of artists' overwhelming passion to create and of the liberation that comes with realizing one's vision. Many of his works dealt with women trapped in empty marriages or by society's restrictive definition of what they can be or can achieve. All these concerns made Maugham's writing appealing to the film industry.

Maugham was a dedicated professional author. More than most writers, he was astute at sensing the literary climate and public tastes of any particular time, and thus, like a chameleon, he was able to adapt to the changing environment. *Liza of Lambeth* appeared in an era when urban misery and poverty in London and other British cities had led to a multitude of realistic slum novels. His autobiographical novel *Of Human Bondage*, published in 1915, joined the flood of *bildungsroman*, or novels of adolescence, being written by James Joyce, D. H. Lawrence, Arnold Bennett, and others. *The Moon and Sixpence* (1919) was one of many artist-hero novels for early twentieth-century readers eager for accounts of rebellious and individualistic creative figures. When the world, through Aldous Huxley, Christopher Isherwood, Gerald Heard, and others, became interested in Vedanta and Eastern mysticism, Maugham produced a novel of spiritual quest, *The Razor's Edge* (1944).

It is not surprising that Maugham and Hollywood would find each other and form a long, productive relationship. In the early twentieth century, the moving picture was becoming the newest of the art forms, embryonic compared to literature, drama, opera, and the visual arts. Initially, audiences were excited just to see moving images on a screen, but soon they wanted to view the figures enacting stories, and producers began scouring the world for plots and characters. The profession of scenario writer or screenwriter was born, but studios also looked to eminent authors for material and for the celebrity of their names. Film producers, said English author Frederic Raphael, "like known quantities; . . . they would often sooner buy the rights of an expensive book than develop an original subject: to buy a bestseller gives them a 'property,' something they can boast of having bought."[2] In his first year as film director, D. W. Griffith adapted Charles Dickens's *The Cricket on the Hearth*, Jack London's *Just Meat*, and Leo Tolstoy's *Resurrection*. In 1919 Samuel Goldwyn created Eminent Authors Pictures, Inc., a company that promised to produce the works of the greatest American novelists of the time: Gertrude Atherton, Rex Beach, Mary Roberts Rinehart, and Gouverneur Morris. Jesse Lasky, of Famous Players/Lasky, looked further abroad and signed up the English authors Henry Arthur Jones, Edward Knoblock, Arnold Bennett, Sir Gilbert Parker, Elinor Glyn, and Maugham.

Maugham was a shrewd enough professional author to recognize the potential of motion pictures, and he had already, in 1915, sold the rights to his play *The Explorer* to Lasky. The producer, however, wanted him to join his stable of authors who would write new scripts on demand, and so in 1920 he visited Hollywood at Lasky's invitation. He quickly discovered, however, like so many other respected authors over the next few decades, that he was not cut out to be a screenwriter. It was one thing to pen a novel or play in the seclusion of his study; it was quite another to write as part of a team made up of producers, directors, cameramen, actors, and editors, all of whom would have a part in shaping the work. Screenwriting, noted Margaret Kennedy, "is no more a work of literature than is a recipe for a pudding";[3] it is not simply another genre of literature but a distinct form of storytelling with its own language. "The novel," explains George Bluestone, "is a linguistic medium, the film is essentially visual. . . . The governing conventions of each medium are further conditioned by different origins, different audiences, different modes of production, and different censorship requirements. The reputable novel, generally speaking, has been supported by a small, literate audience, has been produced by an individual writer, and has remained relatively free of rigid censorship. The film, on the other hand, has been supported by a mass audience, produced cooperatively under industrial conditions, and restricted by a self-imposed Production Code."[4]

In the history of screenwriting only a minority of respected serious authors—Graham Greene and Eric Ambler, perhaps—were able to adapt to the demands of the craft. Edward Knoblock, in contrast, seemed to forget his task when he turned in a script with the direction "words fail to describe the scene that follows." Another author wrote that "not by accident they found themselves alone in a cabin in the mountains," leaving the director to devise dramatically the way by which the characters became so isolated. Nothing, though, better reveals the gulf between the work of serious writers and the demands of film than the example of the Nobel Prize–winning Belgian author Maurice Maeterlinck. When Goldwyn invited him to Hollywood and asked him to create scenarios from his most famous works, he turned in an adaptation of *The Life of the Bee*, a poetic work as much about human beings as about insects. Goldwyn was delighted until he started reading the script, and then he burst out of his office shouting, "My God, the hero is a bee!"[5]

Maugham, himself, for all his versatility in fiction and drama, was never able to master the craft of screenwriting. On his Hollywood sojourn in 1920, he got a $15,000 commission for a script, but it was never used. A decade later, when Samuel Goldwyn sailed to Europe to persuade him, along with Michael Arlen and others, to join his studio as screenwriters, Maugham declined. As part of his war work in 1941, he was reluctantly drawn into writing a screenplay for *The Hour Before the Dawn*, but David Selznick rejected it, and in 1945 he devoted himself to an adaptation of *The Razor's Edge*, only to have Darryl Zanuck prefer the work of veteran Hollywood screenwriter Lamar Trotti. Maugham never believed that screenwriting was particularly difficult, but he confessed to a friend that it "happens to be a knack that I do not possess."[6]

Nothing conveys Maugham's attitude to the film industry better than his comment to Knoblock on leaving Hollywood in 1920 that "I look back on my connection with the cinema world with horror mitigated only by the fifteen thousand dollars."[7] For the rest of his life, though he found many friends—such as George Cukor, Ruth Gordon, Charlie Chaplin—among movie people, he regarded the industry with disdain. At the same time, his income grew very substantially when he became one of the most cinematically adapted authors in history. To date, if television films are included, more than ninety of his individual works—novels, short stories, and plays—have been filmed, which is more than the works of any other author except the Belgian novelist Georges Simenon. Some of his writings, notably *Of Human Bondage*, "The Letter," *The Painted Veil*, "Rain," and *The Razor's Edge* have been put on the screen a number of times. Many of his characters—Mildred Rogers (*Of Human Bondage*), Sadie Thompson (*Rain*), Leslie Crosbie (*The Letter*), Elliott Templeton (*The Razor's Edge*), and Charles Strickland (*The Moon and Sixpence*)—became some of the most sought-after roles in movie history. So influential was Maugham in the film industry that Gore Vidal could write in 1990 that "he dominated the movies at a time when movies were the lingua franca of the world. Although the French have told us that the movie is the creation of the director, no one in the Twenties, Thirties, Forties paid the slightest attention to who had directed *Of Human Bondage, Rain, The Moon and Sixpence, The Razor's Edge, The Painted Veil, The Letter*. Their true creator was Somerset Maugham, and a generation was in thrall to his sensuous, exotic imaginings of a duplicitous world."[8]

There is a great irony in the impact of Maugham's writing on the film industry since he, himself, did not believe that published literature—fiction or drama—made for good movies. Writing in the *North American Review* a year after his first Hollywood experience, he stated that "screenwriting is a technique of its own, with its own conventions, its own limitations, and its own effects. For that reason I believe that in the long run it will be found futile to adapt stories for the screen from novels or from plays— we all know how difficult it is to make even a passable play out of a good novel—and that any advance in this form of entertainment which may eventually lead to something artistic, lies in the story written directly for projection on the white sheet."[9]

If, however, a studio does film a novel or a play, he said, the adaptation should be done not by a professional screenwriter but by the author himself: "That is work that he alone can do. No one can know his ideas as well as he, and no one can be so intimately acquainted with his characters."[10] Maugham reiterated this belief in 1929 when the advent of sound and the addition of dialogue significantly changed the art of filmmaking. When the British company Associated Talking Pictures announced its intention to make sound pictures, Maugham joined Arnold Bennett, Noel Coward, and John Galsworthy in making a public statement: "If talking films are to be made, it is natural and right that British authors should wish, and, if possible, insist that they be made in Britain. It is vital that the authors should themselves supply every word of the dialogue to be used or at the worst, personally supervise it."[11] Despite this injunction, the film industry made only modest moves toward including the authors of adapted works in production teams, and Maugham himself never succeeded in converting his own works into screenplays that were acceptable to studios.

Maugham's works themselves were attractive to film producers for a number of reasons. Like many famous writers, his name alone—that of an author of celebrated plays on London and New York stages and a creator of widely read fiction—attracted moviegoers even in small American towns. Such was his appeal that in 1933 the name of Douglas Fairbanks Jr. was left out of many newspaper and radio advertisements of *The Narrow Corner* on the grounds that it was less of a draw than Maugham's, which was widely publicized. In 1936 *Variety* summed up the situation by saying that "a dramatization of any Somerset Maugham story is almost certain to command attention."[12] Studios were thus eager to attach his name to films, even those that had been so extensively refashioned as to bear little resemblance to his original work.

On the screen itself, many of Maugham's works, both fiction and drama, made for striking film settings, particularly important in the silent era when the emphasis was far more visual. He was one of the most widely traveled authors of the twentieth century, making long expeditions through the South Pacific and Asia in search of material for his writing. Film companies, whether shooting his stories on the actual location or on a lot in Hollywood, worked to persuade filmgoers that they were on a Malayan rubber plantation, on a remote South Pacific island, in an African jungle, or in a Himalayan ashram.

Like multitudes of readers, filmmakers found a rich source of cinematic material in Maugham's characters, and scriptwriters often had to do little more than repeat what he had put on the page or hand the actors a copy of the original story. Describing one of her greatest roles, the Cockney waitress in *Of Human Bondage*, Bette Davis said that "Mr. Maugham so clearly described Mildred it was like having a textbook to go by."[13] As a young writer, he had been strongly influenced by the realism that dominated British fiction in the late nineteenth century and by the French

Naturalism of authors such as Guy de Maupassant and Émile Zola. Their emphasis on the external details of environments and people was much more easily re-created in the visual medium of film than were the interior monologues and stream of consciousness writing of the Modernist authors such as Virginia Woolf and Wyndham Lewis.

As much as his literary influences shaped Maugham's approach to character description, his medical training was probably as influential. As a young student at St. Thomas's Hospital, he learned to diagnose a patient's condition from a close study of his or her outward, physical traits: height, weight, bone structure, shape of face, complexion, eyes, cheekbones, and other observable features. Young doctors recognize these revealing external signs of internal medical problems, but young authors like Maugham soon learn that they are also excellent indicators of emotional and psychological states. From the thin, anemic, greenish-hued Mildred to the "gibbering hideous mask" of Leslie Crosbie's features ("The Letter") to the "strange blue-white, ghastly" pallor of Elliott Templeton on his deathbed (*The Razor's Edge*), Maugham's characters moved easily from the page to the movie screen.

Doctors, however, are more than shrewd observers; they are, as Frederic Raphael said in his discussion of three writer-doctors—John O'Hara, Sinclair Lewis, and Maugham—careful listeners. Raphael explained that "they were free, or seemed to be free, of literary affectation. Their mode was literal rather than metaphorical. They were impatient of the metaphysical and of humbug. They were unshockable, and so they could afford to be accurate. The medical mode led them to observe and to listen—hence the importance they gave to dialogue."[14] Maugham's dialogue, from the sparkling wit of his comedies to the idiom of his colonial administrators or that of his working-class Cockneys, was one of the strengths of his fiction and drama, and it became a much-desired element with the arrival of sound films (they were, after all, initially called "dialogue pictures").

Perhaps most attractive for the film industry were the plots, several hundred of them, of Maugham's works. He was, before all else, a storyteller in the tradition of the tale spinner captivating his listeners around a fire, a conservative author who adhered to the idea of a narrative having a beginning, a middle, and an end. "All of his books," observed Anthony Curtis, "are constructed on the principle of a sequence of events that first of all arouses, and then prolongs and ultimately satisfies the reader's curiosity. Maugham clung tenaciously to the linear logic of narrative at a time when his colleagues appeared to be abandoning its consecutiveness in favour of a much greater psychological immediacy and were experimenting with ways of expressing inward irrational confusion in works that deliberately left curiosity unsatisfied."[15] Filmmaking in the early decades was much less experimental than the works of modernist writers, and its audiences were broader and less sophisticated than the readers of avant-garde literature. Maugham's more conventional stories were thus better suited to an industry that needed to attract millions of viewers.

They were not, however, perfectly suited to the film industry. Maugham once wondered aloud why, if Hollywood liked his plots so much, the studios always changed them. As early as 1929, he confessed to being surprised by this, telling Sewell Stokes: "I'm amazed at the way in which producers buy my stories and then change the plots. If they like their own plots best, why bother to buy mine?"[16] In 1935 he told a *New York Times* reporter that he was not eager to view films of his works because "they change your story and I am not crazy to see something I have written done by a film director in another way."[17] Nineteen years later he told Garson Kanin that "for some reason, not a single one of my works has ever . . . translated well into the cinema,"[18] and in 1977 his companion Alan Searle confirmed to the present author that Maugham disliked most of the films made of his works. Maugham, however, was wrong in saying that none of his works translated well to the screen: he did like *The Moon and Sixpence*, and from time to time he publicly praised the performances of actors such as Bette Davis in other films. But he was right about movie producers and directors usually making major changes to his plots and characters.

The alterations necessary to make Maugham's stories suitable to the movie screen were driven by two forces: the tastes of the moviegoing public as determined by film studios and the demands of film censorship imposed on the studios. In the first case, though film viewers were engrossed in the plots and fascinated by the characters, Maugham's outlook was ultimately too cynical and his attitude to humanity too unforgiving for them. William Dean Howells summed up his countrymen's aesthetic preferences by saying that "what the American public wants is tragedy—with a happy ending."[19] So many of Maugham's works, though, ended with the protagonists failing to achieve happiness and with disreputable and dishonest people thriving. Maugham always believed that the human being was a mixture of good and evil, strengths and weaknesses, nobility and ignominy, and this was not a formula for sending moviegoers home with warm and positive feelings. Thus many of his characters were softened, made more admirable, and made more often to triumph.

From the early 1920s until the latter part of the century, film adaptations of Maugham's works were always constricted by the heavy hand of censorship. Ironically, it was the murder of William Desmond Taylor several days after he started directing a Maugham story, *The Ordeal,* that helped push the Hollywood film industry to try to regulate itself and present a more respectable front to the public. Implicated in the events surrounding Taylor's death were well-known movie figures such as Mabel Normand and other actresses, and the suggestions of lurid sex in Taylor's circle were sensationalized by the popular press. In response the United States Postmaster General, Will Hays, was made president of the Motion Picture Producers and Distributors of America (MPPDA) in 1922 and given the mandate to advise studios about how to produce inoffensive and tasteful movies. In 1924 he created "The Formula," which asked them to submit synopses of novels and plays for vetting, and in 1927 a document called "The Do's and Don'ts and Be Carefuls" listed eleven subjects that should not be treated in films and twenty-five themes that should be handled delicately. Among the "don'ts" were use of profanity, nudity, miscegenation, scenes of childbirth, and ridicule of the clergy.

While the Hays Office, as the censoring body became known, dampened and restricted filmmaking, it could only influence rather than require studios to follow its guidelines. That began to change in 1930 when the MPPDA adopted the Motion Picture Production Code, a formalized prescription of what films should and should not do. Meanwhile, across the United States the Catholic Legion of Decency was developing its own form of censorship, and so in July 1934 the MPPDA took a draconian step. After that, all its members—that is, the Hollywood studios—had to submit their films for approval, and if they were not given a Purity Seal, they were not to be shown in any movie theaters in the country.

Maugham was already familiar with censorship before his works began to be filmed. Even in the freer, more liberal arena of published literature, he pushed the limits of what was acceptable and learned to exercise self-censorship to satisfy publishers. The works of modernist authors such as D. H. Lawrence and James Joyce were often too explicitly about sex and, seen as pornography, were banned. Maugham, however, while dealing with sexual matters in most of his writing, was discreet enough to go beyond Victorian prudery without incurring proscription. His 1904 novel *Mrs. Craddock* explored a woman's sexuality with an openness much ahead of the time, triggering a minor sensation among readers and requiring its author to assure his agent and publisher repeatedly that his next works would offend no one. Ten years later his contract with William Heinemann for *Of Human Bondage* contained an unusual clause, rarely seen in contracts of the period, requiring Maugham to indemnify the publisher if the lending libraries refused the book on grounds of improper material.

The theater was more controlled than literary publication, and in Britain his works were regularly modified and bowdlerized by the Lord Chamberlain's Office, particularly in matters of sexual behavior and religious beliefs. In *The Unknown*, a 1920 play about a widow whose only son has been killed in the war, he got away with having her exclaim, "And who will forgive God?" but audiences were stunned. Movie audiences, however, would not have been allowed to hear the widow's remark. In all its forms, the Hollywood censorship code prohibited such heretical views and any ridicule of the clergy and churches, and so characters such as Rev. Davidson in *Rain* had to be changed to mere do-gooders. Similarly, Maugham's sympathy for—or at least understanding of—criminals ran counter to the code's injunction against showing lawbreakers thriving from their offences or going unpunished. Thus, Warner Bros. had to add an additional scene showing the acquitted murderer, Leslie Crosbie, being killed by a woman who is then herself arrested. Even when an unpleasant character like Charles Strickland, in *The Moon and Sixpence*, is presented much as Maugham wrote him on the page, the filmmakers had to add disclaimers at the beginning and end to indicate their disapproval of him. Prostitution was not to be shown as anything but immoral, and so audiences never saw *Rain*'s Sadie Thompson practicing her trade, and in the end she is shown retiring to the life of a housewife in Australia. Prohibitions of profane language, inferences of unconventional sexual behavior, and marital infidelity going unpunished further meant that Maugham's works had to be modified to

gain the approval of the Hays Office. Little wonder, then, that he was satisfied with so few film adaptations.

Most of Maugham's works could be adapted to satisfy the tastes of the
public and the demands of the censors, if not the expectations of their
author. Some, however, proved to be very difficult for the studios, and
some ultimately proved to be impossible to translate to the movie screen.
Shortly after its publication in 1919, *The Moon and Sixpence* was sold to
a film company, but it was decades before a satisfactory script could be
written. The novella *Up at the Villa* was optioned by Warner Bros. in 1939,
but after numerous attempts, the studio abandoned the project, and a film
version was not made until sixty-one years later. Shortly after the publication of *Then and Now*, Maugham's 1946 novel about Machiavelli with
political implications for the post–World War II world, the Hungarian
producer Arnold Pressburger bought its film rights for $200,000. He had
created a small company called Regency Films in partnership with George
Sanders, though control eventually fell to Two Cities Films. Sanders was to
play the lead under the direction of Douglas Sirk, and a script was written by
Charles Bennett. Submitted to the Hays Office, it was returned with thirty-
seven fundamental objections, and Two Cities, concluding that it would
be too expensive to make so many alterations, abandoned the project.

It is hard to know how many plans for film adaptation were dropped
because it was impossible to create a script that would satisfy the censors
while retaining the integrity of Maugham's stories. There is, however, one
glaring omission in the lengthy catalog of his works that made it to the
screen: his 1930 novel *Cakes and Ale*. Considered by many critics to be the
best of his fiction, it is both a wicked satire about English literary society
and a warm celebration of the pleasures of life and love. At the heart of the
story is Rosie Gann, described by Laurence Brander as "one of the most
real women in English fiction because she is natural . . . and beautiful and
good, . . . the greatest portrait in the Maugham gallery."[20]

Cakes and Ale was published to much praise—and considerable controversy because of its satiric portraits of British authors—and it would have
attracted film studios. Nothing was ever done with it, however, though in
1939 Alfred Hitchcock expressed a desire to make a version with Claudette
Colbert, in a blonde wig, playing Rosie. Fifteen years later an enthusiastic
Garson Kanin talked to Maugham and some British filmmakers about a

project, but nothing came of it, and in 1960 Christopher Isherwood was approached by Peter Viertel to write a screenplay for a production that never got off the ground. Around the same time, director George Cukor, a good friend of Maugham, talked to him about a film possibility, suggesting that Shirley MacLaine would be ideal in the lead because she could be "raffish, funny and moving."[21] Again, the project remained dead in the water, though Cukor continued after Maugham's death to pursue it even to the point of working on it with the author's lover, Alan Searle.

The absence of a film version of *Cakes and Ale* is a glaring omission akin to there being no version of Ernest Hemingway's *For Whom the Bell Tolls* or Jane Austen's *Emma*. The barrier to its production was in fact the novel's greatest strength, its protagonist, Rosie; as Maugham explained to Cukor, she is a nymphomaniac. While that might be an exaggeration, throughout the story she generously gives herself to a number of men, claiming the freedom to live a sensuous life without being imprisoned by them. You must take me as I am, she says, and even in her seventies she has a roguish sensuality. To remove her sexuality to meet the demands of the Hays Office would have severely altered the plot and it would have robbed Rosie of the very characteristics that make her such a memorable and unique character.

Knowing that Maugham was disappointed with most of the film adaptations of his works, how should we judge them? As Raphael has observed, he was hardly alone in his dissatisfaction: "No novelist of whom I have ever heard has had anything favourable to say about the adaptation of his book for the screen."[22] Writers are inevitably distressed by lengthy omissions to novels, subtle or nuanced thoughts represented by an actor's momentary glance or movement of the head, and subplots and minor characters eliminated entirely. Predictably, too, the reimagining of their story through the eyes and attitudes of directors and actors, often influenced by changing cultural and historical settings, can exasperate writers. When Maugham declared that it would be futile to adapt novels and plays for the screen, he was really saying that such adaptations cannot fully re-create the vision of the writer. The wise authors accept that translation to a different art form will give their story a different impact, with loss of some important elements but, in some cases, the gaining of powerful communication beyond that of the literary. A good case, for example, can be made that the film versions of *The Bridges of Madison County*, *The Godfather*, and *Death in Venice*, among others, are superior to the fiction on which they are based.

Readers who have been captivated by the stories on the printed page frequently go to movies to see how a story has been reproduced, to observe how a particular actor embodies a beloved or despised character. This concern with fidelity to the original, shared by authors and readers, became the dominant criterion by which movies in the twentieth century were judged, even by critics and academics (most of whom were trained in literary studies). "Fidelity criticism," says Brian McFarlane, "depends on a notion of the text as having and rendering up to the (intelligent) reader a single, correct 'meaning' which the film-maker has either adhered to or in some sense violated or tampered with."[23] This is, of course, an absurd notion because no text, certainly no work of serious literature, has a single meaning that is recognized and understood by every reader. No filmmaker could possibly satisfy more than a few moviegoers who are looking for absolute fidelity to their unique readings of a text. Besides, notes McFarlane, if you want the identical experience that you had in reading the novel, "why not simply reread the novel? It's much more likely to produce the desired effect. Fidelity is obviously very desirable in marriage, but with film adaptations I suspect playing around is more effective."[24]

With the inception of film adaptation studies in the 1950s—notably started by André Bazin's essay "In Defense of Mixed ["impur" in the original] Cinema" and George Bluestone's *Novels into Film*—fidelity has been widely challenged as the bedrock of film adaptation criticism. Increasingly, the concept of intertextuality, not just of written texts but of other films and influences outside literature and film, has replaced the idea of there being a single source for an adapted film. And as Robert Stam has observed, the term "adaptation" really encompasses "a whole constellation of tropes . . .—translation, reading, dialogization, cannibalization, transmutation, transfiguration, and signifying—each of which sheds light on a different dimension of adaptation."[25] Thomas M. Leitch has argued for replacing the dominance of fidelity in film criticism with a new series of questions: "How has a given adaptation rewritten its sourcetext? Why has it chosen to select and rewrite the sourcetexts it has? How have the texts available to us inevitably been rewritten by the very act of reading? and How do we want to rewrite them anew?"[26]

The effect of these arguments about adaptation, most of them raised by the new breed of academics educated in film rather than literary studies, have served to establish a healthier balance between loyalty to the original text and respect for the quality and creativity of the film adaptation. In the end, of course, such questions are irrelevant to the many moviegoers who have never read the original text and, coming to the film with no preconceptions, are seeing it as an independent work of art, one whose unique elements will entertain them or not. In this book I have tried to keep those moviegoers in mind while, as a literary scholar with a lifelong interest in Maugham's works, I have delineated the ways in which films have presented them. In any case, if Vidal is right, those who value Maugham as a writer must recognize the importance of the film adaptations to his creative reputation. "Maugham," he asserts, "will be remembered not so much for his own work as for his influence on movies and television."[27]

CHAPTER 1

A New Industry
Finds Gold in Somerset

The Silent Era

On July 5, 1915, Maugham sold the film rights to his play *The Explorer* to Jesse Lasky, a pioneering film producer who had created the Jesse L. Lasky Feature Play Company two years before. Maugham had begun his writing career with a well-received novel, *Liza of Lambeth*, in 1897 and followed this with ten less remarkable ones in the next decade. His real fame as a novelist was yet to come—in fact it began six weeks after he signed his contract with Lasky, when the publication of his greatest work of fiction, *Of Human Bondage*, would make him one of the most popular authors in the English-speaking world. In early 1915, however, it was as a well-known dramatist, one whose plays were staged in London and New York and in repertory theaters on both sides of the Atlantic, that he had drawn the attention of filmmakers. In 1908, after years of struggling to break into the theatrical world, he suddenly had four plays running simultaneously in London, an achievement rarely matched in British theater history. He would remain a dominant figure in English-speaking theater until the early 1930s.

Of the ten films made from Maugham stories in the silent era, only one—the novel *The Magician*—was not a play. Producers could choose from a dozen of his dramas, but some were comedies of manners whose main strengths were sparkling, witty dialogue and thus unsuitable for films without sound. Silent movies relied heavily on plot—the more melodramatic the better—and scenery, particularly that of dramatic foreign settings or the still relatively untamed and unspoiled American West. It is thus no surprise that Lasky chose *The Explorer*, a play that, though unsuccessful when mounted in London in 1908, featured scenes in the wilds of Africa. Moreover, in the early twentieth century, the figure of the explorer, whether braving the harsh polar regions or striking deep into the heart of the African jungles, was still a heroic character celebrated in newspapers and in lecture halls. Portrayed by the right kind of actor, he was a dramatic screen presence.

If there was a name on the movie house marquee more important than the author's, it was that of a renowned actor or actress, and Lasky chose such a leading man for his explorer, Alex Mackenzie. The Dutch performer Lou Tellegen was billed as an internationally famous romantic star, known for having played opposite Sarah Bernhardt on several tours. His striking good looks—a "celluloid Adonis," gushed one reviewer[1]—equipped him to portray the lead's necessary virility, strength of character, and understated power. The *Los Angeles Times* described it as "a wild West part," requiring Tellegen to "wear puttees," but in fact he plays the leader of an expedition into northeast Africa.[2] Mackenzie left his intended fiancée, Lucy Allerton, in London, but reluctantly agreed to take her weak and feckless brother, George, with him. George misbehaves in the jungle and kills a Native woman, antagonizing the local tribes and igniting several spectacular battles; later, however, he sacrifices himself to save the rest of the exploring party. Back in London, Mackenzie tries to shield Lucy from the knowledge of her brother's disgrace, even at the cost of her love, but the details are revealed and their betrothal is saved.

Reviewers noted that Tellegen's burned and tanned look was that of an African explorer, and they praised a battle scene at the ford of a river as realistic and exciting. The hero's appearance was at least authentic since numerous episodes were filmed in the burning heat, sand dunes, and arid mountains of southern California's Imperial Valley, into which fifty personnel traveled by horseback for three weeks of shooting. Viewers were entranced by the illusion that the river skirmish was taking place in deepest Africa, and one reviewer observed that "the view of a tribal village, showing the life and surroundings of the savage in his native haunts, is a good example of the careful detail with which the picture is worked out."[3] High praise indeed for an African village constructed on Lasky's ranch outside Los Angeles.

The second Maugham play that Lasky put on the screen, *The Land of Promise*, was advertised as "Maugham's great drama of the Northwest," that part of North America then still seen as a frontier of vast plains, forests, and red-coated Mounted Police. And unlike the contrived settings in *The Explorer*, viewers were offered authentic shots of western Canada, leading one reviewer to praise the director's "remarkable work in securing realistic and beautiful effects. . . . The wheat fields of Canada, the Rocky Mountains, the farming lands of the Dominion, form the picturesque background for the story of life in a comparatively primitive location, . . . and the result is said to be nothing short of exquisite."[4] The setting of Maugham's play was actually a farm on the southern Manitoba prairie several thousand miles from the Rockies, but no one seemed to object to the insertion of some striking mountain scenery.

The human drama in *The Land of Promise* was provided by a play Maugham had written at the suggestion of theater producer Charles Frohman. The dramatist should, he said, adapt the central idea of Shakespeare's *The Taming of the Shrew* to a modern setting, and so in 1912 Maugham made a research trip to Manitoba. He spent some time on a farm, fascinated by the intensity of frontier life, and he gathered enough background to provide an effective contrast between life in the New World and that back in England. On one level the play is about the narrow claustrophobic and restrictive life in the old country and the opportunity and freedom of colonial living. This was a theme particularly appealing to North American audiences, and so the play premiered in New York rather than London.

The Taming of the Shrew story is presented in Nora Marsh, a lady's companion in Tunbridge Wells who has been left with no income after the death of her mistress, and Frank Taylor, a hired hand on her brother's farm in Canada. Forced by economics to emigrate there, she is unhappy and soon quarrels violently with her sister-in-law, a Canadian who sees her as a lazy, pampered English woman. In a rage, Nora agrees to marry Frank, thinking that theirs will be a union in name only, but she discovers that she must cope with a powerful, seemingly insensitive male in a setting of isolation and struggle against the elements. When she refuses to do housework and share his bed, he, like Shakespeare's Petruchio, resorts to physical force. In the end, though, Nora abandons her English detachment and class consciousness and learns respect for her husband's honest strengths.

For Nora Lasky chose Billie Burke, a decision that might have lessened the artistic impact of the film but helped sell it to moviegoers. Burke was then one of the leading silent film actresses, rivaling Mary Pickford and

Lillian Gish, and she was a veteran of live theater in London and New York, one whose name alone would bring people into movie houses. In terms of acting skills and stage persona, however, she was far from the best actress to portray Nora. When she did the part on stage in New York, the run ended after 76 performances, whereas the London production, with Irene Vanbrugh, ran for 185 nights. Vanbrugh was more skillful in conveying the complexities of the heroine's change from shrew to a woman who recognizes the values in her husband and in their life on the land. Burke, though, was famous for her delicate beauty and her lightness in performance—qualities that would later make her perfect as *The Wizard of Oz*'s Glinda the Good Witch—and she played Nora as a romantic ingenue.

Maugham hated Burke's stage performance, telling his friend Gerald Kelly that his play was being "rottenly acted . . . by that little slut,"[5] but he had no voice in the casting of the film version. Lasky wanted Burke's star power, and he not only hired her husband, the Broadway impresario Florenz Ziegfeld, to produce the movie, he also made sure that the camera's main focus was on her. Thomas Meighan, suitably handsome, tall, and masculine for the part of Frank, was as big a film star as Burke, but he played the implacable heavy to her maiden in peril. "You see," said the *Chicago Tribune*, "the heroine most cruelly put upon from the beginning to the end bearing upon her countenance—from beginning to end—an expression of smug, sweet and patient martyrdom."[6] But not entirely patient, according to the *Los Angeles Times*: "Irresistible humor is afforded in the scenes where the temper of little redhead Nora flares up to white heat, only to beat vainly against the impenetrable exterior of her lord and master."[7]

Maugham's play, however, resolved the conflict between Nora and Frank in much starker terms: on their first night as a married couple, he tells her that she is his wife and he wants her and, with no alternative, she reluctantly goes into the bedroom. The next scene opens with Nora, now tamed, happily doing housework in their shack. In contemporary terms, Frank's action is marital rape, similar to the famous scene of Rhett Butler carrying Scarlett O'Hara up to bed in *Gone with the Wind*. Maugham's play's scene has such raw sexuality that it surprised even the London *Times* reviewer when shown on British television in 1958. "It comes as a shock," he wrote, "to realize that in *The Land of Promise* . . . Mr. Maugham was broaching as early as 1914 a subject which still restricts D. H. Lawrence's most celebrated work to Paris bookstalls. There is something invincibly erotic in the idea of feminine gentility being subdued by coarse male virility. The idea is powerful because it simultaneously outrages sexual and social convention."[8]

The power, or the outrage, of Frank's sexual demand of Nora was apparently too intense for the Lasky Company in 1917, either because it was unbecoming for its leading lady to be treated that roughly or because it thought that such behavior would offend moviegoers in the hinterlands. In its version, when Nora rejects Frank's advances on their wedding night, he obediently gives her the bedroom upstairs (this in a prairie shack) and sleeps on the living room floor. After six months of this arrangement, he ventures to embrace her, and when she slaps him he backs down, hanging his head shamefacedly. Eventually, without much further conflict, Nora yields, and she becomes happily reconciled to being a farm wife on the prairies.

This revision of the play's ending did not go unnoticed by film critics, and some, like the reviewer in *Variety*, concluded that it patronized the intelligence of the filmgoing public: "The only possible reason that can be imagined for tinkering with the original story . . . is that, though he may not admit it for publication, the producer believes pictures is the poor man's entertainment and the poor man must have his drama sweetened with more or less idealism. . . . If it be necessary for the picture manufacturer to so distort a very human depiction of a situation in life, then the film is not entertainment designed for other than the crudest minds."[9] This question of the tastes and sophistication of the ordinary filmgoer was thus raised early in the development of the film industry, and it would be fought over by film studios and critics forever after. It would be raised with the efforts to control what studios could produce—that is, censorship—and it would be repeated with many of the adaptations of Maugham's writings.

Whether it arose from disappointment with its film or from the idea that *The Land of Promise* could yield an even greater harvest, the Famous Players-Lasky studio remade it nine years later as *The Canadian*. Despite the appeal of Billie Burke, audiences had found it difficult to like Nora, finding Frank more sympathetic, and so the new version told the story through his eyes, those of a committed New World man rather than of an English immigrant woman. In the words of Mae Tinée, it is "the tale of a Canadian rancher who takes unto himself a sulky wife, weathers many domestic storms, and ends up basking in the sunshine of her love."[10] Thomas

Meighan returned to play Frank Taylor, but where the earlier film had given Billie Burke the top billing and essentially reduced him to a supporting role, he was now the central figure both on the screen and in the advertising. The shift in emphasis was signaled both by the new title and by posters in which Meighan's name appeared above it in even larger letters. Nora was played by Mona Palma, one of the Lasky studio's young actresses in her first role, and her name appeared in only a few of the advertisements.

Like *The Land of Promise*, *The Canadian* offers the viewer a wide array of scenic shots of the Canadian northwest and the foothills of the Rocky Mountains. The setting of the story was moved from the flatland of Manitoba to Alberta, perhaps because shots of the Rockies seemed obligatory in a film set in Canada, but more likely because the screenwriter, Arthur Stringer, was a Canadian author who had gone broke running a wheat farm in Alberta. Stringer was chosen to adapt *The Land of Promise* on the strength of the social realism of his "Prairie Trilogy" of novels, which told of a New England socialite who marries a Scots Canadian farmer and copes with wilderness living. Stringer claimed that he had seen the story firsthand on a visit to Winnipeg, but he was living with an actress in New York when Maugham's play premiered in 1913 and may have thought that a Canadian could tell the story better than an English playwright.

For authenticity, filming of *The Canadian* was done on location in southern Alberta, and as soon as Meighan and the rest of the cast got off their Canadian Pacific Railway car in Calgary, they headed to a nearby secondhand clothing store and bought their costumes. Thus outfitted in some real cowboy's castoff clothes, the handsome Meighan looked every inch the rugged, indomitable tower of strength touted in film posters. The public was accustomed to seeing him in dramatic action, though, and the review in *Film Daily* was typical in complaining that *The Canadian* "lacks action and its dramatic moments are few."[11] *Variety* warned its readers that the film had "no battles, no snow avalanches, cyclones, or Indian stuff. . . . It's just a study of Canadian wheat fields."[12] For *Photoplay*, the story was "pointless."[13]

Among the complaints about lack of action and dramatic scenes in *The Canadian*, there is no mention of Frank forcing himself on Nora sexually. It seems that when the emphasis of the story shifted from the antagonistic relationship of the principals to their struggle to carve out a life in a difficult setting, their sexual struggle was downplayed. The creation of the Hays Office in 1922 to influence what could and could not be shown on the screen, particularly in marital relationships and sexual matters, almost certainly caused the Lasky studio to tread more carefully than it had done in 1917. And in doing so, of course, it moved further away from Maugham's original story.

Not all the early, silent era adaptations of Maugham's works drew on his plays with picturesque outdoor settings, but the screen versions of his drawing-room comedies usually did not fare as well. *Smith*, a long-running London stage success in 1909, is the story of a maid working for a family of superficial, selfish people, a young woman whose contrasting honesty and decency wins the heart of the young man of the household. In 1917 Maurice Elvey, the most prolific British film director in history, made a cinema version for the London Film Company, with the well-known Elizabeth Risdon playing the lead. Unfortunately, no copies of *Smith* exist, and its invisibility in the records of the time suggest that it made no impact on the public or critics and, indeed, that it was never released in North America.

Another lost Maugham film of the silent era, the negative of which perished in the 1965 fire in the MGM vaults, was the 1919 production of *The Divorcée*. Based on *Lady Frederick*, the play that ignited Maugham's dramatic career in London in 1907, the story is set in Monte Carlo and focuses on a pleasure-loving widow who is being ardently courted by a wealthy young marquess. Too honorable to accept the hand of a man she does not love, she sets out to disillusion him by letting him see her as she is and then watch her putting on her makeup and wig in the morning. In an era when actors carefully guarded their public image, no one would play the part until Ethel Irving took it on. When the play became a triumph for her, selling out for 422 performances, Ethel Barrymore re-created the role to great acclaim in New York.

Reviewers of the American production found the plot conventional and the central character hackneyed: "the pseudo-adventuress who is so much better and kindlier than everyone about her."[14] The production was worthwhile, however, because of Barrymore's engaging stage presence and the script's sparkling epigrammatic dialogue. When Metro Pictures made the film version in 1919, they were careful to cast Barrymore and remind moviegoers about her theatrical triumph in a work by an eminent British playwright. Always more interested in the stage than the screen, she made the transition successfully, causing the *Film Daily* critic to comment that "it would be difficult to imagine anyone more suitable than Miss Barrymore in the part."[15] Her lines were abridged and supplied by titles, but the script by June Mathis and Katherine Kavanaugh retained much of the drawing-room comedic style of Maugham's play. It would, sniffed the *Motion Picture News*, "appeal to the better class of movie-goers,"[16] and *Moving Picture World* observed that "it has the air of good breeding and culture called for by its locale" (some scenes were filmed on a luxurious eastern American estate).[17]

Jack Straw, made by Famous Players-Lasky in 1920, was an even lighter comedy that did not translate well to the screen. First performed on stage in London in 1908, it was satire about a family from Brixton that suddenly comes into money, pretentiously hyphenates its name to Parker-Jennings, and moves to a country estate in Cheshire. There these parvenus meet a waiter who, falling for their daughter, ingratiates himself with them by pretending to be a Pomeranian archduke; in the end, he turns out to be a real archduke and the play ends happily. This is all enacted with a lot of farce but there is also a good deal of typical Maugham epigrammatic wit and wordplay, a verbal cleverness that was the strength of John Drew's portrayal of Jack Straw in the New York production in 1908. He was, said the *New York Times* reviewer, "the mouth piece of many sprightly speeches. . . . It would be absurd to assume that without [Drew's] adroitness in turning a point or enforcing the value of a line the result would mean as much."[18]

Olga Printzlau wrote the script of the film version of *Jack Straw*, and she moved the setting from England to the United States, making the Parker-Jennings a Harlem, New York, bourgeois family that suddenly comes into money and moves to California. This change drained the story of much of the satiric humor about English class attitudes that had amused London audiences and, in the view of many critics, left only a flimsy, well-worn plot. The story "goes stale as soon as it is uncorked,"[19] said *Picture Play Magazine*, and was not imaginative enough to survive translation to a silent medium. "If the original was a gem of its kind," added *Motion Picture News*, "then the adaptation is proof again that physical action and subtitles cannot take the place of pointed dialogue."[20]

For its next Maugham film, *The Ordeal*, in 1922, Paramount made several extravagant claims: that the author had written the script specifically for the screen and that he had personally supervised the production. "When a great author writes directly for the screen," its advertisements proclaimed, "you realize what a screen story can be. 'The Ordeal,' Somerset Maugham's first original screen story, is one of the most dramatic and powerful ever written."[21]

In reality, Maugham was home in London during the filming, and the script was based on a 1917 play called *Love in a Cottage*, the rights to which Lasky had acquired for $25,000 in 1920. The piece had been written on commission for the English actress Marie Löhr, who did well with it in England, but it had not been produced in New York and so the name meant nothing to American filmgoers. The story, moreover, was flimsy, so Lasky turned to Paramount's veteran screenwriter Beulah Marie Dix, in whose hands Maugham's play became almost unrecognizable. She gave the heroine a crippled sister and a feckless brother, and a Black maid (played by a White actress) becomes a murderer and perishes in a fire. The point of Maugham's play, that human values and intimacy are more important than money, barely survives in the ashes of Dix's alterations.

Paul Powell directed *The Ordeal*, but he was not the studio's first choice. It was supposed to have been directed by William Desmond Taylor, a respected craftsman who had done fifty-nine films, but two days after he was scheduled to begin filming, he was found shot to death in his home. His assailant was never identified, though there were several suspects, but his murder had a wide-ranging, lasting impact on the Hollywood film industry. Along with other scandals, it so alarmed film studio executives that they quickly set up the Hays Office, which, in its evolving forms, inhibited American moviemaking for the next forty-five years.

The Ordeal received mostly negative reviews, and Maugham bore the brunt of much of the criticism, accused of writing down to the American public with clichés. One commentator sarcastically praised the film for its brevity, and another claimed that the distress of the heroine was nothing compared to the suffering of those watching *The Ordeal*. Those familiar with Maugham's writing and drama noted the absence of wit and clever dialogue. "Where are the lance-like Maugham satire, breezy, whimsy, fresh angles on life? All absent, alas," said the *Los Angeles Times*, "Oh, W. Somerset, how could you?"[22] The answer, of course, is that he didn't.

Maugham's play *Caesar's Wife*, first performed in London in 1919, has held an unusual attraction for Hollywood filmmakers, unusual because the characters are all virtuous and the plot has few fireworks. Set in Cairo, it tells of a beautiful young woman, Violet, who, married to an older man, the British consul, becomes bored and falls in love with a handsome young attaché. Her husband is aware of the young people's passion but, for the good of the British mission in Egypt, he refuses to send his attaché away. Violet, too, realizes that the work of both men is essential to their country, and her scruples overcome her emotion when she reluctantly breaks off her relationship. The play ends with her realizing that she actually does love and need her husband, and she falls asleep in his arms. Everybody has behaved admirably, and allegiance to the empire rules the day. It is hardly surprising that in the London stage production the consul was played by C. Aubrey Smith, who would go on to become the embodiment of Britishness in countless films.

The theme of Maugham's play is clearly signified by its title, "Caesar's wife" being a term to describe someone who is required by position to be above public suspicion. The appearance of absolute rectitude and integrity was a foundation stone of British colonial rule throughout the world, and unlike so many of Maugham's other characters, Violet suppresses her feelings in order to remain respectable. Maugham did not believe that American audiences would accept such a sacrifice being driven by concern for the greater public good (though of course they later did with *Casablanca* in the patriotic days of the Second World War). Apparently First National Pictures agreed with him and abandoned the title for its 1925 film version, much to the disappointment of the actress who played Violet, Corinne Griffith. She understood its significance but was forced to choose from pages of alternates, some options being as silly as "Flirtation," before finally settling on *Infatuation*. It was suggested that this switch would prevent filmgoers thinking that they were being offered a spectacle of ancient Rome, but it is more likely that it signaled a shift in emphasis. Instead of portraying personal sacrifice for the greater public good, the story was reduced to being one of a restless wife's attraction to an illicit romance.

This theme, the basis of hundreds of films, was later explored with great effect in *Brief Encounter* and *The Bridges of Madison County*, but reviewers of *Infatuation* found it merely trite and bland. *American Film Daily* said that the film "moves as slowly as a turtle with a sprained ankle,"[23] and Martin Dickstein dismissed it as a "procession of drivel."[24] *Variety* observed that it was "one of those British parlor complexes switching to the Far East but still indoors, . . . and minus the dialogue of the play it's something of a nicely produced dud."[25] Movie house managers were advised to sell *Infatuation* on the presence of Griffith, whose legendary beauty was said to have elicited the phrase "the camera loves her."

Despite the poor reviews of *Infatuation*, Warner Bros. believed that its plot could make a successful film, bought the rights, and in March 1936 announced that Errol Flynn and Bette Davis would star in their version, *Another Dawn*. Screenwriter Laird Doyle would produce the script and the story would be set in Iraq during the British occupation. Several months later, however, Davis became embroiled in a dispute with the studio and was suspended; after Tallulah Bankhead was considered, the role went to Kay Francis. Filming took place at the Lasky Ranch at the end of the San Fernando Valley, where its rolling hills and mesas augmented footage of the sand dunes of Yuma, Arizona, to suggest the terrain of Iraq.

Another Dawn seems to have been plagued with lack of commitment from the beginning. William Dieterle directed the film reluctantly and only as a favor to Hal Wallis, and Flynn, who did not like working with Dieterle, was no more enthusiastic. Shooting was interrupted for a length of time when Francis was overcome with exhaustion—or perhaps it was boredom, since she spoke dismissively of her role: "I don't do much in it. Things just happen about me; I am just a wife who has been unfortunate in love."[26] For much of the filming the screenwriter and director were not certain how to resolve the heroine's romantic misfortune, so six different endings were shot, the one finally chosen reversing the Maugham conclusion. Rather than having the woman reject her lover in favor of her more staid but honorable husband, *Another Dawn* ends with the husband nobly flying to his death in a suicidal bombing mission. The young lovers thus are given "another dawn," and the point of Maugham's original play is abandoned.

Another Dawn received generally poor reviews—Philip K. Scheuer referred to its "English preciosity, of stout-fellowship and all that sort of thing, . . . a kind of 'Charge of the Light Brigade' without the charge."[27]

The plot of *Caesar's Wife*, however, continued to interest filmmakers, and in 1939 Warner Bros. announced that it would be remade as "The Outpost." Flynn was to return to the role, opposite Geraldine Fitzgerald, though his name was later replaced by that of Cary Grant; the English author James Hilton was reported to have completed a script, and Michael Curtiz would direct. This project was mentioned again in an article about upcoming Warner films in early 1941, but it was eventually shelved. Shelved but not completely abandoned, because in 1945 the press reported that screenwriter Leopold Atlas had devised an adaptation of *Caesar's Wife* to reflect current history. Political unrest was on the boil in India and was likely to become intense in the near future, and since the British had ruled India for a century, in part by the appearance of superior moral and civil conduct, it was an excellent setting for the story. In the end nothing came of this project, perhaps just as well for Warner Bros., considering that the film would have appeared around the time that the viceroy of India's wife, Edwina Mountbatten, was conducting what many people believe to be an affair with the prime minister, Jawaharlal Nehru.

East of Suez, a seven-scene play that began a run of 209 performances in London in 1922, has the most complicated plot of all of Maugham's dramas. Set in Peking, its central figure, Daisy, is the daughter of a White man and a Chinese mother, and the plot focuses on the tension in her—and around her—of European and Asian elements. A decade before the play begins, her lover, George Conway, broke off their relationship because marriage to an Asian woman would have killed his professional career. Her mother then sold her to a rich, unscrupulous Chinese merchant, Lee Tai Cheng, from whose clutches she eventually escaped. As we see her in the present, she marries a pleasant Englishman, Harry Anderson, but a year later she tires of him and yearns to renew her affair with George.

Daisy is aided in her attempts to win George back by her wily old amah, who soon is revealed to be her mother. The amah and Cheng, who also has reappeared, plot to free Daisy of Harry through assassination, but this fails when George is wounded instead. Daisy herself contrives to have George's love letters sent to Harry, suggesting to George that Harry will divorce her and they will be free to marry. George is appalled, pointing out that marriage to her would destroy his career, whereupon Daisy says that she will live with him as his Chinese mistress, making him opium pipes and teaching him the Asian way of happiness. George then goes into another room and shoots himself, and Daisy is left to confront her husband about the letters. Defiantly, she dresses and makes up her face in the Chinese style so that Harry confronts someone he hardly recognizes: a Chinese woman. His exclamation, full of meaning, ends the play: "Oh, Daisy, for God's sake say it isn't true!"

Maugham was more familiar than most Westerners with China, having made a very long trip along the Yangtze River in 1919–20, which he wrote about in *On a Chinese Screen* (1922). He was fascinated by Asian culture, but he also saw how difficult it was for Westerners to understand and adapt to a foreign and alienating culture. The gulf between East and West shows up in several of his works of fiction and drama, and it is central to *East of Suez*. It appears in the attitude of the Western community to biracial people like Daisy, who can never be an appropriate wife to a respectable Englishman. It is present, too, in the portrayal of the amah and Lee Tai Cheng as devious, cunning plotters working cleverly against the vulnerable, trusting foreigners. And ultimately, of course, it is powerfully represented at the end when the Chinese part of Daisy's personality becomes dominant, both in her appearance and in her character.

In addition to presenting the conflict between East and West, Maugham wanted to re-create the atmosphere of China for the audiences who had never experienced it. *East of Suez* was, he later wrote, "a play of spectacle," and the first scene is thus an overture that portrays a street in Peking full of laborers, water carriers, shops, people, and even a Mongolian caravan with ponies and camels. More spectacle is offered in the attempted assassination scene, when the stage is crowded with a mob of chattering, noisy Chinese citizens, monks, and neighbors. Adding to the ambiance was atmospheric incidental music written by the composer Eugene Goossens.

When Famous Players-Lasky filmed the play in 1925, the colorful atmosphere of Asia, easily re-created on the screen, no doubt was a strong drawing card, and reviewers praised the detail of the beautiful and striking foreign settings. "The picture," said *Variety*, "is screened in lavish fashion, holds one's interest throughout [with] delightful Chinese atmosphere and color."[28] According to *Moving Picture World*, "the outstanding point of this picture is its oriental atmosphere, and this has been effectively played up. . . . 'East of Suez' will have its greatest appeal for patrons who are fascinated by Oriental atmosphere and intrigue. For the general public we doubt it will prove altogether satisfying entertainment."[29]

Moviegoers in fact liked the film, and it did well at the box office, likely on the strength of its visual attractions, on the allure of the title, and on the actress who played Daisy, the celebrated Pola Negri. More discerning critics, however, found the plot problematic, largely because its screenwriter, Sada Cowen, had made large and significant changes to Maugham's script. Some alterations were a healthy simplification of an overly complicated plot: Abandoning the back story of Daisy's earlier life, the film begins with her arriving in Peking after years in England. It is then that she is kidnapped by the treacherous mandarin, Lee Tai, and rescued by Harry Anderson, whom she marries in gratitude. Cowen turns Anderson into a cad and, when he learns that marriage to her has made him an outcast in the foreign enclave, he treats her cruelly and she turns to George Tevis, a former lover. Other alterations, unfortunately, go beyond merely streamlining the plot: the ending is almost entirely changed. Anderson, threatening to kill Tevis if he comes near Daisy, dies after drinking poison that Lee Tai intended for Daisy's lover. Tevis and Daisy are then free leave together for England, and Lee Tai is executed according to Chinese law.

The film adaptation of *East of Suez* tells a love story that ends happily, but the plot change robs Maugham's play of many of its original—and more subtle—points about Eastern and Western culture and attitudes. More important, it turns another of the author's notable scheming antiheroines into a bland and relatively passive victim of the men and the racial prejudice around her. Maugham's Daisy is a complex character in whom two races battle for supremacy as she tries to survive in a world made complicated by the clash of East and West. The screen Daisy is reduced to a woman who happens to have an Asian mother but who is essentially and dominantly white and European, a passive victim who needs to be rescued by the ethical Englishman. As more than one reviewer noted, this transformation in her character deprived Negri of the chance to ignite the screen with a portrayal of a cynical, devious plotter. Mae Tinae summed it up in the *Chicago Tribune* by saying:

One wonders what Somerset Maugham thought when he witnessed 'East of Suez,' adapted for the screen from his play. The title is about the only thing in the picture that resembles his play. The latter was a brilliant and most unpleasant thing, with the heroine a villainess. The former makes her pure as the driven snow and sweet as honey in the honeycomb. Miss Negri plays the adapted heroine sympathetically—but how she COULD have played the woman of the original story! If honestly transferred to the silver sheet 'East of Suez' might not have been a pleasant picture, but it would probably have been a brilliant and unforgettable one.[30]

East of Suez's portrayal of China and the Chinese was not without controversy. Played by the Japanese actor Sojin Kamijama, Lee Tai was the familiar screen figure called by *Variety* a "scheming Chink." His long fingernails seemed designed cruelly to pry into the most private places, and his evil glare dominated the film posters. So offensive was this portrayal that Chinese Americans in Rochester, New York, asked the city's police to censor the film. The police declined to intervene, but *East of Suez* seems to have been trimmed by the intervention of the Hays Office. Its director, the first great one to handle Maugham material, Raoul Walsh, had ended the film with Daisy and Tevis marrying, but he was shocked to see that the version playing in movie houses was without its full final reel. Portrayal of miscegenation was discouraged by the Hays Office code, and Walsh always resented Paramount's allowing the censors to damage his work.

The Circle, first performed in London in 1921, is generally considered the finest of Maugham's thirty-two plays. Nearly flawless, it has been compared to the works of eighteenth-century satiric masters like Richard Brinsley Sheridan and William Congreve, and it puts Maugham in the company of Oscar Wilde and Noel Coward. Its clever comic structure offers two love triangles, one whose drama has played out in the past and the other whose crisis is to be confronted in the present. It concerns the revolt against social convention and the marriage contract by a romantic young woman, Elizabeth Champion-Cheney, whose marriage to a dull, conventional, and lifeless member of the English upper class has left her bored and feeling trapped. Not surprisingly, she has fallen in love with—and plans to elope with—Teddy Luton, an energetic young man on leave from his post in the

Federated Malay States. All of this is conveyed in witty, sparkling dialogue that, spoken by skilled stage actors, entertained sophisticated audiences on both sides of the Atlantic.

The play gets its title from the added complication of the arrival of Elizabeth's mother-in-law, Kitty, who thirty years earlier ran away from her husband with the dashing young Lord Porteous. Elizabeth is intrigued to meet them because she is enthralled by the romance of their past, but she discovers that, far from being alluring figures, they are old, faded, and quarrelsome. Despite this disillusionment, however, she asks her husband, Arnold, for a divorce, and he consents, hoping that the spirit of his sacrifice will cause her to reconsider. This strategy does not work and, even with the example of the rheumatic and cranky old lovers in front of her, she elopes with Teddy, who has promised her not happiness but love, excitement, and freedom.

Elizabeth makes her choice knowing that there may be a large price to be paid. The older runaways have suffered from years of ostracism from their upper-class society for having so blatantly broken its rules. Lord Porteous warns that, being a gregarious animal, men and women are members of a herd, and "if we break the herd's laws, we suffer for it. And we suffer damnably."[31] Years of living as outcasts have turned them into trivial people and, worse yet, not the romantic couple that Elizabeth had expected. They were once young, attractive, and passionately in love; time has turned them into a bickering geriatric couple, complaining about each other's failings and lamenting what they had given up in their elopement. They sacrificed everything for love, and that love—at least the all-consuming romantic passion for each other—has not endured. "The tragedy of love," laments Kitty in one of Maugham's most famous lines, "isn't death or separation. One gets over them. The tragedy of love is indifference."[32] Elizabeth is thus faced with the possibility that history will repeat itself, that she and Teddy will become Kitty and Porteous. The question becomes whether they will have the character to avoid that fate or, if not, will their youthful love have been worth the inevitable decline?

The success of *The Circle* on London and New York stages, as well as the name of its author, persuaded Metro-Goldwyn-Mayer to produce a screen version in 1925. It would feature Eleanor Boardman as Elizabeth, be directed by Frank Borzage, and Kenneth B. Clarke would write the screenplay, but they could hardly have chosen a more unsuitable work for adaptation to silent film. The plot revolves around a decision, with very little action outside of the conversations of the older and younger couples, speeches conveyed in clever satiric dialogue that could not be conveyed in subtitles. The *Evening Standard* reviewer noted that "sparkling dialogue cannot be picturized,"[33] and thus the cast turn it into broad comedy. The *Daily Mirror* said that "as a play, 'The Circle' sparkled, enchanted, amused with its sophisticated lines and daring action. As a picture 'The Circle' plods through many reels, burdened by wholesale supply of cheap subtitles and little action."[34]

The "daring action" of Maugham's play refers to another problem faced by Metro-Goldwyn-Mayer. Elizabeth's elopement with Teddy shocked even some members of the sophisticated London theater audiences, and they booed; and in 1935 the BBC permitted a radio dramatization only if some passages were deleted. MGM was operating in the shadow of the Hays Office, created three years earlier, one of whose stipulations was that films should uphold the sanctity of marriage and the home. People conducting love affairs outside of matrimony were not to be portrayed as happy or successful.

MGM dealt with this problem by radically altering the ending of the play. In their version, the limp and ineffectual Arnold suddenly develops courage and vigor and disguises himself as the chauffeur so that he can intercept the fleeing lovers, punch out Teddy, and in a show of masculine proprietorship, force his wife back to the marriage bed. The ending is highly implausible given that Arnold has shown no potential for manly heroics, and of course it strips the story of Maugham's point about marriage and romance and daring to defy convention. The absurdity of this alteration was not lost on reviewers, who suggested that the final scene should be cut because, as the *Morning Telegraph* said, "it completely defeats the intention of the author. . . . Between the censors and the adapter, all the irony has been zealously plucked out."[35]

MGM remade *The Circle* in 1930 under the title of *Strictly Unconventional*, and the addition of sound brought Maugham's dialogue into play. This led reviewers to label it a sophisticated drama for mature audiences, but they still lamented the lack of screen action. According to the *Film Daily*, "it is the story of English society life that will find little appeal to American audiences. . . . On the stage this was a clever satire on married life, but in its screen version it falls pretty flat."[36] Surprisingly, this adaptation, by Sylvia Thalberg and Frank Butler, went back to Maugham's original ending with Elizabeth and Teddy running away together. The Hays Office, it turned out, did not have the teeth to put the bite into offending filmmakers, and studios that defied its code sometimes remained unpunished. The new Hays Code had come into effect in March 1930, and several months later Morris Dickstein pointed out that *Strictly Unconventional* was one of several films breaking the rules, particularly the injunction against presenting adultery positively. According to film reviewer Welford Beaton, "The nice manner in which David Burton directs the picture robs the elopement of offensive qualities, but the fact remains that it breaks one of the Hays laws and shows how absurd the whole code of morals is."[37] Absurd, yes, but four years later the Hays Office would become very much more powerful and tighten its grip on American filmmaking for decades.

When Maugham delivered the manuscript of *The Magician* to his literary agent, J. B. Pinker, in 1906, he attached a note: "I have come to the conclusion that it is very dull and stupid, and I wish I was an outside broker, or Hall Caine [a highly successful author of popular fiction], or something equally despicable."[38] William Heinemann nonetheless published the novel in 1908, and it sold well enough to warrant a second edition six years later. When Maugham put together the collected edition of his works in 1934, however, he omitted *The Magician*, explaining that what he had written was "all moonshine. I did not believe a word of it. A book written under these conditions can have no life in it."[39]

It was not until 1956 that Maugham agreed to a new edition of *The Magician*, and this change of heart occurred largely because of the circumstances of its writing rather than the book itself. His career as an author had begun auspiciously in 1897 with *Liza of Lambeth*, but the next decade saw seven more novels and one collection of short stories make little impact on the reading public. Looking around for a genre of fiction with which he might have some commercial success, he became aware of the growing popularity of literature of the occult, horror, and science fiction. Joris-Karl Huysmans's *Là-bas* (*Down There*, 1891) had fascinated him as well as many readers on the continent, but numerous works in English had also captured the public imagination: Robert Louis Stevenson's *The Strange Case of Dr. Jekyll and Mr. Hyde* (1886), Oscar Wilde's *The Picture of Dorian Gray* (1891),

George du Maurier's *Trilby* (1894), Arthur Machen's *The Great God Pan and The Inmost Light* (1894), H. G. Wells's *The Island of Dr. Moreau* (1896), and E. F. Benson's *The Image in the Sand* (1905).

Maugham's story focuses on a young innocent Englishwoman and Parisian art student, Margaret Dauncey, and her psychological enslavement and ultimate destruction by a grotesque but hypnotic magician, Oliver Haddo. She lives with a friend, Susie Boyd, and is watched over by her fiancé, a medical doctor called Arthur Burdon. When Arthur assaults the magician over his cruelty to a dog, Haddo takes revenge by hypnotizing Margaret into eloping with him. He does not, however, force himself on her sexually because he intends to use her virginal blood in an experiment to create life in the form of a homunculus. Margaret is in thrall to him, and Arthur and Susie are unable to prevent her death in Haddo's horrific experiment, but Arthur kills the magician, and his laboratory in the English countryside is destroyed by fire.

The Magician was written with liberal borrowing of situations, characterizations, imagery, and pseudoscientific jargon from the abovementioned books and other accounts of the occult and mysticism. For his central figure, the sinister black magician, however, Maugham needed to go no further than his own experience. In early 1905, he had spent several months among the writers and artists drawn to Paris, and the oddest of this bohemian set was an eccentric English poet and satanist, Aleister Crowley. A sharp-tongued, flamboyant dabbler in the occult, Crowley was largely a charlatan, but he was reputed to conduct supernatural rituals, called himself "the Beast 666," and genuinely frightened people he met. Before he died in 1947, the British press commonly called him the wickedest man in the world.

Writing in 1956, Maugham claimed that Oliver Haddo was not a portrait of Crowley. "I made my character," he said, "more striking in appearance and more ruthless than Crowley ever was. I gave him magical powers that Crowley, though he claimed them, certainly never possessed."[40] Indeed, Haddo is a repulsive figure, a large, excessively obese man with piercing eyes, an irresistible hypnotist and frightening necromancer, an intimidating figure who seems to have power over everyone around him. Despite the exaggeration, however, Crowley recognized himself and the sources of much of *The Magician*'s occult trappings, and he struck back with an article titled "How to Write a Novel! After Somerset Maugham" in the December 20, 1908, issue of *Vanity Fair*. Crowley proved conclusively that Maugham had plagiarized a variety of books about magic and the supernatural, but he did not pursue the matter in the courts and, in fact, liked occasionally to call himself "Oliver Haddo."

Despite Maugham's claim that *The Magician* has "no life in it"—indeed, the novel lacks the allegorical or thematic substance of the best of occult or science fiction literature—it does contain several motifs that recur throughout Maugham's writing. In Haddo's Svengali-like enslavement of the young woman, Margaret Dauncey, one can recognize the lifelong concern for individual freedom that became pronounced in works such as *Of Human Bondage* and *The Razor's Edge*. And the emotional suffering and despair of her fiancé, Arthur Burdon, resembles that of so many of Maugham's protagonists and most fully represented in *Of Human Bondage*'s Philip Carey. Lying behind and in the shadow of Arthur's relationship with Margaret is the enduring love for him of their friend, Susie Boyd, a passion that may be consummated with Margaret's death at the end of the novel.

The ghoulish plot of *The Magician* would have been excellent material for German film makers of the 1920s, who had given the world *The Golem* (Paul Wegener, 1915), *The Cabinet of Dr. Caligari* (Robert Wiene, 1920), and *Nosferatu* (F. W. Murnau, 1922). Instead, it was produced by Metro-Goldwyn-Mayer studios in 1925, at a time when American film companies were making few horror films. The writer/director was the highly regarded Irish Rex Ingram, whom Erich von Stroheim called "the world's greatest director."[41] Margaret was played by Ingram's wife, Alice Terry, and Arthur by Ivan Petrovic, a Serbian actor whose handsome features led some people to see him as the successor to Rudolph Valentino. Terry conveyed her character's vulnerability well, though not memorably, but Petrovic contributed little more than a handsome face to the part of the brilliant surgeon and lover. In the words of the assistant director, Michael Powell, he "wandered through the . . . scenes in the manner of an innocent bystander caught up in an insurrection."[42]

It was the central role of Haddo, however, that most interested Ingram, so much so that he bought the rights to the story in order to work with Paul Wegener, a well-known German actor who had impressed him in the lead role in *The Golem*. Maugham had made Haddo grotesquely fat, but Wegener was merely a large burly man, ironically probably closer in appearance to Aleister Crowley than to the fictional magician. His costume was stereotypical: a floppy black hat, a large black cape (which he dramatically swirled about him at every opportunity), and an ebony walking-stick—leading to a wonderful bit of meta-criticism when Arthur exclaims, "he looks like he stepped out of a melodrama." Wegener's acting, too, is clichéd, relying heavily on grimaces of his downturned mouth and glares from bulging eyes. As Powell described it, "We were saddled with a pompous German whose one idea was to pose like a statue and whose one expression to indicate magical powers was to open his huge eyes even wider, until he looked about as frightening as a bullfrog."[43]

If his actors were mundane, Ingram imported several other artists to convey the atmosphere of an occult and licentious world. The film begins with a shot of the gargoyles of Notre Dame cathedral looking down on Paris and moves to Margaret's studio, where she is completing a giant statue of a faun. To create this large corrupting figure, Ingram hired Paul Dardé, a noted French sculptor whose "Faune" had been put in the Musée Rodin a few years earlier. Later, when Haddo hypnotizes Margaret with an erotic vision in which the faun comes alive and leads her through a scene of debauchery and her near rape, the scene was choreographed—and the faun danced—by the American painter and ballet dancer Hubert Stowitts. Having danced with Anna Pavlova for several seasons, Stowitts had a striking physique and a creative vision, an imagination that would be employed again in *The Painted Veil* in 1934.

These effects were not enough to save *The Magician*. Ingram had aspired to make a horror film to stand with the best of the German ones, but as Powell explained, he made a fundamental mistake in filming it naturalistically, rather than using the expressionistic elements that made films like *Nosferatu* and *The Cabinet of Dr. Caligari* so mesmerizing. Instead of making the décor disconcertingly unreal through exaggerated sets, tilted camera angles, and shadowy chiaroscuro lighting, said Powell, Ingram took "a tall tale and made it taller by telling it in real exteriors and natural settings."[44] Indeed, the one use of chiaroscuro had Haddo's face lit from below, the effect serving only to make him resemble a campfire ghost storyteller bottom-lit by a flashlight. Ironically, expressionism does appear in *The Magician*, but only in a passing glimpse of a painting of a bridge over the Seine, a Picasso-like landscape created by a student artist.

Some of the most effective scenes of the film come at its conclusion, when Arthur saves Margaret from the clutches of the mad scientist/magician. For both economic and artistic reasons, Ingram moved Haddo's laboratory from his English country home to southern France, to a "sorcerer's tower" high on a craggy rock. Constructed in a village in the hills near Nice and filmed as if at night and during a violent thunderstorm, it has the sense of atmospheric "unreality" that Powell thought would have enhanced the story overall. If the final scenes there were not innovative for the period, they certainly joined a long line of horror film clichés. The local townspeople will not go anywhere near Haddo's forbidding tower, which is guarded by a hunchbacked dwarf with absurdly large feet. The laboratory is full of strange devices and bubbling and steaming concoctions, and Margaret, strapped to an operating table, is every bit as helpless as a heroine on the railway tracks. Just in the nick of time, Arthur bursts in and grapples with Haddo, eventually hurling him into a furnace, whereupon the tower catches fire and explodes, and with the destruction of Haddo and his evil schemes, the world is normal and safe again.

The magician's death also breaks the spell cast on Margaret, and she is reunited with her lover. This conclusion, the "happy" outcome so often tacked onto Maugham films, blunts the effect of the original story in which the young woman is sacrificed in Haddo's experiment. To reach this end, Ingram substantially revised Maugham's novel, relegating Susie Boyd to being a minor observer rather than an undeclared lover of Arthur. He, too, is reduced from being a somewhat interesting, vulnerable figure to a one-dimensional traditional hero. Lost in these changes is the idea that love between the plain but loyal Susie and a sensitive Arthur may ultimately be stronger and deeper than that of Arthur's infatuation with the beautiful but shallow Margaret.

During production of *The Magician*, MGM touted it as "daring, colossal, magnificent" and "Ingram's most dramatic work, . . . a theme of startling nature."[45] Louis B. Mayer is reputed to have liked the final cut. It did not, however, win over general audiences or critics. Powell attributed its failure to its being a hybrid, an American film made in Europe (Ingram's studio was in Nice) with a script that did not satisfy viewers on either side of the Atlantic. In 1930 film historian Paul Rotha blamed Ingram, writing that the film was "a bad adaptation of Somerset Maugham's novel."[46] For his part, Ingram declared that he had done his best but was hampered by working with a poor story. "I changed the ending," he said later, "because it had to be changed. Maugham's story wasn't much good anyway. Just a melodramatic plot ending in the death of the heroine. I gave it a happy ending. It was the only thing to do. . . . You must have a first-rate story, one big enough to lead up to an unhappy ending." But, he said, he was working with "that cheap melodrama of Maugham's."[47] For his part, Maugham claimed to be unaware that Ingram was filming *The Magician*. He might well have privately agreed with the director's assessment of his novel, but reportedly Ingram's defense of his changes rankled him.[48]

CHAPTER 2

Swanson, Crawford, and Hayworth

Rain

In the winter of 1920–21, Maugham was in Los Angeles and at dinner with some of the brightest lights of the Hollywood film community: Douglas Fairbanks, Mary Pickford, and Charlie Chaplin. He held the table spellbound by a tale, "Miss Thompson," which he was about to publish, a somewhat lurid story of an American prostitute and her encounter with a strait-laced, sin-obsessed missionary. He had fashioned the short story, as he did with so many of his works, from his own observations of people, in this case passengers on a ship from Honolulu to Pago Pago in 1916. One was a cadaverous medical missionary with a look of "suppressed fire,"[1] and another was his rigidly moral wife. The third was a twenty-seven-year-old woman who had been driven out of the red-light district of Honolulu and was heading for Apia, where she hoped to get a job in a hotel bar. Her name was Miss Thompson,[2] and she would become the raw material for one of the most colorful and notorious female characters in twentieth-century literature, drama, and film.

The missionary, given the name "Davidson" in Maugham's story, became an equally memorable and notorious fictional character. There are echoes in him of the central figure in Anatole France's 1890 novel *Thaïs*, a holy man who ultimately succumbs to the beauty of a penitent courtesan. And the religious fervor of his attempt to reform the fallen Miss Thompson resembles the ferocity of the inquisitor's battle for the soul of Joan in Bernard Shaw's *Saint Joan*, written three years later. But as Graham Greene said, it was Maugham's minister who most vividly embodied the rigidity and

40

hypocrisy of many religious crusaders: "Maugham has done more than anyone else to stamp the idea of the repressed prudish man of God on the popular imagination."[3] It was not, however, an idea or a figure that Hollywood film producers were prepared to put on the screen.

In that spring of 1921, Maugham was on his way to Singapore with his companion, Gerald Haxton, and had stopped in California largely at the invitation of Jesse Lasky, head of the Famous Players-Lasky film studio. On a trip to Europe the year before, Lasky had signed several eminent authors, and he was hoping to rein in Maugham. Distinguished authors' names on a film poster were guarantees of increased ticket sales, but Lasky also wanted articulate new scripts. A number of writers adapted to the demands of creating film scripts, of essentially working for producers, directors, actors, set designers, and other studio employees, but Maugham was not one of them, and after only a few weeks in Hollywood, he decided to move on to East Asia and to submit screenplays from there.

There was, however, an entirely unexpected bonus to Maugham's weeks in the film community. One of the other guests in his hotel was the playwright John Colton, also in Hollywood to write screenplays, and unable to sleep one night, he borrowed the galley proofs of "Miss Thompson" that had arrived in the mail that day. At breakfast the next morning, Colton confided to Maugham that he had lain awake thinking what a wonderful play it would make, and could he adapt it? Maugham was skeptical: *The Smart Set* had agreed to publish the story only after several other magazines considered it too lurid for their pages, and Maugham doubted that it could be presented on stage. He nonetheless agreed to let Colton have a try at it. When the story appeared in *The Smart Set* in April and then again as "Rain" in book form in *The Trembling of a Leaf* in September, one of several dramatists wanting the rights offered Maugham's agent, Elizabeth Marbury, $7,000. Colton did not have that kind of money, nor did he have anything more than Maugham's handshake on their agreement, but when Miss Marbury's cable reached Maugham in the South Pacific, he replied that the handshake still stood.

Colton's adaptation, written along with Clemence Randolph, opened in New York in November 1922 and was a smashing triumph that ran for 648 performances. Seen by several million people, the play grossed $3 million. It was driven by the superb performance of Jeanne Eagels as Sadie Thompson, in the words of Gloria Swanson, "a great actress in a great role that suits her perfectly." Swanson saw the play twice, the second time just to study Eagels's technique and because, as she said, "every actress in America with a brain and a figure . . . wanted to play Sadie."[4] Eagels, though, had a justifiable sense of proprietorship over the role, telling a *Los Angeles Times* reporter in 1928: "She's mine, mine. No one can play Sadie but me. I have lived and breathed Sadie for years. I know her very soul. She's mine, only mine."[5]

Among the many other actresses who coveted Sadie was Marion Davies, but her lover and de facto manager William Randolph Hearst would not allow her to play a prostitute. Indeed, actresses were prepared to die for the role, if the story of Tallulah Bankhead's pursuit of it across the Atlantic is to be believed. When she was turned down for the London production of *Rain*, she went home, donned her Sadie costume, took a modest number of aspirins, and left a suicide note reading, "It ain't goin' to rain no mo'." It was, as critic Brendan Gill said, "the smallest possible attempt at suicide."[6] But, referring to Maugham's recently published story "The Man Who Wouldn't Hurt a Fly," she wired to her manager, "The Man Who Wouldn't Hurt a Fly is crucifying me."[7] In the end, she survived her rejection, and when she drew mixed reviews in a New York revival of *Rain* in 1935, she made sure that the good notices were sent to Maugham.

Swanson later recalled that it was more than just actresses who fell under the allure of Sadie Thompson: every Hollywood producer had secretly dreamed of filming *Rain*. But while the play was triumphing in New York, film studios were blocked from tackling it by the restrictions established a few years earlier by the Hays Office. In response to the damage believed to have been done to the film industry's reputation by the murder of director William Desmond Taylor and the alleged rape of an actress by Roscoe Arbuckle, the studios sought to show that they could control the moral content of its work. Hays's "The Formula" required a film company to submit a provocative text to a committee of studio officials, and if it was judged to be morally offensive, it would be put on a list of works to be avoided. Hays soon bragged that "more than a hundred and fifty books and plays, including some of the best sellers and stage successes, have thus been kept from the screen."

The Hays Office's control of what was permitted to be filmed was strengthened in 1927 when a committee comprising Irving Thalberg, Sol

Wurtzel, and E . H. Allen drew up a list of "Do's and Don'ts and Be Carefuls" to which studios were expected to adhere.

The inventory of "don'ts" covered a lot of material:

1. Pointed profanity—by either title or lip—this includes the words God, Lord, Jesus, Christ (unless they be used reverently in connection with proper religious ceremonies), Hell, SOB, damn, Gawd, and every other profane and vulgar expression however it may be spelled;
2. Any licentious or suggestive nudity—in fact or in silhouette; and any lecherous or licentious notice thereof by any other characters in the picture;
3. The illegal traffic in drugs;
4. Any inference of sex perversion;
5. White slavery;
6. Miscegenation (sex relationships between the white and black races);
7. Sex hygiene and venereal diseases;
8. Scenes of actual childbirth—in fact or in silhouette;
9. Children's sex organs;
10. Ridicule of the clergy;
11. Willful offense to any nation, race or creed.

In addition to these proscriptions, the committee advised that "special care be exercised in the manner in which the following subjects are treated, to the end that vulgarity and suggestiveness may be eliminated and that good taste may be emphasized." Among these subjects were two that seemed to rule out any filming of *Rain*: "the sale of women, or of a woman selling her virtue" and "excessive or lustful kissing, particularly when one character or the other is a 'heavy.'"[8]

In Swanson the Hays Office had a formidable challenger: an actress determined to play Sadie, one who had her own company, Gloria Swanson Productions, which distributed films through United Artists. As Janet Staiger has noted, Swanson formed her independent company in 1925 to change her star persona from "clothes horse" to mature actress.[9] She was not deterred by the Hays restrictions, and she began a campaign to film *Rain* that was part diplomacy and part deception. She invited Hays to lunch, took him aside, and attempted to negotiate a means of producing *Rain* that might satisfy his rules. She pointed out that her film company was not yet a member of the Association of Motion Picture Producers and Distributors, and thus not being a signatory to the Hays code it was not actually bound by its restrictions. She did not, though, wish to contravene the rules, and a new script could change the missionary from a clergyman to a secular reformer. She talked, not of *Rain*, the notorious play, but of "Miss Thompson," the short story by the eminent author, W. Somerset Maugham. "Miss Thompson" was not on Hays's register of banned works, so he did not think to object to Swanson devising a screenplay from it.

To avoid antagonizing jealous film studios, Swanson embarked on an undercover campaign to secure the rights to both "Miss Thompson" and *Rain*. She arranged for Joseph Schenck, chairman of United Artists, to work through a Los Angeles dramatic agent to negotiate surreptitiously with Maugham's agent and with Sam Harris, who was representing Colton and Randolph. So secretive were these maneuvers that *Rain* was always referred to merely as the "Maugham-Colton-Randolph play,"[10] and all correspondence was written in code, including the triumphant telegram of Schenck's agent: "YOU ARE NOW OWNER OF THE TWO MOLEHILLS OF NEBRASKA WHICH COST YOU SIXTY THOUSAND."[11]

Swanson revealed her filming plans to the newspapers in what she thought was a discreet announcement that she would be putting Maugham's "Miss Thompson" on the screen. Neither *Rain* nor "Sadie" were mentioned, but people quickly connected the dots and the headlines soon proclaimed that she was going to play Sadie in a production of *Rain*, a play banned by the Hays Office. Before long Schenck received a long telegram of protest from Hollywood's most important studio chiefs and the country's largest chains of movie houses. Swanson, it said, was endangering the film industry's newly established reputation for not making movies from salacious books and plays. The group forwarded the telegram to Will Hays with an equally strong plea that he use every power that he possessed to prevent *Rain* being filmed under any title, even with significant changes to characters. Hays in turn sent this wire to Schenck and Swanson, urging them to reveal whether the situation had been misrepresented.

Diplomatically choosing not to fight the battle through the press, Swanson responded to her antagonists with a skillfully worded telegram. She emphasized again that she would be using the magazine story rather than the stage play and that she had an agreement with Hays that she could go ahead if she did not portray a missionary or clergyman. The story could then be told "IN A CLEAN MANNER WITHOUT OFFENDING THE CLERGY. . . . YOU KNOW VERY WELL THAT AS FAR AS THE PUBLIC IS CONCERNED SADIE THOMPSON CAN BE PRODUCED IN SUCH A MANNER THAT THERE WILL NOT BE THE SLIGHTEST OBJECTION TO IT BY ANY CENSOR BOARD OR ANY RELIGIOUS BODY." It is hard to imagine Swanson drafting these claims with an entirely straight face, but she was on more solid ground when she declared that Maugham's story was "A GREAT LESSON IN TOLER-ANCE."[12] She omitted to say that the voice of tolerance in "Miss Thompson," Dr. Mcphail, would have a greatly reduced part in her film, but she hoped that the film studios would show the same tolerance toward her project.

Though Swanson was not negotiating with the studio heads through the newspapers, she used the trade journals, read by movie house managers all over the United States, to put pressure on them. On June 17, 1927, *Motion Picture News* carried the story "No Preacher in 'Sadie Thompson,' Says Schenck": "Declaring that there will be no preacher in the cast of charac-ters in Gloria Swanson's next film, 'Sadie Thompson,' Joseph M. Schenck, president of United Artists, releases the information that Miss Swanson does not desire to have any minister or missionary of any church in the picturization of the W. Somerset Maugham story, and is particularly anx-ious of having this point understood."[13]

Swanson's telegram to the committee of studio heads elicited a response from only one of its members, but he was its most powerful and influential one. Marcus Loew was the owner of a network of movie houses stretching from coast to coast, and he had founded the Metro-Goldwyn-Mayer stu-dio. If Hays had made an agreement with her, he said, he would ensure that the agreement was upheld. Loew, who was to die two months later, seems to have been as good as his word; Swanson was never given an official approval, but after ten days of silence she began shooting her film without any further objections from the Hays Office. Nevertheless, thinking of a possible sequel and to maintain good relations with everyone, she wrote Maugham to ask for a new, original story of Sadie's life after Pago Pago. The author's reply is interesting in light of his reputed disinterest in writ-ing for the screen. He had, he said, an agreement with the Fox Film Com-pany to write an account of Sadie beginning a new life in Australia, but that deal was now dead. "So if you would like me to do a picture for you on these lines I am not only at liberty to do it, but should be very glad to. I think I have abundant material to make a scenario full of colour and action. The price I had arranged with the Fox Film Company was $25,000."[14]

By the time Swanson received Maugham's response, she had lost her enthusiasm for further films about Sadie Thompson. Indeed, despite what she told Hays, her intent had always been to make a film extension of the stage version of *Rain* rather than faithfully reproduce the published story. For diplomacy's sake, she used the title "Sadie Thompson," but Raoul Walsh's screenplay was clearly an adaptation of the play. Moreover, argues Staiger, Swanson was responsible for three significant plot changes from the short story and play: the romance between Sadie and a marine, the conventional Hollywood happy ending, and the shift in point of view from Dr. McPhail to Sadie.[15] Where Maugham's story had only a passing reference to several American sailors, with whom Sadie does no more than exchange greetings, the film, like *Rain*, adds the substantial presence of Sergeant Timothy O'Hara and a detachment of US Marines. Indeed, the action begins with marines looking longingly at a docking ship, and a title reminds us that these men have spent weary months of exile from "white women." Soon a group of them are escorting Sadie ashore, telling her that she has time to meet the whole detachment—"the whole army," they say—but in fact there are no scenes of any sexual interaction between her and the men. She quickly develops a relationship with O'Hara, but there is no suggestion that it is sexual; it is instead a conventional romance in which he quickly suggests that he imitate a friend who married a woman like her, that is, a worker from the red-light district of San Francisco. At the end of the film they do indeed intend to sail to Sydney and forge a new life.

Most film critics agree that this "happy" ending robbed even the play version of much of its potency. *Picture Play* claimed that "much of the original power of 'Rain' was lost in the screen 'Sadie Thompson' by the utilization of a felicitous ending."[16] Paul Rotha agreed: "The contrived ending, which may have fitted in with United Artists' idea of picture-sense, was mediocre."[17] On the other hand, *Motion Picture News*, which called the film "rattling good entertainment," argued that the story of Sadie's romance with O'Hara "saves it from being carried along a single groove."[18] Years later Walsh's biographer, Marilyn Ann Moss, maintained that the marine's presence in the story immediately softens Sadie as a character: "She can express love and be loved."[19]

Swanson had guaranteed the studio chiefs that she could make a film to which no censor board or religious body could object, and this involved removing many of Sadie's rough edges. The addition of O'Hara, played by the handsome Walsh himself, made her a much more conventional and sympathetic figure. Moreover, Sadie is given a speech in which she pleads her innocence before an unyielding Davidson, claiming that she is innocent of the charges that await her in San Francisco. The door is thus opened to the film viewer seeing her as a misjudged victim, in the words of one reviewer, "a giddy girl in search of romance."[20] Maugham's Sadie, though, is a hardened, cynical prostitute trying to avoid being sent back to San Francisco where, as she almost casually admits, she faces a three-year prison sentence. Shoved almost to one side by the film's changes is the heart of Maugham's tale: Sadie's apparent conversion by the fervent Davidson and her reversion to the brash woman of the street when he tries to exploit her sexually like everyone else.

The shock, too, of Davidson's fall from grace, so dramatically revealed in the last line of the story, is diminished. To be permitted to make her film, Swanson promised Hays that Sadie's antagonist would not be identified as a clergyman or missionary, and so the religious references were dropped and he is described as a "professional reformer." According to journalist Frank Scully, Maugham claimed that the removal of "Reverend" from Davidson reduced the profits of the film from £20,000 to £12,000.[21] Perhaps that is true, perhaps the public were eager to see a bullying man of the cloth revealed as a hypocrite and moral weakling, but Davidson is nonetheless a fierce and repugnant figure. Even without the church behind him, says the hotel owner, he is said to be able to earn a living and wield sweeping power: "Politicians all scared of him—bosses these islands like he owned them." He is going to bring, by coercion and intimidation, a sense of sin to the Indigenous islanders who have been living in amoral freedom.

Much of the power of the Davidson of *Sadie Thompson* comes from the excellent casting of Lionel Barrymore. In physical makeup and psychological demeanor, he is very close to the sullen and morose figure described on the page by Maugham:

His appearance was singular. He was very tall and thin, with long limbs loosely jointed; hollow cheeks and curiously high cheek-bones; he had so cadaverous an air that it surprised you to notice how full and sensual were his lips. He wore his hair very long. His dark eyes, set deep in their sockets, were large and tragic; and his hands with their big, long fingers, were finely shaped; they gave him a look of great strength. But the most striking thing about him was the feeling he gave you of suppressed fire. It was impressive and vaguely troubling. He was not a man with whom any intimacy was possible.[22]

Barrymore was forty-nine when he was filming *Sadie Thompson*, still relatively slim, with an almost haggard look that was perhaps the result of an illness, an injured leg, and a reliance on painkillers. His sharp facial features, which fitted his numerous roles as villains, military officers, and in later years, amiable curmudgeons, were well suited to Alfred Davidson. Standing five feet, ten inches, he played the part with a stoop, leaning over Swanson like an angel of doom. Most striking, though, were his eyes, blue in real life but conveying an unsettling intensity in black-and-white film. Avoiding the exaggeration that had made Wegener's wide-eyed magician a ludicrous figure, Barrymore excellently conveys the "suppressed fire" of Maugham's original missionary. This is particularly dramatic in a scene where, grilling the cowering Sadie about her San Francisco life, he is shown in a full face-on shot glaring at her and shouting: "Sadie Thompson, you are an evil woman!"

As Sadie, Swanson gave one of the finest performances of her career as she matches Barrymore's demonic intensity with a variety of emotions ranging through disdain, evasiveness, apprehension, and fear to fragile vulnerability. Some of these feelings are conveyed by the dialogue titles, but far more is communicated, in close-ups, through her eye movement and other facial gestures, none of which has the exaggeration of so many silent films. This is particularly effective in the scenes where, having fallen under the control of Davidson, Sadie has thrown off her brassy persona and become a quieter, less assertive woman. Plainly dressed and without heavy makeup, she stands with her reformer to confront O'Hara, and declares, "I'm different now!"—and we believe her.

Sadie's conversion, however, is not the end of the tale, and the film treats the denouement differently from that of the printed story. Maugham concludes "Miss Thompson," as he does so many of his short stories, by following Guy de Maupassant's practice of hitting the reader with a shocking—

and usually unexpected—last line. This *coup de canon* compels the reader to view the story differently and perhaps reevaluate earlier judgments; it can also reveal aspects of characters that had been deeply hidden behind their public faces and behaviors. This device is particularly effective in conveying Maugham's strong conviction that people are strange mixtures of qualities and that the well-mannered social facade can often mask shocking impulses and compulsions.

The last line of "Miss Thompson" is such a cannon shot. It represents an awakening in Dr. Macphail, who plays a much more prominent part on the page than in Swanson's film. He is a common figure in many of Maugham's works: a *raissoneur*, a humane, generous, and conventional person who witnesses and comments on the actions of the main character. Macphail is roused in the early morning and taken to the beach, where Davidson's body has been found; he has inexplicably cut his own throat. Returning to the hotel, he hears the gramophone playing loud ragtime music, and Sadie has reverted to her garish makeup and gaudy clothes, "the flaunting quean that they had known at first." When Macphail confronts her about her disrespect to the grieving Mrs. Davidson, Sadie spits out a disdainful answer.

> No one could describe the scorn of her expression or the contemptuous hatred she put into her answer.
> "You men! You filthy dirty pigs! You're all the same, all of you. Pigs! Pigs!"
> Dr. Macphail gasped. He understood.[23]

The reader, too, understands: while Davidson has pursued Sadie's soul, intent on converting her from her sensual behavior, he has succumbed to his own carnal desire for her. He has proven to be no better than the men from whom Sadie earns her living—worse, in fact, because of his hypocrisy—and she has returned to being the tough, coarse woman who stepped ashore at the beginning.

Maugham does very little to prepare his readers for the fall of Rev. Davidson and the reversion of Sadie, though a careful reader with a knowledge of Freudian psychology might be tipped off by Mrs. Davidson's comments that her husband had been having strange dreams. They were "about the mountains of Nebraska," which Dr. Macphail recalled seeing on a trip across the United States. "They were like huge mole-hills, rounded and smooth, and they rose from the plain abruptly . . . like a woman's breasts."[24]

This almost casual reference takes on much greater significance when Dr. Macphail and the reader understand that Davidson, driven by a rigid ascetism and tormented by his repressed sexuality, has assaulted Sadie.

Sadie Thompson, closely following the play *Rain* rather than the short story, eliminates the surprise at the ending, and this softens the impact of the revelation about the missionary. Not trusting the viewer to recognize the significance of the "mountains of Nebraska," Dr. Macphail responds to the news of Davidson's strange dreams by looking directly into the camera and commenting, "I'm beginning to think that our friend's dreams about Miss Thompson are not altogether unpleasant!" Moreover, the film takes us beyond the story's limited perspective of Macphail to see Davidson's succumbing to Sadie, the whole process in fact, except his actual assault. When she says that she is haunted by visions, he replies fervently, "I, too, have been seeing things in the dark—flaming hot eyes—Aphrodite—Judas! . . . Sadie, you are like one of the Daughters of the King! . . . You are radiant—you are beautiful!" As Sadie retreats into her room, his eyes gleam with much more than missionary zeal. Having seen this, the viewer can hardly be surprised at Davidson's moral collapse.

Swanson had promised Hays that the Sadie Thompson story could be filmed in such a way that there would be no objection from censors or religious bodies. The final scenes are thus a departure from Maugham's stark cynicism to a softened and sentimental conclusion. Sadie's disgusted retort is shortened to "You men are all alike—pigs—PIGS!" But she doesn't, of course, mean Tim O'Hara, and she agrees to accompany him to Sydney, where, presumably, she will abandon her profession and settle into a conventional life as his wife. Her disillusionment with Davidson and the damage of his actions has not, after all, left her irretrievably hardened and cynical.

Swanson's Sadie, however, does more than merely look to a positive future: she dispenses a wisdom that is supposed to bring closure to the characters who witness Davidson's fall and to the viewers of the film. In the original story, Mrs. Davidson remains "hard and steady," and hurries away when Sadie spits at her. In the film, she approaches Sadie and shows a generosity previously hidden in her, saying, "I understand, Miss Thompson—I'm sorry for him and sorry for you." Sadie responds, not with spittle, but with an expansive forgiveness: "I guess I'm sorry for everybody in the world—life is a quaint present from somebody." This is a sentiment that would never have come from the pen of Somerset Maugham, and *Sadie Thomson* ends not with a bang but with a mawkish whimper.

Swanson had succeeded in making her film but only by distorting many of the elements of the original story to satisfy the Hays Office. Even in the editing process, the Hays people demanded changes, employing lip readers to look for obscenities and scouring the titles for transgressions. The film's launch was thus delayed by several months, but some movie reviewers like the *New York Times*' Mordaunt Hall approved of Hays's restrictions. "It is quite evident," he wrote, "that Will H. Hays's action concerning the picturing of the play 'Rain' has had a salutary effect upon this production, for a good deal of the restraint may be traced to Mr. Hays's stand."[25] Welford Beaton, on the other hand, did not find the sanitizing process useful, and he warned of the damaging effects of censorship on art: "[*Sadie Thompson* is a picture] that the United Artists people had the greatest difficulty in cleansing sufficiently to make it fit to be released. A picture that has to be put through such a delousing process as *Sadie Thompson* was subjected to cannot emerge as a good example of screen art. In removing the filth it is not possible to avoid scraping off some of the healthy substance. . . . Quite apart from considerations of good taste, it is the greatest economic folly to peddle rottenness to shoppers for screen entertainment. The producers who chafe under the restraint of censorship have only themselves to blame for it."[26]

In the end Swanson's faith in Sadie's story and her ability to put it on the screen was rewarded. The film did very well at the box office, and she was nominated for Best Actress in the newly created Academy Awards, losing out to Janet Gaynor, who had been put forward for roles in three films. Maugham, who always claimed that no one could touch Jeanne Eagels's performance in *Rain*, was gracious about Swanson's evocation when he met her shortly after a preview showing. "Just as I imagined her," he said. But, he added to Walsh, "why do those johnnies always cut the best scenes? They're worse than God."[27]

Maugham had offered to write a sequel to *Sadie Thompson* for Swanson, but the struggle to put it on the screen left her little appetite for doing another. In 1931 she sold the film rights to Schenck and United Artists, which were planning a blockbuster sound version. It would be headed by the hottest director of the time, Lewis Milestone, winner of Best Director

Oscars for *Two Arabian Knights* in 1927 and *All Quiet on the Western Front* in 1930. The distinguished dramatist and screenwriter Maxwell Anderson, who had adapted *All Quiet on the Western Front* and would win a Pulitzer Prize in 1933, was commissioned to do the screenplay. Walter Huston would play Mr. Davidson, and the supporting cast included many of Hollywood's most capable actors and actresses, among whom were Guy Kibbee as Horn and Beulah Bondi as Mrs. Davidson. For Sadie, the studio had considered Ann Dvorak and Jean Harlow—Tallulah Bankhead, favored by many, was under contract to another company—and so it chose Joan Crawford. As for the threat of censorship, Schenck did not see a problem: "The Depression has sobered the Hays Office. We'll sail through like a breeze."[28] He might have added that *Sadie Thompson* had broken the ground and made things easier for a sound remake.

Like Walsh's screenplay for *Sadie Thompson*, the plot of Anderson's adaptation closely follows that of Colton and Randolph's *Rain*, rather than Maugham's original story. The marine, Sergeant O'Hara, is prominent, and played as a decent, caring suitor for Sadie by William Gargan, making his film debut after a successful career in New York theater. Dr. Macphail has a larger part than in *Sadie Thompson*, largely because the sound dialogue allows him more fully to express a generous, humane viewpoint. Whether intended or not, the mustachioed Matt Moore's quiet observant demeanor, implied in part by his thoughtful drawing on his pipe, gives him a resemblance to the middle-aged Maugham himself. Beulah Bondi capably embodies the shriveled, rigid, judgmental Mrs. Davidson.

One significant difference between this adaptation and its predecessors is some depth given the storekeeper, Joe Horn, portrayed with energy and originality by Kibbee. In *Miss Thompson*, he merely reports on Davidson's missionary work and his repressive power in the islands; here he joins Dr. Macphail in offering a humanist's commentary on the persecution of Sadie. It seems, moreover, that Anderson had read beyond "Miss Thompson" in *The Trembling of a Leaf*, because there are echoes of the protagonist of "The Fall of Edward Barnard" in Horn. Like Barnard, Horn has left Chicago to settle in the South Pacific; both men have rejected American materialism and pressures to conform. Barnard spends much of his time reading; Anderson gives us a bibulous storekeeper who not only reads but also walks around quoting Nietzsche's *Thus Spake Zarathustra*.

Though *Rain* ends much the same as Swanson's *Miss Thompson*, with Sadie leaving for Australia with O'Hara, Anderson made a number of minor adjustments along the way. Instead of the pointed signal of Davidson's repressed sexuality in his "mountains of Nebraska" dream, Dr. Macphail reports only that the reformer has been having "uneasy dreams." On the other hand, viewers are put on the alert early when, on their first meeting, Sadie and Davidson exchange a long, intense gaze, and she exclaims, "He just gave me the filthiest look." And Davidson's fall is made more explicit when, in our last view of him, he tells Sadie that she is "a Daughter of the King . . . radiant . . . beautiful," and a closeup reveals his face beginning to contort. In the final scene, when Sadie has returned to being the hardened woman of the street, the truth of Davidson's nature is driven home when she says sarcastically, "I'm radiant, beautiful, apparently." Her abbreviated reference, "You men, pigs!" is hardly necessary after that, and Crawford delivers it almost casually.

Rain repeats the implausible magnanimity of the conclusion of *Miss Thompson* with Mrs. Davidson's offer of forgiveness and Sadie's response that she is "sorry for everyone in the world." Anderson's script, however, goes beyond this when, on learning of Davidson's suicide, she says, "Then I can forgive him." Does anybody really believe that this would be the response of a woman who had been raped by the man only a few hours earlier? Certainly not Somerset Maugham.

With such an excellent cast, an Oscar-winning director, and an acclaimed screenwriter, *Rain* should have been a success, and viewed today it stands up well in several ways. On its release, however, it quickly became seen as a failure: the box office returns were disappointing, and reviews were lukewarm or damning. The heads of United Artists were unhappy and for some years believed that Crawford's career had been damaged, and so did she. In part the lack of success of *Rain* is a classic case of being measured against a bar set too high, a standard built on exaggerated expectations.

For decades afterward, Crawford blamed herself for the failure of *Rain*. She was, she claimed, "simply awful [in an] unpardonably bad performance. . . . I was wrong every scene of the way."[29] "I did it badly," she said, "I know it. I would have given anything to recall it. What was the matter with me? Why had I gone so wrong?"[30] Film reviewers, who had seen Sadie as the plum role of the season, agreed with Crawford: "*Rain*, intended to climax her claim for supremacy, drifted into mere drizzle. No one was more amazed at the weak appeal of Pago Pago passion than Joan herself. And she was mortified."[31]

Crawford, however, had to confront more than simply the expectations of a talented production team: she was haunted, she said, by the two ghosts of Sadie Thompson. The third actress to take on the role in less than a decade, she had the nearly impossible task of following the legendary performance of Eagels and the acclaimed one of Swanson. As her actor friend William Haines said of her playing Sadie, you "couldn't find a sharper razor to cut your throat with." And early in filming, a member of the cast, Walter Catlett, cautioned her: "Listen, fish-cake, when Jeanne Eagels died, *Rain* died with her."[32] These warnings were confirmed by the comments of many reviewers and of some fans like Jacqueline Laurence, writing in to *Picture Play Magazine*: "To put this girl in a part made immortal by the genius of the late Miss Eagels is something of a sacrilege. Miss Eagels was a genius. Miss Crawford is not."[33]

For many of Crawford's fans, unable to separate the actress from the role, the part of a woman of the streets was demeaning and repulsive. Some took to writing vicious letters to movie magazines, often attacking her appearance: her large eyes, her prominent eyebrows, and her large mouth. This reaction was exacerbated by her costume and makeup in the early scenes, exaggerated to ensure that viewers would have no doubt about Sadie's profession. Abel Green, in *Variety*, wrote that "Joan Crawford's get-up as the light lady is extremely bizarre. Pavement pounders don't quite trick themselves up as fantastically as all that."[34]

If there is a flaw in Crawford's performance, it is the near caricature of the gaudy costuming and the overdone tough talking of the opening scenes. However, the excessiveness in this portrayal serves to give greater impact to the later scenes, when Sadie, under the relentless moralizing of Davidson, decides to change her life. In plain clothes, without the extravagant makeup, and with a subdued earnestness, Crawford is beautiful and convincing, her face almost luminescent in the lighting. This follows a powerful scene where she verbally attacks Davidson for his rigid, unforgiving, and unyielding moral righteousness. As Sadie spits out her contempt, the reformer is unmoved, repeating the Lord's Prayer over and over until, beaten down and kneeling below him on the stairs, she too begins to join his invocation.

Crawford effectively portrays this surrender and in the subsequent scenes, as in Swanson's film, the viewer is convinced that she has truly changed. And she is equally persuasive as the Sadie who reverts to her original hard-boiled persona, proving the inaccuracy of Abel Green's comment that "the dramatic significance of it all is beyond her range."[35] It is a performance that has drawn the admiration of more recent critics such as Molly Haskell, who wrote that "her performance in *Rain* is one of her loveliest and most appealing. . . . Her twisted relationship with the zealous reformer played by Walter Huston—her spiritual conversion, his guilty surrender to the lust against which his whole life's work has been a fortress—is one of those heady, erotic encounters that only the pre-code thirties could produce."[36]

If there is a significant weakness in *Rain*, it is not Crawford but Walter Huston. Where Barrymore's Davidson seemed driven by true religious zeal, Huston's is merely pompous and wooden, like a petty power-loving bureaucrat with a stubborn sense of propriety. In the words of Mordaunt Hall, "He walks as if he had spent years as a private in the Prussian Army,"[37] and for Norbert Lusk he "discards the sable of the cleric to wear the string tie of the reformer whose only creed is meddlesomeness. Something of the force of his encounter with Sadie Thompson is lost thereby, Mr. Huston managing to seem argumentative rather than zealous."[38]

The most damning evidence of the problems in Huston's performance were the responses of the filmgoers. According to Hall, the dramatic effect on New York audiences of the discovery of the reformer's body was nullified, and "the lines, coupled with the way in which Mr. Huston speaks them, so weakened several sequences that many in the crowded theater giggled and laughed when they should have been held in silence."[39] Abel Green, reporting for *Variety* and corroborating Hall's description of the audience response, noted that the seriousness of the story had been damaged. That "they laughed in the wrong spots at this and other points tells the story."[40] British viewers were no different when *Rain* was screened a month later at a London trade show.

Green's censure of Huston's lines and his delivery of them were part of a broader criticism; perhaps nostalgic for the silent era, he found *Rain* "all too talky."[41] For its director, Milestone, the talk may have been of the wrong sort. Trying to account for the disappointing attendances, he suggested that by 1932 stock theater productions of the stage version across the country had made people familiar with the sensational lines and, already aware of the plot, they were not interested in seeing a euphemistic version on the screen. It may have been that audiences in the American hinterland were more sophisticated than the Hays Office and the studio heads were able to recognize.

Crawford's *Rain* may have been seen as a failure in 1932, but interest in Sadie Thompson continued for decades. For several years after the film's launch, Hollywood studio heads frequenting the Coconut Grove nightclub were confronted by a stream of aspiring young actresses dressed up and made up as Crawford had portrayed her. Broadway still wanted Sadie and in 1935 Bankhead finally got her chance to play her on stage. Eleven years later, Vernon Duke, Howard Dietz, and Rouben Mamoulian turned it into a musical, complete with ballet interludes, for Ethel Merman. When Merman withdrew after a week and a half of rehearsals, claiming that the lyrics didn't suit her style of singing, June Havoc took over, but the production was panned by the critics and folded after only sixty performances.

Havoc's Sadie was able to call Davidson a "psalm-singing son of a bitch" and deliver other lines expunged from the film versions. For television and radio, however, Maugham's story remained problematic. As late as 1948, a BBC radio producer warned that *Rain* was "a rather ticklish (moral) job,"[42] and in CBS Television's "Somerset Maugham TV Theatre"—comprising forty-seven episodes in 1950–51—*Rain* was conspicuously absent. In 1970 the BBC did televise *Rain* as part of a twenty-six episode, two-season run of Maugham stories, none of which, unfortunately, have been preserved. Sadie was played by Carroll Baker, famous for her erotic performance in *Baby Doll*, and Michael Bryant portrayed Davidson. Baker called it "a part I'd have gone to Timbuctoo to do."[43]

Hollywood had never lost interest in putting Sadie back on the big screen, and in 1940, when May Pickford owned the rights to *Rain*, she was approached by three studios. RKO wanted the story for Ginger Rogers, MGM had Ann Sothern in mind, and Warner Bros. saw it as a vehicle for Bette Davis, but none of these projects came to fruition. Sadie Thompson did appear in two more feature films, but neither approached the quality of *Miss Thompson* or *Rain*. *Dirty Gertie from Harlem USA* was a "race" picture, comprising an all–African American cast and made to be shown on the race movie circuit. Directed by Spencer Williams, one of the few noted African American film directors of the 1940s, its Sadie was played by Francine Everett, called by many the most beautiful woman in Harlem but whose film career was brief. Done on a shoestring budget, the sets are unremarkable and the acting is frequently amateurish.

Maugham was not credited with providing the story for *Dirty Gertie from Harlem*—it was claimed to have been an original tale written by the ironically named True T. Thompson—but the plot is essentially an adaptation of "Miss Thompson." Gertie LaRue is not a prostitute but a stripper from Harlem who flees to a Caribbean island to escape from Al, a sugar daddy whom she has wronged. On "Rinidad" she is hired to do a strip performance at a nightclub, but a missionary, called "Jonathan Christian," staying at the same hotel, is offended and tries to reform her. When this fails—she calls him a "dirty Psalm-singing polecat, you want me like all the rest"—he stops the show by attacking her onstage. Returning to her room late at night, she is surprised by Al, who kills her with a pistol. If there is a central theme to this version of Maugham's tale, it is buried in such additions as Al and a fortune-telling woman astonishingly played by Williams (with mustache) himself.

Miss Sadie Thompson, produced by Jerry Wald for Columbia Pictures in 1953, went back to adhering more closely to the plot of *Rain*, but it is the most watered-down of all the film versions. A semi-musical filmed in Technicolor and in 3-D, its tone is inconsistent, alternating between being a colorful rollicking tale of post–World War II goings on in the South Pacific and Maugham's darker story of religious hypocrisy and repressed sexuality. Rita Hayworth's Sadie is portrayed as a free-spirited party girl, a singer-dancer rather than the prostitute whom Davidson appears to imagine that she is. A seemingly misunderstood gal with a heart of gold, she is shown playing with one group of local children and singing—a ditty better suited to Mr. Davidson, "Hear No Evil, See No Evil"—with another, as if she has stepped out of *The King and I* or *The Sound of Music*.

Davidson has even fewer trappings of religion than in the earlier films, here deriving his power from heading the board of directors of the island hospital. Gone is the whiff of fire and brimstone from the earlier portrayals, as Davidson's quarrel is now with modern psychoanalysis—"men of science like Freud and Adler and Jung," he complains, "are destroying moral values by denying individual responsibility." Ironically, his incantation of the Lord's Prayer to a subdued Sadie is done not with the power of Huston's but in the soothing tone of a therapist. Indeed, Jose Ferrer's performance is so low-keyed and expressionless that there is little suggestion that anything at all is going on in Davidson's mind except for an irritation with a noisy party in Sadie's room. Only in his final moments, when his assault of her is shown more directly than in the earlier films, does he convey much emotion, and here it seems too sudden, more surprising than revelatory.

Miss Sadie Thompson ends much as did the earlier versions, with Davidson's suicide and Sadie's reversion to her previous high-spirited self. Her dramatic comment on the nature of the human male is toned down to "You men, you're all alike. You pigs." Despite this cynicism, she accepts O'Hara's proposal that they meet in Australia, a development all the more surprising since, in a new addition to the story, he had firmly rejected her in a fit of moral outrage when he learned that she might have worked at a notorious nightclub in Honolulu. Forgiven and revitalized, she ends the film escorted to her ship by a pair of marines, the unsinkable Sadie Thompson.

In 1950 on arriving in New York on the Queen Mary, Maugham declared that Jeanne Eagels's portrayal was the best of the Sadie Thompsons; no other actress, he said, came close to her performance. Gloria Swanson described Eagels as "a great actress in a great role that suits her perfectly," and nobody following her was able to match that high standard. Worth considering, though, is a version of *Rain* that was never made, one that would have matched the most recognizable and iconic sex symbol of the twentieth century with the role of one of the century's most memorable female characters.

In 1956, three years after *Miss Sadie Thompson*, the *Ottawa Citizen* newspaper informed its readers that Marilyn Monroe had beaten out Linda Darnell for the role of Sadie in a television production in the spring. That did not happen, but in 1961, the television producer Ann Marlowe told the *New York Times* that she had been negotiating with Monroe: "I started to work on the idea of 'Rain' and Marilyn Monroe a year ago," she said. "Although her agents had never been able to get her to do television, I talked to her about it and she said she was interested but would have to wait until she had finished a picture and came back to New York. When she returned from the coast, we started working on it and now the lawyers are drawing up contracts."[44] Marlowe added that she hoped to get Frederic March to play Davidson and his wife, Florence Eldridge, to portray Mrs. Davidson, but March said that they would have to see a script before joining the production. Several respected authors—notably Rod Serling and Paddy Chayefsky—were mentioned as screenwriters. The project had the approval of Maugham himself, judging by a gracious note he sent Monroe in January 1961: "I am so glad to hear that you are going to play Sadie in the TV production of 'Rain.' I am sure you will be splendid. I wish you the best of luck."[45]

Despite the flurry of publicity sparked by Marlowe's announcement, negotiations with Monroe had been lengthy and not smooth. On June 10, 1960, Marlowe had telegraphed the actress to say that "before I make final arrangements with another star I would like to again offer you 'Rain' for television spectacular. Lee Strasberg told me you were a superb Sadie Thompson. I have excellent sponsor. Taping depends on your availability. Please wire me 1160 Park Avenue, New York." Monroe read the telegram and then scrawled a note at the bottom: "I would only consider it if Lee Strasberg directed it."[46]

It may be that this demand is what killed the production since some people believe that NBC would not accept Strasberg, or it may be that Monroe's Sadie was sabotaged by her growing mental and physical deterioration that led to her death only two years later. Did the world lose a great performance? Who knows? Monroe's difficult childhood in various foster homes and her career as a sex object might have given her a special insight into Sadie Thompson's situation. But though she was a skilled actress, her talents seemed to lie in comedy rather than serious subjects. She might have been a laughable Sadie, and *Rain* is anything but a comedy.

CHAPTER 3

Eagels and Davis
Evil behind the Smile

Like *Miss Thompson* and *Rain*, the film versions of *The Letter* had their origin in a Maugham short story that then became a highly praised stage hit. And like "Miss Thompson," the story had been inspired by a real-life event, in this case a murder trial in Kuala Lumpur that became a sensation throughout the British Southeast Asian colonies. In 1911 Ethel Proudlock, the English wife of a schoolmaster, killed her lover, the manager of a tin mine, and was sentenced to hang for murder. After receiving a petition signed by her friends and many sympathizers, the Sultan of Selangor pardoned her, and she returned to England and then to North America.

Ten years after the trial, Maugham was traveling through Southeast Asia and heard an account of it from Proudlock's lawyer. From the bare bones of the incident, he fashioned a short story, "The Letter," which was published in *Hearst's International* magazine in 1924 and reprinted in a collection, *The Casuarina Tree*, in 1926. It begins with Robert Crosbie, a big, good-natured rubber planter enlisting the service of a Singapore lawyer named Howard Joyce on behalf of his wife, Leslie. She is standing trial for murdering a friend, Geoffrey Hammond, having shot him on the verandah of their home. Robert was away that night and Hammond, Leslie said, had come around and tried to rape her; she was only defending herself. Joyce, a shrewd, experienced lawyer is concerned by one detail: Leslie had fired all six bullets of her revolver into him. Still, the woman he sees before him is delicate, fragile even, and graceful, "a quiet, pleasant, unassuming woman. . . . She was the last woman in the world to commit murder."[1]

Leslie's testimony throughout the trial has been calm, careful, and consistent, and she is likely to be acquitted in an English-controlled court. Joyce, however, soon discovers a complication that is pure Maugham invention:

a damning letter that she had written Hammond imploring him to come to her on that fateful evening. It is in possession of Hammond's Chinese mistress, and the unsuspecting Robert borrows funds so that it can be bought and destroyed. This is done, Leslie is cleared of the charge, and then in the quiet calm of the Joyce household, she reveals to her attorney and to the reader of the story the real person behind the proper English woman. Hammond had been her lover for years but when he was about to leave her for his Chinese mistress, she killed him in a rage. In exposing her real self, she stuns Joyce, her face "no longer human" but "a gibbering hideous mask." The real shock, though, comes with her response to Mrs. Joyce's hospitable summons: "Mrs. Crosbie's features gradually composed themselves. Those passions, so clearly delineated, were smoothed away as with your hand you would smooth a crumpled paper, and in a minute the face was cool and calm and unlined. She was a trifle pale, but her lips broke into a pleasant, affable smile. She was once more the well-bred and even distinguished woman. 'I'm coming, Dorothy dear. I'm sorry to give you so much trouble.'"[2]

"The Letter" is a brilliantly constructed story, among the best written in English in the twentieth century. Maugham keeps the reader in doubt about Leslie's true nature until the last page, and her final comment, dripping with irony, is as shocking as Sadie's at the end of "Miss Thompson." It conveys one of Maugham's most recurrent themes: that people are mixtures of good and bad, and that a genteel and civilized facade can often hide a flawed and violent personality. Furthermore, like so many of his colonial tales, "The Letter" is a revelation of the underside of British imperialism, the success of which was largely built on the illusion that English culture and social behavior were superior to those of the colonized peoples. In V. S. Pritchett's words, "Maugham succeeds [Kipling] as the debunker of the white man's burden which usually turns out to be his wife's adultery. Maugham is Kipling turned inside out."[3] Leslie's actions are all the more shocking because they are played out against that imperial facade: a social structure and legal system controlled by the British and a deeply ingrained and pervasive racist attitude to the Asian population. Much of her rage at Hammond boils up not simply because he no longer wants her; she is disgusted because he prefers his Chinese mistress.

Maugham was aware of the dramatic appeal of "The Letter," and when no film studio was interested, he turned it into a play in 1927 that was hugely successful on both sides of the Atlantic. Gladys Cooper played the lead for 338 performances in London, and a production with Katharine Cornell ran for 104 nights in New York before going on tour. As it had with *Rain*, the stage success of *The Letter* made it a hot property. Maugham's original asking price of $5,000 for the film rights following the publication of each story had attracted no interest; but Jeanne Eagels had pushed the price of *Rain* up to $60,000, and Paramount then paid $30,000 for *The Letter*.

Eagels should have had the opportunity to repeat her performance of Sadie Thompson in the screen version of *Rain*, but Swanson, with her own production company, was able to buy the rights for herself. Eagels, though, got a part almost as coveted by actresses, that of Leslie Crosbie, in the 1929 film version of *The Letter*, and she made it her own. With her was a cast more experienced on the stage than on the screen, but it was capable: the Australian O. P. Heggie as the lawyer, Mr. Joyce, veteran English actor Reginald Owen as Robert Crosbie, and Herbert Marshall as Geoffrey Hammond. Marshall had appeared on stages on both sides of the Atlantic for a decade, and *The Letter* was his first American film; it was also the first of five roles in films based on Maugham works.

Produced by Monta Bell and directed by Jean de Limur, *The Letter* was made to exploit the reputation and genius of its leading lady, and it succeeded. Eagels's performance earned almost universally glowing reviews: "a magnificent piece of work" (*New York Daily News*);[4] "one of the most gorgeous portrayals ever caught upon the silver sheet" (*New York American*);[5] "a splendid performance" (*Variety*).[6] *Picture Play* proclaimed that "from now on every appearance of Jeanne Eagels on the screen will be a major event, no matter how many stars spring up to compete with her. For who will forget her in 'The Letter' and the history she made with eloquence such as the screen had never given us before?"[7] Eagels's performance earned a nomination for an Academy Award, but sadly, she died a few months after the release of *The Letter* and so she became the first person to be considered for an Oscar posthumously (she lost to Mary Pickford).

Eagels's performance is in fact uneven, with scenes in which she is very much the stage actress who has not yet learned how to tone down her gestures for the more intimate medium of film. Sound movies were in their infancy—*The Letter* was only Paramount's second foray into sound—and actors were still adapting to the revolutionary change. With the exception of Marshall, who played Hammond with unaffected ease, the cast performed as if they were still on stage, but in a number of places Eagels demonstrated that she could be a great film actress. One such scene is when Joyce tells her about the letter, and she reacts with a range of shifting emotions from defiance, surprise, fear, panic, and resignation. An even finer one is a sustained shot of her testifying in court, the effect of which led film critic Andrew Sarris to rate it as one of the great pieces of film acting:

> Where Eagels attains her epiphany of emotion is in the trial scene in which she gives testimony to her defense attorney played by O. P. Heggie. Here de Limur holds down the reaction shots so as to give Eagels sufficiently long to establish an intense lyricism in elaborate lying. With Eagels we know all before she opens her mouth on the witness stand, but she nonetheless succeeds in leaving our mouths open with a passionate duplicity that verges on sociological schizophrenia. Indeed, she leaves us suspended helplessly in that ironic limbo between the inferno of her private passions and the paradise of her public protestations. And, irony of ironies, it is when she is reciting the litany of nice girl fending off the male predator that she becomes most lascivious to all the patriarchal types on the bench and the jury box. It is here the actress first and foremost taking off on her own into those indeterminate realms where a very marginal art is enriched by a very powerful myth. This one sequence alone constitutes one of the greatest passages in the history of screen acting.[8]

To focus more attention on Leslie and to make her more sympathetic, screenwriter Garrett Fort made substantial changes to Maugham's story, revisions that significantly change its meaning. Most immediately obvious is that any mystery about Leslie's relationship with Hammond is removed at the beginning by the viewer being shown their argument, Hammond's attempt to break things off with her, and her impassioned shooting of him. For this opening scene, Fort used material from Maugham's stage adaptation, published in book form in 1925. In an appendix to that volume, the author explained that, to avoid having Leslie give a second lengthy narration of the shooting, he wrote an alternate ending that was used in the London production: a flashback in which we see the argument and the shooting. This scene, intended to end the play, became the action that begins the film.

With the circumstances of Leslie's liaison with Hammond made clear at the beginning, the film's emphasis shifts from a revelation of the shocking truth of her real nature to an exploration of what drew her to an affair she wanted desperately to maintain. Her plight is suggested even in the opening scene, where she is idly doing lacework and knitting while her husband is examining his guns. While he claims to be grateful that she has come out to a rubber plantation, where there is little social life and few interesting planters' wives, he seems unable to take any real interest in her or offer any real intimacy. Answering her desperate summons, Hammond, played as a smooth but shallow cad by Marshall, devastates her with the announcement that he wants out of the affair. Equally as—or perhaps even more—wounding is his admission that he prefers his Chinese mistress to her.

Hammond's Chinese lover is much more prominent in the film than in the original story, serving both as a rival for Leslie and an embodiment of the Asia that the British despise and find incomprehensible. On the page she is only ever referred to as the "Chinese mistress" and seen just briefly when she accepts payment for the letter. In the film she is given a name, "Li-Ti," and she plays a significant part in a number of scenes: embracing Hammond when he is called away by Leslie's note, observing Leslie's trial and acquittal, and most dramatically, confronting Leslie herself. In Maugham's tale, the two women never meet, but the film treats them as antagonists, both humiliated by Hammond's behavior and each contemptuous of the other, and it brings them together in a dramatic confrontation. Instead of the payment being made by Joyce and Robert, the film has Li-Ti insist that it be delivered by Leslie in circumstances as humiliating as possible for her.

Where Maugham's story had the exchange being made in a room above a shop, Eagels's Leslie has to meet on the mistress's turf, a shadowy basement opium den/nightclub/brothel. In a scene worthy of the best film noir, she is shown fearfully descending a long, dark stairway, as if she were entering an infernal underworld. Almost every manner of depravity is available below, including Indian snake charmers who stage a fight between a mongoose and cobra (this is, astonishingly, represented by crudely inserted footage from the 1928 documentary *Killing the Killer*, a borrowing that drew laughs from viewers who immediately recognized the source). Li-Ti, it turns out, is a madam, and she relishes the chance to have one of her customers, having rejected the young women on display in a bamboo cage, look over Leslie with a lascivious leer.

Maugham's writings are full of descriptions of racist attitudes among the British colonial officials, but Eagels's *The Letter* goes far beyond his depictions. This is most pronounced in the portrayal of the Chinese mistress, whom Maugham describes as "stoutish," with "a broad phlegmatic face," "wearing a pale blue jacket and a white skirt," a "costume not quite European nor quite Chinese."[9] Lady Tsen Mei, who played Li-Ti, could easily have depicted her as a biracial woman, being herself born in Philadelphia to a Chinese father and a White mother and identified as white in a 1910 census. As a young woman, Josephine Moy adopted the name Lady Tsen Mei, claimed she was born in Canton, China, and achieved some fame performing as a Chinese woman on the vaudeville circuit.

It was this exaggerated show business impersonation—one could call it a caricature—of an Asian that Lady Tsen Mei brought to *The Letter*. Throughout the film, she is dressed in elaborate Chinese costume, heavily bejeweled, equally heavily made up, with her hair pulled tight in an Asian fashion and her lips painted in a rosebud shape. She is presented in this guise in the opening episode with Hammond, in the courtroom scenes where she stands out from the moderately dressed crowd like a performer who has wandered in from a stage show, and of course in the confrontation with Leslie in the brothel. In all these scenes Li-Ti is anything but phlegmatic, reacting to events with a smirk and a shifting of her eyes from side to side to convey a devious, calculating—and by implication, Asian—sensibility.

This presentation of a "crafty" Chinese mind is repeated in Li-Ti's accomplice, Joyce's clerk, Ong Chi Seng, played by a Japanese American actor Tamaki Yoshiwara. In a strange scene, Chi Seng discusses the letter and the money demanded for it, all the while standing not in front of his employer's desk but beside it, stealing sidelong glances rather than making direct eye contact. The effect is that of an illicit transaction being conducted surreptitiously, an illegal act being initiated by the Chinese and entered into only reluctantly by the upstanding British lawyer. Maugham describes the clerk's attitude as respectful but with a hint of mockery, but Yoshiwara positively smirks when he knows he has the upper hand over the English. When Chi Seng leaves to arrange the exchange of letter and money, Joyce stares ahead and mutters, "Damned clever, these Chinese." For "clever" the viewer is meant to read "devious," "wily," and "cunning."

The tension between the British colonial society and the local Chinese population, always simmering beneath the surface, explodes in the climactic

meeting between Leslie and Li-Ti. The English community had been re-
pulsed by Hammond's living with a Chinese woman, and Li-Ti knows that
this has given Leslie a great deal of public sympathy. She is also aware that
the English woman is viscerally revolted by the idea of sharing her lover with
someone she considers racially inferior. Thus, in their final confrontation,
Li-Ti gleefully reminds Leslie that she had to share her man with a Chinese
woman, and she deliberately drops the letter on the floor. As Leslie kneels
to retrieve it, Li-Ti triumphantly points and declares, "White woman at
Chinese woman's feet," to the derisive laughter of her group of prostitutes.

Li-Ti has her moment of exultation but, with the suppression of the
letter, Leslie is quickly exonerated by the court. In Maugham's story, she is
able to return to being a sociable, respected member of the British colonial
community, her life troubled only by Robert's knowledge of her infidelity.
The reader can only infer what direction her life will take in the future,
but she has got away with murder. Eagels's film, though, substantially alters
the ending, eliminating Maugham's point that people can betray others
and commit brutal murders yet calmly go on with a seemingly decent and
respectable life. It ends, not with Leslie's confession to Joyce but with an
explosive confrontation with her husband. Maugham's Robert is an open,
frank, and gentle man, quiet with no fierceness, and very much in love with
Leslie. His reaction to learning of her infidelity is to leave her at the Joyces'
house while he returns to the plantation, presumably to absorb the news.
Reginald Owen, however, plays him as a heavy-handed, angry, wronged
husband out of a poor Victorian melodrama. With fist clenched and face
twisted in a grimace, he demands to know what the letter means, as if he
does not already know, and splutters at Leslie that "I gave you my name"
and "I worked and slaved for you." She replies that all she wanted was love,
and that, while all Robert ever talked of was "rubber, rubber, rubber,"
Hammond spoke to her of love, romance, and music.

The effect of this transformation of Robert is to make Leslie a much
more sympathetic figure than she is in the story. But, unlike Maugham's
Leslie, this one is going to pay for both the infidelity and the murder. She
hopes that Robert will send her back to England, but he sneers that they
have no money and that her punishment will be having to "stay right here
with your memories." Hurt by Robert's attack, Leslie replies with her own
wounding verbal assault, culminating in a line that never appeared in the

published story but that Maugham used to end the stage adaptation. The film closes with her deeply felt exclamation, "With all my heart and all my soul, I still love the man I killed!" In the play, though, the line is spoken to Joyce, while Eagels says it twice, the first time in anger as a lacerating spear directed at Robert's pride. Having fired this wounding shot at him, she falls back to considering her own future, and when she repeats the comment, Eagels's facial expressions subtly suggest that, if the sentiment is true, she will be the one to feel its pain for the rest of her life.

Few films end with such a powerful and indelible final line. Years later movie producer Walter Wanger said that "Somerset Maugham's *The Letter* was a tremendous innovation because of the last line. . . . Pretty strong stuff for those days."[10] Film critics in 1929 immediately recognized its originality, agreeing with playwright Robert Sherwood that "it is more than a milestone in motion picture history. It is the herald of a new order."[11] The *New York Morning Telegraph* declared that "it marks a new epoch in the talking screen."[12] For Norbert Lusk, "talking pictures are vindicated and justified as never before. . . . To miss it is to ignore a milestone in the progress of the new art, for surely the history of audible films must ever give a glowing chapter to this."

Lusk maintained that *The Letter* was not "a sweet fairytale" but a "civilized" picture, and "civilized" is how movie house managers advertised it across America. It signified that a film might not end happily, that it might be dark, unsettling, and challenging of an audience's comfortable assumptions. Spoken dialogue now allowed films to explore complicated social and psychological issues and, as in life, the resolution of the problems might not always be happy. *The Letter* had such an ending, but for Lusk it heralded a bright future for talking films: "According to movie conventions this is a darkly unhappy ending, but it is a bright augury of the future of the talkies. For if at this early stage of their development they can flout convention and dare to be courageous, then it means the coming of age of the movies."[13]

The Letter rather daringly challenged the assumed tastes of the viewing public, but it also flew in the face of the guidelines of the Hays Office. One of its prohibitions was "willful offense to any nation, race or creed," and the film emphatically portrayed the Chinese as devious, conniving, and immoral. The hatred of Leslie and Li-Ti for each other, so central to the story, seemed to be grounded more on racial aversion and disgust than on sexual jealousy. That such racism escaped the prohibition of the Hays Office can be attributed only to its being merely an advisory body in 1929. It seems, however, that the film's Sinophobia as well as its portrayal of British colonial decadence led to its being banned in the United Kingdom and throughout the British Commonwealth. In April 1938, Joseph Breen, director of the Production Code Administration (the Hays Office), told Jack Warner that *The Letter* had been "rejected, in toto, in England, in Canada, and in Australia, and the company had much difficulty in securing permission to exhibit it in a number of foreign countries. The British objection seems to hinge upon the characterization of the several British people, engaged in an illicit sex relationship, and, more importantly, in the suggestion that Hammond, the murdered man, maintained a China woman as his mistress. We have no reason to believe that the official attitude throughout the British Empire will be any different now than it was in 1929 and 1930."[14]

Breen's letter was a shot across the bow of Warner Bros.'s plan to make a new version of *The Letter*, which had been a desirable property for several studios. Paramount owned the rights to the story at the beginning of 1938, and the distinguished screenwriter C. Gardner Sullivan was preparing an adaptation for a film to be produced by William LeBaron. The project stalled, however, and by August, there were rumors that Selznick International was interested in *The Letter* for the English director Robert Stevenson. By December, however, Paramount traded it to Warner Bros. for the rights to Harold Bell Wright's *Shepherd of the Hills*.

Any studio wanting to make a new version of *The Letter* had to face the heavy artillery possessed by Breen. While the Hays Office had exerted a strong inhibiting influence on American filmmaking, it never had the power to force studios to adhere to its guidelines, and many films, Swanson's *Sadie Thompson* and Eagels's *The Letter* among them, slipped by its rules. In 1934, however, in response to the creation of the Catholic Legion of Decency, whose power across the United States frightened the studios, the Hays Office established the Production Code Administration (PCA) to enforce the new Production Code it had adopted in 1930. At its head was Breen, a Catholic zealot who declared that Hollywood, "the pest hole that infects the entire country with its obscene and lascivious moving pictures must be cleaned and disinfected."[15] Beginning on July 1, 1934, the new Production Code was enforced by draconian practices not seen before, and there was not, as there had been with Hays, much room for studios to negotiate. All screenplays had to be submitted to the PCA, excisions could be demanded before production was allowed, and completed films frequently had large and small segments deleted. Only when a studio had satisfied the requirements of the PCA and secured its Seal of Approval could its film be shown in an American theater. The effect of this new control of film production was immediate and obvious. The sound films of what is now known as the Pre-Code Era, from 1929 to 1934, dealt with all manner of sensational subjects: sexuality, drug usage, prostitution, infidelity, abortion, violence, homosexuality, heroic gangsters, strong and independent women, women's issues, and miscegenation. After 1934, these elements vanished from movie screens or appeared only by implication or as suggestions.

Breen's 1938 rejection of the Warner Bros. proposal for *The Letter* was not based on a submitted screenplay but only on Maugham's dramatization and a memory of the Eagels film. As we read the play, he wrote:

> This is the story of a wife, who murders her lover, but who, by lying, deceit, perjury, and the purchase of an incriminating letter, defeats justice, and gets off "scot free." In the development of this story we have the murder of the lover; all the sordid details of the illicit sex relationship between the married woman and her lover; and very pointed and very numerous references to the second mistress of the murdered man, who is characterized as a Chinese woman. . . . Because of all this, we could not, of course, approve a motion picture based upon this story.[16]

Despite this firm rejection, Warner Bros. were determined to make *The Letter*, thinking that director Edmund Goulding could devise a way to get Breen's approval. On December 20, 1939, however, screenwriter Robert Lord wrote the producer, Hal Wallis, to report that Goulding's ideas were "a trifle radical," and so he had agreed that Lord should try to write an acceptable screenplay. Lord respected Maugham's play very much, and he thought that he could write a script that would remain faithful to it while satisfying Breen. "In my opinion," he said, "if we can follow the play very closely and manage to get by the censors, we will have one of the most powerful and different motion pictures ever made."[17]

Lord, together with Howard Koch, who became the credited screenwriter, did indeed succeed in creating a script that allowed the production to go ahead in 1940. Responding to Breen's letter as they would to a senior editor's challenges to a manuscript, they dealt with each of the objections. In the murder scene, which, as in Maugham's story and play takes place at the beginning, Hammond is barely visible, the focus being almost entirely on Leslie firing the gun. Their illicit affair is described, but without "sordid details," and the Chinese mistress is given respectability by being made Hammond's wife and biracial rather than Chinese. Most important, though Leslie is exonerated in court, she does not go "scot free": in the final scene she steps out into the moonlit garden and is stabbed to death by Hammond's widow.

The screenwriters, in collaboration with the director, William Wyler, did much more than simply adapt the script to meet Breen's objections; they made some judicious additions to the story, making their film thirty minutes longer than the earlier version. The final scene in the garden accounts for some of the added footage, but most of it resulted from the expanded roles given Leslie's husband, Robert, and her lawyer, Howard Joyce. In both cases, their developed characters remain faithful to Maugham's story, and in fact enrich it. On the page, they are typical short story supporting characters represented almost as stock characters in a few lines: the faithful but unperceptive husband and the cool, imperturbable lawyer. In this screen version, they are each revealed to have depths of suffering and complex emotional states, and acted superbly, they provide a balance to the intensity of the focus on Leslie.

Warner Bros. considered George Brent and Raymond Massey for the role of Robert but finally settled on Herbert Marshall, who had played the part of Hammond in the 1929 production of *The Letter*. While he was effective as the caddish lover, his screen persona—and, indeed, his real-life personality—made him much better suited for the sympathetic part of Robert. When Gloria Swanson met him in 1934, she said he was "a handsome man in his early forties with a gentle face and soft brown eyes," and he had "one of the most perfect musical voices I had ever heard. . . . Beside him all the other cultivated men I had ever known seemed just a bit coarse."[18] When transferred to the screen, these features made Marshall one of the best-known romantic leading men of the 1930s, popular with audiences and sought after as a co-star by numerous actresses. Norma Shearer described first seeing him in a romantic scene on the screen: "I thought I had never seen a lady so thoroughly and convincingly loved. He is both manly and wistful. He wins the sympathy of women because his face expresses tenderness and silent suffering."[19]

The English critic C. A. Lejeune described Marshall's frequent screen roles as "a man who was always taking his coat off in the hall while his wife was concluding her big scene with the lover in the parlor." Graham Greene was less kind, referring to Marshall's "characteristic act. dumb suffering."[20] But in *The Letter*, the tenderness and silent suffering, and one might add the integrity and trusting nature that Marshall so effectively projected, were the perfect qualities for Robert Crosbie. Brent had turned down the role in the belief that it would not give him a chance to act, but Marshall excelled in a number of scenes that take Robert beyond the briefly sketched character of Maugham's story. The effect, suggests Michael Anderegg, is to make him more sympathetic and attractive than Maugham intended, thereby intensifying the cruelty of Leslie's betrayal.[21] In any case, it shifts some of the audience's attention away from the psychology of the adulterous and murderous wife to the agony of the betrayed husband.

Claudette Colbert, who played opposite Marshall in several films, said that "he has a miraculous quality of sincerity and great sympathy, . . . absolutely no artificial note."[22] This makes him the perfect yardstick by which to measure those around him in what John Thomas McGuire has characterized as a world of deception: "*The Letter* encompasses the rending of four veils of human illusion: the existence of a happy marriage between Robert and Leslie Crosby [*sic*], the reserve and impregnable self-control of Leslie, the professional probity of lawyer Howard Joyce, and most significant, the apparent moral and social superiority of the British colonists in Malaysia over the 'natives.'"[23]

The sincerity, the strong sense of authenticity, made Marshall perfectly suited to play the only major character in *The Letter* who is sincere, who is not willfully hiding behind an illusion. Hammond's widow, heavily made up in an Asian style, is often referred to as presenting a facade to the world, but then too does Leslie, superbly played by Bette Davis, coolly hiding her guilt; Joyce, whose unruffled, expressionless face disguises his professional and personal disquiet; and Ong Chi Seng, hiding his contempt for the English behind a facade of smirking obsequiousness. All these characters reflect Maugham's belief that people hide their true natures behind veneers; in their midst, Robert stands out as unguardedly being who he really is: an

honest, loving, and loyal man. He is also trusting and naive, and up to
Leslie's confession of her infidelity he sees her uncritically as a victim rather
than an adulterer and murderer. It is easy for such a character to be laughable, but Marshall portrays Robert as a sympathetic, and even admirable,
figure. And in a line worthy of Maugham, Joyce suggests that Robert's
imperception is hardly unique: "It's strange that a man can live with a
woman for ten years and not know the first thing about her."

Rushing home after learning of Hammond's death, Robert immediately
moves to comfort Leslie but does not notice that she briefly steps back
from that embrace before collecting herself and then hugging him as she
begins to fabricate her story of Hammond's assault. He is always solicitous
of her, which Marshall skillfully conveys with his eyes, putting his arms
around her, and clasping her hands. Leslie accepts his attention as if it is
her due and offers little in response. When Joyce tells her that she will be
charged with murder, she shows no sign of alarm; it is Robert who is distressed and apprehensive. After Leslie has been in custody for several weeks,
she looks as fresh and composed as she would be attending an afternoon
tea; Robert, however, living at home and deeply troubled, is unshaven and
rumpled. Joyce suggests that he collect himself, and he tells Leslie, accurately, that "he's much more anxious about you than you seem to be about
yourself." Leslie then uses this as a lever, suggesting that Joyce buy the
incriminating letter for Robert's sake not hers.

Marshall is at his finest in the scene in which Leslie, with Joyce present,
shows Robert the letter, admits her adultery, and describes Hammond's
shooting. Wyler places the focus on him as he registers shock, disbelief,
rising anger, and then a shattering collapse into tears. As he rushes out of
the room, Joyce comments, "He's going to forgive you," and Leslie replies
matter-of-factly, "Yes, he's going to forgive me." Robert does indeed reach
the point where he is prepared to look beyond his wife's behavior and
begin again with her, but this comes after seeing the end of his dream of a
plantation in Sumatra and the crushing of his illusions about her. Leaving
the party thrown for them by the Joyces, he steps into their bedroom and
looks around with a gaze that brilliantly conveys a mixture of emotions:
grief, despair, resignation, and loss. Though severely wounded, he offers
Leslie a way back, saying "If you love a person you can forgive anything."
But for Leslie there is no return to a satisfying marriage to him, and he
surrenders, a thoroughly beaten man.

As good as Marshall's performance is, James Stephenson's as Leslie's lawyer, Joyce, is even better, earning him an Oscar nomination for Best Supporting Actor. According to the *Chicago Tribune* reviewer, he "completely dominates 'The Letter.' . . . I have never seen a quieter performance. Never one that was more reticent, more completely revealing—more effective."[24] It was the high point of a career that began on British stages and took Stephenson into English films at the age of forty-eight. In 1938 Warner Bros. brought him to the United States, where he made forty films in four years, specializing in suave, urbane villains of the George Sanders sort. Wyler looked beyond this stereotype, seeing Maugham's lawyer in the tall, dapper, crisp-talking, mustachioed Englishman with a quiet authoritative manner. Stephenson responded with the performance of his career, a career sadly cut short after four more films when he died of a heart attack in July 1941.

Maugham's Joyce is a composed, precise, specialist hired to defend Leslie in court, and in doing so he calmly dissects—for Leslie and Robert and for the reader—her situation in the eyes of the law. Stephenson's performance is a triumph of minimalist acting, portraying him as a professional man who betrays little of his deepest feelings. His clothes are precise: throughout the film he wears a tropical white suit jacket, which he keeps buttoned, even when working alone at his office desk. In the opening scene, when Leslie weaves her account of Hammond's death, Joyce's equanimity stands out among her other listeners, the overwrought Robert and the naive young assistant district officer Withers. He is the one who examines Hammond's body, notices that he was shot six times, and begins to doubt Leslie's explanation. His cool composure is superbly shown in the scene when Ong Chi Seng reveals the startling and damaging news about the letter, the camera focused on Stephenson's face, on which there is only the slightest hint of disquiet. The men are engaged in a high-stakes poker match, Ong acting like the dutiful and concerned legal assistant, but nonetheless hinting at the powerful card in his hand, and Joyce revealing none of his concern. Similarly, and at greater length, Joyce works efficiently and apparently dispassionately to deconstruct what lies behind Leslie's own inexpressive public face.

Behind the professional facade, however, Joyce becomes a troubled man, shocked but fascinated by Leslie and concerned by his own breach of ethics in aiding the recovery of the letter. Both elements go beyond the original story, where Maugham writes that Joyce "had lived in the East for a long time and his sense of professional honor was not perhaps so acute as it had been twenty years before."[25] The brilliance of Stephenson's performance lies in his skill in revealing Joyce's troubling emotions without shattering the veneer of the cool and urbane lawyer. This restraint adds weight to the two occasions when Joyce does betray his inner turmoil, the first and more effective being his hurriedly ordering a second gin sling while meeting with Robert at their club. The second, and somewhat overdone, is Stephenson's stumbling over the words "truth" and "justice" in Joyce's overly hesitant summation at the trial.

The film interaction between Joyce and Leslie goes far beyond that of the strictly lawyer-client relationship of the original story, and much of this is conveyed to the viewer only by subtle hints. They are at times antagonists, the determined inquisitor trying to draw the truth out of a reluctant and guarded subject. Joyce is appalled by her adultery, dishonesty, and evasiveness, but he is also captivated by her strength of will and her skill in manipulating the people around her. It has been suggested that he feels a kind of emotional attraction to her, an idea that is given credence when he tells her that "it isn't important what I feel about you" and the camera lingers on Davis's face. It is nearly expressionless, inviting the possibility that she is thinking, "Oh, really, is that what you tell yourself?" Or at least that she has just realized that she is very much in his mind.

As much as the roles of Robert and Joyce go well beyond their parts in the original story and the 1929 film, the heart of *The Letter* is still Leslie, and Davis plays her superbly. She was, of course, well aware of Eagels's memorable portrayal, and throughout the filming she wore a ring, loaned to her by Helen Broderick, that had been on Eagels's finger throughout her performance. As much as she admired Eagels, however, Davis's Leslie is much different, and much closer to Maugham's original character: not a vulnerable woman verging on hysteria but one who, following the shooting, presents a firmly controlled front to the world. In one of the finest performances of her career, Davis deftly portrays a woman playing a part for those around her while at the same time revealing to the movie audience a calculating but tormented interior. Either through Wyler's direction or the actress's own determination, the infamous Davis mannerisms—darting of the eyes, fluttering of the hands—are largely absent. As a result, as when Joyce confronts Leslie with the existence of the letter, Davis is able to convey alarm by just the slightest glance to the side. And her loss of composure during her confrontation with the formidable Mrs. Hammond is revealed by only a slight expression of apprehension and by a widening of the eyes as her antagonist drops the letter to the floor. The effect is dramatic.

According to biographer Ed Sikov, Davis's Leslie is "a sociopath, a calculating killer and remorseless liar, ceaselessly putting on acts for those around her because authentic emotions—other than murderous rage, that is—are not part of her psychological makeup."[26] Nothing reveals the sociopath better than the close-up of her face as we first see her, emptying her revolver into the prone body of her lover and staring down with no more expression than if she were exterminating a troublesome reptile. But behind this coolness there is strong emotion, not seen but conveyed by a wracking sob heard after she has retreated to her bedroom, an anguish soon skillfully masked on the arrival of Robert and Joyce. She greets the lawyer with the social niceties Maugham had given his character and then, while languidly reclining on a sofa like a society hostess entertaining guests, contrives her account of Hammond's death. Robert and Withers are entirely persuaded—doubts begin to form in Joyce—and Leslie goes on cheerfully to cook breakfast for them all, and for most of the remainder of the film she maintains a rigidly controlled exterior. According to Pauline Kael, Davis offered "what is very likely the best study of female sexual hypocrisy in film history."[27]

Unlike that of Eagels, Davis's Leslie does not invite much sympathy or empathy. Throughout her career Davis was not afraid to play unsympathetic women, and her first widely acclaimed role had been the very unpleasant, dislikable Mildred in Maugham's *Of Human Bondage*. Her portrayal of Leslie is a faithful rendering of the author's creation, but, she said later, its severity worried the studio:

> After Wyler saw *The Letter* completed, he felt the audience would have no sympathy for its heroine. He had many scenes rewritten to give her sympathy. I was heartbroken, as I felt, after reading the rewrites, that my performance could be ruined with these additions. I asked Willie if I could see the film before doing the retakes. To my horror *I* was crying at myself at the end of the showing. There was dead silence in the projection room when the lights came up. I said, 'If we film these retakes, we will lose the intelligent audience. It is impossible to please everyone with any one film.

If we try to accomplish this, we can lose *all* audiences.' Plus, to my shame, even though *I* played the part, I deeply sympathized with Leslie Crosbie. We only made one small addition to the original film. Wyler had agreed with me. Thank God![28]

Davis disagreed with Wyler on another matter but lost that battle. In the final moments, when Robert is prepared to forgive Leslie and rebuild their marriage, she first accepts his offer and then utters the sensational line from the Eagels film: "With all my heart, I still love the man I killed." Davis could not imagine a woman saying such a cruel comment directly to her husband's face and, when Wyler insisted on it, she walked off the set. She eventually returned to follow his direction but remained convinced for the rest of her life that she was right. And she probably was, considering that Eagels spat the line to wound a bullying, mean-spirited Robert, while Marshall's loving and generous husband does not deserve such a brutal assault.

Despite their disagreements, Davis respected Wyler, writing that "*The Letter* was a magnificent picture due to Willie."[29] It may be hyperbolic to call it "magnificent," but of all the film adaptations it is the one that most enriches a Maugham story with the artistic possibilities of the medium. This is largely attributable to Wyler and his production team, which included screenwriter Howard Koch, the highly respected cinematographer Tony Gaudio, and Oscar-winning film composer Max Steiner. With three Oscars—his twelve nominations were the most in history—Wyler was the most acclaimed director ever to tackle Maugham. Under his supervision, *The Letter* showed what can be communicated by film noir—using some of the symbolic devices of German Expressionism—before that genre became so widely adopted.

Wyler's genius is immediately apparent at the beginning of *The Letter*, in a scene that he insisted filming thirty-three times and that Davis called "the finest opening shot I have ever seen in a film."[30] Following the credits, the film begins with an almost incandescent full moon illuminating and casting shadows among the rubber trees and palms of a tropical plantation. A dog lazily scrounges for scraps, and the Native "coolies," restless in the heat, try to sleep in hammocks in their open-sided palapa. An almost seamless series of shots moves among the trees and settles on a sizeable house, the home of the plantation manager; and thus with great economy the viewer is quickly immersed in the Maugham world of the British colonials. Suddenly a gunshot shatters the calm, alarming a white cockatoo into flight, and a man stumbles out onto the porch followed by a woman who shoots him five more times. As the camera rests on Leslie, she is almost expressionless, and then the scene is darkened as clouds shroud the moon. A few seconds later, the moon reappears and she turns to look at it with a look on her face that suggests that she has suddenly been exposed to her deepest core.

Koch had proposed using the moon to suggest the guilt lying behind Leslie's public facade, but it went beyond this to become a dominant motif throughout the film. At key—and always private—moments she gazes at the moon as if to connect with some deeper longing or imaginative life than she has been permitted with Robert and that is now buried in her role as wronged woman. One such scene occurs when she is about to leave for Singapore to turn herself in and her communion with the moon is interrupted by Robert; another takes place near the end when her reverie is broken by Dorothy Joyce's reminder of the party arranged for her. Most powerfully, when Leslie's confession of her enduring love for Hammond has ended her marriage and she realizes that she has no possibility of a happy future, she is drawn by the moon out into the courtyard. She knows that Hammond's widow is waiting with a dagger and, with a sigh suggesting that she welcomes her fate, she goes out, and when clouds block the moonlight, she is murdered. The film then ends as it had begun, with the clouds moving off and the light revealing Leslie's body and flooding into the house and onto her lacework.

The use of the moon enabled Wyler to present dramatic contrasts between light and dark, representing, in the manner of German Expressionism, the two sides to her personality. Shining through the slats in the shutters, the light casts stripes onto Leslie, suggesting to some critics the guilt she feels and the imprisonment that will go beyond merely that meted out by the law. Since many of the key scenes, particularly at the beginning and ending of the film, are set at night, Wyler was also able to make dramatic use of shadows, even to the point of ordering some to be painted on the sound stage floor to make them starker. At times he even creates an ominous effect by focusing on Leslie's shadow moving along the walkway rather than on Davis herself.

The lace shawl that the moon illuminates in the last shot is the other sustained motif of *The Letter*, an object and the making of which can represent various aspects of the story. Leslie is seen several times intensely focused on weaving the delicate threads together just as she has cleverly woven her justification for Hammond's shooting for Robert and the law court. This is emphasized when, on meeting Mrs. Hammond, she seeks to hide herself under a lace shawl, and the widow requires her to remove it. It is further suggested that the very act of creating the lacework is a distraction from her suppressed passion and sexual urges, but it is a diversion that cannot work forever. Just before she leaves the Joyce home to meet Hammond's widow, she steadily works on her lace, her glasses and calm demeanor making her look very much like the delicate Leslie of Maugham's story. At the end, however, when she has returned from the party to her room and looked out at the moon, she is overcome by feeling and frantically begins working on her lace. It is, however, no longer enough to keep her mind off her despair and regret, and she throws it aside and turns to confront Robert.

The Letter is an atmospheric film and much of its mood is well established by Steiner's excellent music score. The rolling of the credits at the beginning is accompanied by intense, ominous music that immediately warns of momentous happenings. As the camera moves from the moon to the trees below and along the ground to the bungalow, the music becomes quieter, with Asian rhythms and plucking of strings, in keeping with the languid atmosphere of the plantation and making the gunshots more dramatic. Later Steiner introduces the theme music, a haunting, throbbing melody that for the rest of the film seems to suggest the longing and torment of its protagonist. Believing that it would be inappropriate for the confrontation scene between Leslie and Mrs. Hammond, Wyler created an eerie effect by shooting the sequence with only the tinkling of Chinese wind chimes in the background.

Later, when Leslie is alone in her room with the party going on and Hammond's widow waiting outside, the story's main threads are brought together with a subtle blend of sound. "Steiner," said John Kinlock, "uses the Davis theme, typical string-saturated mood music; the Eurasian woman theme, replete with Chinese dissonance and plucking rhythm; and the dance orchestra is heard in the distance. The three conflicting tempos are combined in perfect counterpoint, and respectively tell stories of agony, threat, and gayety."[31]

The Asian element in the music is a reminder not only of Mrs. Hammond but also of the Southeast Asian setting of the story. The contrast in the opening scene between the laborers crowded in their open palapa and the plantation manager's spacious house is an emphatic statement about colonialism. The English always call the workers "boys," a patronizing attitude emphasized as well by the waiter's comment to Joyce and Robert at their club lunch: "It's too bad rubber won't grow in a civilized climate." The empire strikes back, though, in the form of Ong Chi Seng, who, though he drives an inferior car to Joyce's, is given control of Leslie's situation through the emergence of the letter. Capably performed by Victor Sen Yung, better known to moviegoers as Number One Son to Sidney Toler's Charlie Chan, Chi Seng is a smiling, ingratiating servant of the English waiting for the time, inevitable perhaps, that he can supplant them.

Like the 1929 film, Wyler's *The Letter* expands the role of Hammond's Chinese lover well beyond that in Maugham's story, and the treatment has invited similar controversy about racism. Changing the character from Chinese to mixed race made it credible to use Gale Sondergaard, a Minnesota-born daughter of Danish immigrants, but critics have seen her portrayal as typical Hollywood stereotyping of Asians. While the bangles and jewelry and form-fitting dress, together with an implacable look of hatred, do give her a dragon-lady aura, Sondergaard adds depth that was absent in Lady Tsen Mei's earlier depiction. She explained, "I don't think Somerset Maugham meant the Chinese woman to be played up. And I know that, as she was written in the original screenplay, she was more disreputable than sympathetic. I thought she should have more dignity. I thought she should be something more than tawdry bangles. I thought she should look like an intelligent, understanding woman who would justify the interest of a lonesome planter."[32] Though she is, in Davis's words, "breathtakingly sinister,"[33] as silent and threatening as a cobra, she is humanized in the scene where she is taken to view Hammond's body. Though, like Joyce and Leslie, she betrays little of her interior life, she is a grieving widow.

Mrs. Hammond, however, is more than a disconsolate widow; in this incarnation, she is an avenging angel. Wyler could well have ended the film with Leslie's exclamation of her continuing love for Hammond and

Robert's desolation, but he had to contend with Breen's strictures. It was
surely the shadow of the Hays Office code that led the screenwriters to add
lines to Leslie's confession of her infidelity that never appear in the original
story. "Every time I met him, I hated myself," she tells Robert and Joyce.
"It was horrible. There was never an hour when I was at peace. When I
wasn't reproaching myself, I was like a person who is sick with some loath-
some disease and doesn't want to get well."

This warning to would-be adulterers in the moviegoing audience was not,
however, enough: a cinematic killer could not go unpunished, and so an
added scene shows Leslie going into the garden where she is stabbed to death
by the widow. Then, because even avenging figures cannot get away with
murder, Mrs. Hammond and her accomplice are immediately escorted away
by a police officer. Despite this absurdity, the fabricated retributive ending
is filmed artistically, and Leslie's implied acceptance of her self-destruction
has emotional power. But it destroys the point of Maugham's story: that in
the dominant British colonial society, a person can commit murder and not
only escape punishment but slip back easily into her social setting as well.

Maugham never commented publicly about the damaging effect of the
twist to his plot. He did, though, praise Stephenson's performance and called
Davis's "incredibly good. She is exactly the woman I had in mind when I
wrote the story."[34] Critics, too, though feeling that the film was too grim
and sharp-edged for the general public, gave it glowing reviews, and it did
well at the box office. It received seven Academy Award nominations—
notably for Davis, Stephenson, Wyler, Gaudio, and Steiner—though it did
not win an award. For her part, Davis recognized that she had done very well
with two Maugham characters—in *Of Human Bondage* and *The Letter*—
attributing her success to her willingness to portray, unsoftened and un-
apologetic, the damaged souls of women. She looked forward, she told a
journalist, to playing "a whole gallery" of his females, such as Rosie in
Cakes and Ale, because there is not "a dramatic dud in the lot. . . . Even if
I had never played any of the women Maugham creates, I'd still be fascinated by them. They challenge me."[35] Warner Bros. were aware of the
potency of the Maugham-Davis combination, and they were rumored to
be buying the rights to the author's other work. Unfortunately, for several
possible reasons, Davis never made another Maugham film.

In light of the acclaim given this rendition of *The Letter*, it is rather
surprising that Warner Bros. made yet another version only seven years

later. Maugham was not credited as the original author of *The Unfaithful*, released on July 1, 1947, but the basic elements of its plot unquestionably are those of his short story. The four screenwriters, the most notable of which was playwright John Van Druten, moved the setting from the Malayan jungle to a contemporary American city, and the protagonist, Chris, played by Ann Sheridan, kills a man in her home after returning from a late-night party. It turns out that he was her lover several years earlier when her husband was away serving in the Second World War, and the affair is revealed, not through a letter but by a lifelike bust of her done by the man. Her husband, Bob, is played by a badly miscast Zachary Scott, a dark mustachioed actor whom audiences were used to seeing as a Mississippi riverboat gambler kind of villain. If anything, his screen presence emphasized how well cast Herbert Marshall had been. Similarly, the lawyer is well played by Lew Ayres but without the cool, reserved panache of James Stephenson, and in the end becomes a mouthpiece for platitudes and generalities.

It is hard to compare *The Unfaithful* to the earlier versions of *The Letter* because its emphases, reflecting the concerns of the postwar years, are so very different. The war had seen millions of married couples separated for long periods, and the resulting loneliness led to infidelities by both husband and wife; the resulting sense of betrayal and distrust in reunited couples led to a rise in divorce rates. *The Unfaithful* emphasizes the loneliness of its protagonist, something implied but not stressed in the earlier versions, and through a long, moralizing speech by Ayres, it argues against hasty divorce. The film ends with Chris and Bob reconciling and remaining together, the Hays Office apparently foregoing its objection to adulterous wives achieving happiness because marriage is championed. The happy ending rang false, and the *Chicago Tribune* observed that "compared to the sensitive and honest portrait of another marital problem in 'Brief Encounter,' 'The Unfaithful' is just another movie."[36]

"The Letter" continued to attract the interest of filmmakers, particularly those working in the new postwar medium of television, and in late 1956 separate productions were shown on each side of the Atlantic. William Wyler returned to the story on October 15, 1956, not as a director, but as a producer of a version for NBC's *Producers' Showcase*. Directed by Kirk Browning and filmed in color, it featured Siobhan McKenna as Leslie, John Mills as Robert, and Michael Rennie as Joyce. Anna May Wong, whom Wyler had decided against casting in 1940 because she was too young and sexy, excelled in the part of Hammond's wife. In England, six weeks later, the BBC *Sunday Night Theatre* presented an adaptation with Celia Johnson in the lead, Norman Wooland playing Robert, and Roland Culver as Joyce. In some bizarre casting, Ong Chi Seng was rendered by Patrick Cargill, whose haughty, world-weary expression brightened many British comic films.

In June 1969, the BBC included *The Letter* in its twenty-six-part series of Maugham stories, this one starring Eileen Atkins, an excellent British actress with "Bette Davis eyes." Then, in June 1982, ABC televised a lavish production featuring Lee Remick and a largely British cast of Jack Thompson (Robert), Ronald Pickup (Joyce), Ian McShane (Hammond), Wilfrid Hyde-White (the judge), and Herbert Marshall's daughter, Sarah (Dorothy Joyce). The Singapore scenes were shot in Los Angeles's Chinatown, and Hammond's Asian lover became again a Chinese mistress. "Our version is different," said Remick, "because we actually show what happened rather than relying on the woman's explanation."[37] Apparently the screenwriter, Lawrence B. Marcus, knew more than Maugham about what really happened because in his adaptation Leslie has had an affair not only with Hammond but also with Joyce. Like "Rain," "The Letter" thus seems infinitely malleable, adaptable to the pressures of censorship, the changing attitudes of the times, and the desires of film creators to leave their mark on a celebrated story.

CHAPTER 4

Rebellious Wives, Secret Agents, and Beach Bums

Early Sound and the 1930s

The Constant Wife, Maugham's 1926 play that has aged well over the years, deals with two of the most recurrent themes in his writing: individual freedom and the importance of money in one's life. A drawing-room comedy, it focuses on Constance and John Middleton, an upper-middle-class London couple whose marriage has settled into comfortable cohabitation. John is engaged in an affair with Marie-Louise, a liaison that Constance knows about and tolerates because she accepts the idea of her class and era that, as long as men pay the bills, their wives have no justification for complaining or demanding similar liberties. In this she is supported by her mother, Mrs. Culver, one of Maugham's older female characters who is given many of the play's wittiest lines. More importantly, she is the voice of English society's sexual double standard, telling Constance that men "can be perfectly promiscuous and remain upright, industrious and reliable. It's quite different with women. It ruins their character. They become untruthful and dissipated, lazy, shiftless and dishonest."[1] Constance does not agree with her mother, but she does maintain that an upper-middle-class wife is nothing but a parasite: "Have you ever considered what marriage is among well-to-do people? Her house is managed by servants, nurses look after her children, if she has resigned herself to having any, and as soon as they are old enough she packs them off to school. Let us face it, she is no more than the mistress of a man whose desire she has taken advantage of to insist on a legal ceremony that will prevent him from discarding her when his desire has ceased."[2]

With this attitude, Constance will neither divorce her philandering husband nor will she run off with Bernard, an old flame who has returned from working in Japan and would like to rekindle their fire. Instead, she decides to gain economic equality with her husband by going into a partnership in a friend's business. After a year she is able to deposit a thousand pounds into her husband's account to pay for her year's keep, and with this economic independence she claims her sexual freedom. She now feels justified in confronting her husband. "I owe you nothing," she says. "I am able to keep myself. For the last year I have paid my way. There is only one freedom that is really important and that is economic freedom, for in the long run the man who pays the piper calls the tune. Well, I have that freedom and upon my soul it's the most enjoyable sensation I can remember since I ate my first strawberry ice."[3] "I am economically independent and therefore I claim my sexual independence,"[4] she tells John, and so she will take a six-week holiday in Italy—as man and wife—with Bernard. John is outraged, but she reminds him that her behavior is no different from his with Marie-Louise. She makes it clear that the trip will be strictly a sexual fling after which she will return to him; she may be unfaithful, she says, but she is constant. She has redefined their marriage contract, destroying the sexual double standard and giving her the same right to philander as he has had. John pauses and then tells her to come back when her fling is over. While the import of Constance's leaving does not have the weight of Nora's slamming of the door on Torvald at the end of Ibsen's *A Doll's House*, it does announce a serious redefinition of marriage—at least among the English well-to-do.

The Constant Wife was first performed in 1926 in the United States, where it ran for 295 nights, but it did badly the following year in London. One explanation offered for such different responses is that the American production played it for light comedy whereas the British version was more serious, and the audiences were not ready for such a radical reinterpretation of marriage. Paramount Pictures—and certainly the Hays Office behind them—were not ready either when they produced their film adaptation, called *Charming Sinners*, in 1929. The *Los Angeles Times* dismissed it as "pleasant summer diversion and certainly not a subject to tax the intelligence."[5]

Paramount considered *Charming Sinners* its most prestigious film of 1929, assembling a strong cast around Ruth Chatterton, who, after a career on Broadway, had started to make films in Hollywood. As Constance (here called Kathryn Miles), Chatterton is the center of the film, and she has adapted her stage-trained manner of speaking and acting very well to one of the earliest of sound pictures. William Powell brings his rich and smooth voice to the part of Kathryn's handsome love interest, Karl Kraley, though his delivery lacks the naturalness he was to display in *The Thin Man* only five years later. Though his part is not large, Powell and Chatterton have one memorable scene together where she plays the piano and sings a pensive song while he, sitting beside her, ardently declares his love. There is a real chemistry between them, and a sincerity in their acting that stands out in an often stagey and stiff picture.

Laura Hope Crews, a longtime veteran of Broadway theater making her first appearance in a sound film, is excellent as the witty and acerbic Mrs. Carr, the first of many successes as a character actress in the 1930s. Mary Nolan, whose Hollywood film career would be cut short by drug abuse four years later, adopts a high-pitched Kewpie doll voice but, perhaps because she was a former Ziegfeld Follies girl named "Bubbles Wilson," is an appropriately flighty and superficial Anne-Marie. A Paramount regular, Clive Brook, plays Kathryn's husband Robert in a stiff and occasionally farcical fashion, and Montagu Love is Ann-Marie's thick-headed husband, George.

Charming Sinners was written by Doris Anderson, who cut the script down to sixty-six minutes, thus losing a good deal of Maugham's sparkling, epigrammatic dialogue and much of the discussion of modern marriage carried on between Constance, her mother, and her husband. Moreover, Constance's financial independence is gained not by going into a business partnership but by betting a large sum on a horse race. Thus the film avoids portraying her as a modern woman succeeding in the financial world, instead showing her gaining her economic independence merely by a lucky choice at the racetrack. Most significant of the changes is the ending, where Karl joins Kathryn on the boat train expecting to travel with her to Italy, but she declines and prefers to make the trip alone. She may be charming, but she is not a sinner, making Paramount's original title *The Marriage Holiday* far more appropriate. It was one of two endings shot by Paramount—the other being Maugham's original—and undoubtedly the one preferred by the Hays Office.

Film reviewer Martin Dickstein rightly said that the Paramount ending, "bathed in moral whitewash," was "a lamentable distortion of the central character."[6] Kathryn remains both constant and faithful and does not truly claim the freedom—the right to have an affair—given her husband; her infidelity is only feigned to chastise, and perhaps reform, her husband. Earlier in the picture both Mrs. Carr and Kathryn refer to men as little boys who occasionally need to be spanked, an observation that could never come from the pen of Maugham. When Robert sends flowers to the train with a card saying, "I'm pretending that you didn't mean it, and even if you did, I'll never love any other woman," Karl observes that "this is the last spanking Robert will ever need." Kathryn is left alone in the rail compartment, clutching Robert's flowers and considering Karl's remark.

The Sacred Flame, first performed in 1928, was one of the last four of Maugham's thirty-two plays. With a few exceptions, he had written light drawing-room comedies, but he decided to wind down his career as dramatist by showing that he was capable of serious, significant work. None of these valedictory plays captured large audiences, but they are among the most powerful things he wrote. In *The Breadwinner* a London businessman allows himself to be bankrupted and plans to abandon his family in a bid for freedom. *For Services Rendered* is a catalog of the horrors of war, and *Sheppey* presents a contemporary Christ figure whose moral behavior is rejected by contemporary society. The central theme of *The Sacred Flame* arose from his observation of a young nephew who had fallen out of a tree at seventeen and was paralyzed for life. The youth's crippled condition and his mother's devoted care of him led Maugham to write a play about maternal dedication and euthanasia.

In *The Sacred Flame* the son, Maurice Tabret, is a war veteran who has been badly paralyzed and confined to a wheelchair, a situation familiar to many people a decade after the Great War. For five years he has been living with his wife, Stella, his mother, and a nurse, Miss Wayland. Faced with a lifetime as an invalid and unable to give Stella the physical love he believes she deserves, he is deeply depressed and, though he keeps it hidden from everyone except his mother, wishes to die. Unknown to him, his wife has been having an affair with his brother, Colin, and is pregnant by him, but before this shocking news breaks, Maurice is suddenly found dead one morning from an overdose of his sedative. Nurse Wayland reveals Stella's pregnancy, and she accuses her of murder. A family friend even suggests that Stella consider suicide, but the play ends with Maurice's mother confessing that, without Maurice's knowledge, she had administered the overdose. She had promised him that, if his life ever became unbearable, she would help him end it, and she knew that learning of Stella's infidelity would shatter him. "What do we any of us live for," she says, "but our illusions and what can we ask of others but that they should allow us to keep them? It was an illusion that sustained poor Maurice in his sufferings, and if he lost it he lost everything. . . . He dreamed his dream to the end."[7] Nurse Wayland, having been, throughout, the rigid voice of conventional morality, yields to Mrs. Tabret's humane understanding and agrees to the coroner reporting Maurice's death as accidental.

In *The Sacred Flame* Maugham not only dealt with the perennially controversial subject of euthanasia; he experimented with language, giving his characters a more formal dialogue than he had used before. The extreme colloquialism that had been adopted by playwrights to create a sense of greater realism, he wrote in *The Summing Up*, had narrowed the range of subtle thought and restricted the themes that could be represented on stage. "It is impossible," he said, "to analyze the complexities of human nature . . . when you confine yourself to a naturalistic dialogue. . . . I thought then that in *The Sacred Flame* I would try to make my characters speak not the words they would actually have spoken, but in a more formal manner, using the phrases they would have used if they had been able to prepare them beforehand and had known how to put what they wanted to say in exact and well-chosen language."[8] This experimentation with language did not harm the play when, after a casting problem cut short its opening in New York, it had a successful run in London. It did, though, make it unsuitable material for the movie version (now considered a lost film) released by Warner Bros. in November 1929. Sound film was then in its infancy, and this adaptation was little more than a copy of the stage play. As such, wrote Philip K. Scheuer, "it is subject to most of the weaknesses that the translated drama is heir to, depending largely on its Maughamish talk to carry it through. And it is surprising how penetrating the ear of the microphone detects artificialities which, coming across the footlights, would sound like eminently respectable British small talk and large."[9] Other reviewers were more blunt: "wordy and slow," said *Photoplay*;[10] "annoyingly flowery," observed Mordaunt Hall;[11] and it suffers from "dialogue excrescence," wrote Mae Tinée.[12]

In addition to the stylistic language, some elements of the plot should have created difficulties for Warner Bros. During its London stage run, the bishop of London had condemned *The Sacred Flame* as "the most immoral play ever produced in London,"[13] a condemnation repeated by the Vatican a year later. Their main objection centered on the euthanasia, carried out and justified by the young man's mother, and then covered up by the doctor, the nurse, and the rest of the family. There was also the illicit affair between Stella and Colin and her pregnancy by him, all of which Mrs. Tabret argues is understandable and forgivable. The Warner Bros. film, however, was made before the Hollywood Production Code became rigidly established, and so it was able to follow Maugham's play fairly closely. In an attempt to break free of the claustrophobia of a merely dialogue-heavy stage play, director Archie Mayo began with a short scene of the wedding of Maurice and Stella (called Taylor here) and then a shot of the accident at the airstrip. And to show off its Vitaphone sound system, Warner's employed a symphony orchestra to accompany Conrad Nagel, playing Maurice in a wheelchair, as he sang "The Sacred Flame," a song that became a repeated motif throughout the film.

Despite these additions, this film version of *The Sacred Flame* remains faithful to the original play by having Maurice's mother confess to the mercy killing of her son. Even here, though, the hand of the censor may have intervened since reviewers reported that, in the preview showing, the sound system was silent, either deliberately or accidentally, during her admission. In any case the bleakness of the ending is softened by the spirit form of Maurice walking down a garden path between Mrs. Taylor and Nurse Wayland, signaling that he will live on through them.

In 1934 Warner Bros. decided to tackle *The Sacred Flame* again, with Claudette Colbert and Warren William, both major film stars, playing the leads. In the end they got neither Colbert nor William, but they assembled a strong cast of Josephine Hutchinson (Stella), Colin Clive (Maurice), George Brent (Colin), Peggy Wood (Nurse Wayland), and Henrietta Crossman (Maurice's mother). C. Aubrey Smith played his usual role as the tweedy Englishman, Major Liconda, and Leo G. Carroll was a persuasive Dr. Harvester. Screenwriter Ralph Block was given the task of producing a script less formal and more naturalistic than had been used in the 1929 film, and William Keighley was assigned to direct.

The 1930 Production Code and the creation of the Production Code Administration under Joseph Breen in 1934 meant that Warner Bros.'s new version of *The Sacred Flame* would be a pale and bland version of the original play. The relationship between Stella and Colin, though shown more fully, is not a full-blown affair, and Stella is not pregnant with his child. Played woodenly by Brent, Colin appeals to her because he can take her dancing and to the opera and garden parties at the palace; she nonetheless rejects his invitation to run off to Brazil with him. "No matter what happens," she tells him, "my life belongs to [Maurice]."

Warner Bros. gave their new adaptation the title *The Right to Live*, but a very important change in the plot makes it more fitting to be called *The Right to Die*. Instead of Maurice's mother admitting that she killed him, she reveals that she discovered him dying from a self-administered overdose. Euthanasia becomes suicide and, since Maurice is now responsible for his own end, the film spends a great deal time preparing the audience for it by focusing on him and his relationships with the others. Colin Clive is excellent at portraying a man shattered by his injuries, hopeful of regaining his mobility, and always concerned that his wife should live a happy and full life. He urges Stella to let Colin squire her around London and, until a final scene, he hides his depression about his condition behind a mask of joviality and cheerfulness.

On the night that he dies, the film gives Maurice a long scene with Stella where he breaks down and tells her that her life is being wasted by being attached to him. Whatever happens, he says, she should go on and live fully and happily, suggesting a tacit approval of her ultimate future with Colin. His final comment to her, "I feel much better," sounds like the freedom that comes with confession or resignation, a state that is repeated in his mother's recollection of his deathbed conversation with her. He has been able to get to his sedative and take an overdose, and as he dies peacefully, he says that Stella must never know about his despair. "I'm more content now," he tells his mother, "than I've ever been since it happened. . . . Free."

Any sense of impropriety in Stella and Colin's relationship or any responsibility they might have in Maurice's suicide is eliminated by Dr. Harvester's suggestion that it was Maurice's realization that he would never walk again that drove him to take his own life. Nurse Wayland agrees to remain silent about the cause of death, and Stella and Colin will eventually leave for Brazil.

Written in 1915, *Our Betters* is one of Maugham's best plays, a witty but acerbic look at English upper-class mores and practices. In particular, it examines a social phenomenon that had developed in the late nineteenth and early twentieth centuries: the marriages of American women to British aristocrats. The play presents these as cynical arrangements devoid of any romance or love: the woman from Chicago or Philadelphia gets an aristocratic title and an entry into British upper-class society; the impoverished English gentleman gets the American dollars she brings with her. For as long as the marriage lasts, they present themselves as happily wedded but in fact go about their own lives and pursue their own emotional and sexual gratification elsewhere.

Most of the characters in *Our Betters* are Americans, including three women who have married into a titled family: Lady George Grayston (née Pearl Saunders), the Duchesse de Surennes (Minnie Hodgson), and the Principessa Della Cercola (Flora van Hoog). A fourth American is Pearl Grayston's younger sister Bessie, who is in London to follow their paths and snag an aristocrat, and indeed she becomes engaged to Lord Harry Bleane. American men are well represented by Thornton Clay, who prides himself on the number of balls he attends and the titled Brits whom he knows; Arthur Fenwick, who has become rich in the food industry and is Pearl's lover and financial benefactor; and Fleming Harvey, an earnest and innocent young man from New York. The only significant non-Americans are Lord Bleane and the Duchesse de Surennes's young gigolo, Tony Paxton. Pearl's husband, important only because of the title he gave her, is absent and never seen.

Our Betters is often called satiric, but Alexander Woollcott more accurately described it as "an uncommonly thoughtful, searching, and withering comedy."[14] That is, Maugham's group of dissolute, mendacious snobs are not exaggerations or caricatures but portraits from life, denizens of a London social milieu that he knew well. Indeed, it seems likely that Pearl was based on his own wife, Syrie Barnardo Wellcome, who moved adeptly through salons and country houses. Arthur Fenwick is a thinly disguised Gordon Selfridge, the wealthy American who built a retail empire in Britain and had been Syrie's lover, and Tony Paxton is a version of Maugham's own kept lover, the handsome scapegrace Gerald Haxton. Maugham's publisher identified an American diplomat, Henry Chalmers Roberts, as the original of Thornton Clay, but Maugham may have been skewering Henry James, another American who eagerly insinuated himself into the English social life. Whether coincidentally or not, the actor who portrays Clay in the film version bears a considerable resemblance to James.

The strength of *Our Betters* lies in the brilliant revelation of these characters rather than its action. The most dramatic moment comes at the end of the second act when Pearl and Tony are discovered in flagrante delicto in the garden teahouse. The others, gathered around the poker table, are shocked, and when the pair appear and realize that they have been found out, she blurts out, "You damned fool. I told you it was too risky."[15] Enraged, Fenwick mutters, "The slut! The slut," language that sent gasps through the audiences of the time. It was, however, a different aspect of the scene that troubled Britain's Lord Chamberlain when the play was mounted in 1923: he demanded that someone other than the young Bessie be the one to discover the infidelity. And so that an innocent young woman not receive a fictional shock in an unseen, off-stage teahouse, Lord Bleane is the one who wanders out into the garden.

Our Betters is one of the very few plays that premiered in the United States rather than London, a result of its caustic portrayal of vulgar, social-climbing Americans alarming the British Foreign Office. The United States was on the verge of entering the war and, not wanting to antagonize its citizens, British officials pulled strings and had the opening night of Maugham's play canceled. The premiere was therefore presented in Atlantic City on March 8, 1917, and the response of at least one reviewer suggests that the British government might have been right that the play could strike an American nerve. *Our Betters*, said the *Brooklyn Daily Eagle*, is "one of the cheapest and most degrading plays that has ever been seen on the American stage. . . . It will be thrown into the theatrical garbage pail."[16] Most reviewers, however, praised the production, but the London premiere did not take place for six years.

In 1933 RKO Pictures filmed *Our Betters* with George Cukor directing from a script written by Jane Murfin and Henry Wagstaff Gribble. Pearl was played by Constance Bennett, whom Cukor described as "a medium-sized talent with an oversized personality." An RKO advertisement promised that she would be "more alluring than ever before—wearing her most gorgeous gowns,"[17] a promise backed up by the hiring of the renowned high-society party giver Elsa Maxwell to advise on costumes and settings. Bennett does indeed slink around in stylish dresses, wearing luxurious pearls and wielding a cigarette holder as long as a stiletto. For much of the film she portrays Pearl as Maugham has written her: calculating, unflappable, seemingly oblivious to morality, sympathy, and sincerity. Playing the people she so skillfully manipulates is an excellent cast: Anita Louise (Bessie), Violet Kemble-Cooper (the duchesse), Gilbert Roland (Tony Paxton, here called Pepi D'Costa to accommodate Roland's accent), Grant Mitchell (Thornton Clay), Charles Starrett (Fleming Harvey), Minor Watson (Arthur Fenwick), and Hugh Sinclair (Lord Harry Bleane).

For much of the film the cast plays the characters as Maugham had written them, but Cukor and the screenwriters felt compelled to soften Pearl's personality for screen audiences. Thus *Our Betters* opens with a brief shot of her wedding, with her looking the most bored and least happy bride imaginable; then there is an additional scene in which she sees her husband with a lover, a revelation that we are to believe started her on her own road to infidelity. Most striking is an exchange with Lord Bleane that takes place late in the film, entirely fabricated for the screen and very much at odds with Maugham's play script.

In the original, Bessie becomes disgusted with the dishonesty and cynicism she observes in Pearl's social circle, and she asks Bleane to release her from her promise to wed him. The film, on the other hand, shows a remorseful Pearl intervening to ask Lord Harry to break off with Bessie, her explanation constituting an admission of her own sordid behavior. "She doesn't love you, Harry," she says. "She likes the glamour that surrounds you. She likes the idea of being a marchioness. She's dazzled by your setting, Harry. . . . She's so young, someone must protect her. . . . I was like her once. On my wedding day, my mother told me I was too soft. I needed hardening. Well, I've hardened. Bessie mustn't get like me. That's what I want to prevent. She mustn't grow hard and indifferent and cynical and common." As the scene ends and Pearl departs, she dabs dramatically at a tear, but whether it is real is uncertain. She immediately goes back to being the cool, calculating woman she was before, and at the end of the film she is standing with Pepi as they exchange a glance that suggests they will continue to betray the duchesse.

Another departure from, or at least an exaggeration of, Maugham's play presents perhaps the most bizarre performance in any of his film adaptations. *Our Betters* ends frivolously with the dancing master Ernest arriving to give impromptu lessons to the duchesse. Maugham describes him as being a small dark man with hair plastered down, dressed like a tailor's dummy, and speaking in mincing tones. No doubt with Cukor's approval, or perhaps encouragement, Tyrell Davis, who had appeared in *Strictly Unconventional* three years earlier, takes "mincing" beyond anything suggested in Maugham's text. He flounces into the room limp wristed, wearing exaggerated lipstick kewpie-doll style, eye shadow, and liberal eyebrow penciling. It is, in fact, more makeup than worn by any of the actresses. In an effeminate lisp and with an affected manner, with pouts and eye rolls, he pretends to chastise the duchesse's dancing while persuading her to stay for Pearl's evening party. In the coded words of one reviewer, he is "the most broadly painted character of the kind yet attempted on the screen."[18] And he is given the last words of the film when Pearl and the duchesse embrace in a pretense of reconciliation, clasping his hands together and exclaiming: "That's what I like to see. Two ladies of title—*kissing*."

The film version of *Our Betters* was not successful in the theaters or in the eyes of the critics. Its dialogue, sparkling and witty when delivered by skilled performers on stage, did not translate well when spoken by Americans unused to the required cadences and deliveries. Perhaps the most capable member of the cast, Violet Kemble-Cooper, was nonetheless miscast as the opulent, sensual duchesse. Reviewers found the film excessively talky, without enough movement in the plot to retain their interest. Experienced director King Vidor told Cukor, "I would never have tackled a subject with so little locomotion. . . . I feel that the picture is on the border edge of being static but you get away with it beautifully."[19] Cukor, however, was not convinced, saying, "It was a brilliant play of Maugham's, of a milieu that a large part of the movie-going public didn't know. . . . I don't think we did it at all well. . . . I think it was ill-advised to do the picture."[20]

One of Maugham's most underrated—and perhaps misunderstood—novels, *The Narrow Corner*, was published in 1932. Its plot revolves around the travels in the South Pacific of Dr. Saunders, an Englishman who has been struck off the medical register for unethical procedures and has subsequently built a successful practice among the native population. On a lugger taking him home from a distant island, he meets the unscrupulous rogue Captain Nichols, who is transporting a young man, Fred Blake, from Australia, where he has committed a murder. When the ship stops at Kanda-Meira, this trio meets a dreamer-scholar, Frith, his coolly beautiful daughter, Louise, and her fiancé, the young Erik Christessen, who as his name suggests is the personification of idealistic goodness. The handsome Blake is attracted to Christessen and they become friends, but when Christessen discovers that Blake has slept with Louise he feels betrayed and kills himself. Saunders continues his travels, and he learns later that Blake was lost at sea, likely pushed overboard by the disreputable Nichols.

Despite being a story of murder, love, jealousy, and suicide, *The Narrow Corner* is one of a number of Maugham's novels, beginning with *Of Human Bondage*, that is primarily about philosophical and spiritual growth. Much of it is an exploration of Buddhism, elements of which Maugham included in *The Painted Veil* and would employ again in *The Razor's Edge*. Saunders is interested in the mystical experience from the beginning, when through opium he escapes his bodily ties. At the death of a Japanese pearl diver, he considers Karma, and through the middle section he listens to Frith's elucidation of mystical faith, coming at the end to accept some of the basic Indian beliefs. The novel ends with him considering Louise's future in terms of a Buddhist tenet: "He sighed a little, for whatever it was, if the richest dreams the imagination offered came true, in the end it remained nothing but illusion."[21]

Dr. Saunders is one of Maugham's choruses and *raisonneurs*, a more fully developed version of Tim Waddington, in *The Painted Veil*, and he shares so many of the author's own beliefs that he can nearly be considered an autobiographical sketch. The title of the novel comes from a quotation of Marcus Aurelius—"Short, therefore, is a man's life and narrow is the corner of the earth wherein he dwells"—and it reflects Maugham's belief that humans have little room to maneuver to find physical or spiritual freedom. Having concluded long ago that life has no meaning, Saunders is comfortable with pessimism, but like Maugham, he regards goodness as the highest value in people. This he sees in his servant Ah Kay's selfless devotion to him and in Christessen—"Through the oddness of the huge, ungainly Dane, lighting up his complete sincerity, giving body to his idealism and charm to his extravagant enthusiasm, shone, with a warm, all-embracing glow, pure goodness."[22]

In the triangle of Christessen, Louise, and Fred, the strongest attraction is the Dane's appeal to Fred, and indeed there are unmistakable elements of homosexuality in the novel. In addition to Saunders's recognition of the nature of the relationship between the two young men, there is his own admiring glances at his slim, comely young Chinese servant, with his skin as smooth as a girl's. Together with *The Razor's Edge*, this is the closest Maugham came to dealing with homosexual matters, and he once told his nephew Robin that *The Narrow Corner* was his queer novel, but the general public had not recognized it. Robin himself even entertained the idea of writing a screenplay that would properly emphasize the bisexuality at the heart of the novel and make the queer elements quite clear.[23] In 1956 Christopher Isherwood, who knew Maugham well and understood the homosexual consciousness, discussed making a film version with director Fred Zinneman, but unfortunately nothing came of this project.

Most of the focus of *The Narrow Corner* is on men, and one might think that Louise, whose betrayal of Erik drives him to suicide, is merely a selfish, destructive young woman. Maugham, however, complicates her in a conversation she has with Saunders where she explains that Erik had actually been in love with her mother, who died some years ago, and she had promised her mother that she would eventually marry him. Thus she was trapped by other people's wishes: her mother's desire that Louise be her surrogate lover of Erik and his love of her mother in her. "Erik killed himself," she says, "because I'd fallen short of the ideal he'd made of me. . . . He didn't love me. He loved his ideal."[24] Even Fred, in the night they spent together, talked of settling on the island with her, thus imprisoning her in his dream, but now she is free to pursue a future of her own designing.

When *The Narrow Corner* was acclaimed by the critics and the reading public, Warner Bros. quickly bought the rights and assigned Robert Presnell to create a suitable screenplay. Producer Hal Wallis assembled a talented cast: the young and handsome Douglas Fairbanks Jr. (Fred), Ralph Bellamy

(Erik), Dudley Digges (Dr. Saunders), Hans Hohl (Captain Nichols), and Reginald Owen (Frith). The studio wanted Kay Francis to play Louise, but when she was unavailable they chose Patricia Ellis, a young actress used so often in decorative roles that she came to call herself "Queen of the B Pictures at Warner Bros." In the end it was the performances of Digges and Hohl that drew substantial praise from reviewers, overshadowing the superficial acting of Fairbanks and Bellamy.

The Narrow Corner had two things that particularly interested Warner Bros.: the beguiling South Pacific setting and the tale of two men competing for a woman on a remote island. Maugham had made a very long voyage through the Dutch East Indies in 1928, and he turned his careful observation of one small island, Banda-Neira, into the Kanda-Meira of the novel. Nowhere else in his Southeast Asian stories are the natural settings and the atmosphere of tropical heat and lushness more vividly evoked. When Maugham sold the rights to Warner Bros., he strongly urged them to film on location in Banda-Neira, but worried about the budget, they persuaded him that Catalina Island would suffice. It was a poor substitute.

Screenwriter Presnell and director Alfred E. Green stripped Maugham's novel of almost everything except the melodramatic story of Fred's hasty departure from Sydney, his arrival on the island and seduction of Louise, and Erik's suicide. They paid lip service to Dr. Saunders's philosophical observations, primarily his belief in resignation to a fate one cannot control, but gone are the lengthy ruminations on Buddhism and human behavior. Digges is excellently cast, but much of the complex character of the Saunders of the novel is lost, as is the wonderfully written Captain Nichols. Not surprisingly, there is little hint of homosexuality—Ah Kay is not the slender, attractive young man of the novel but a rotund, nondescript figure—and even the ordinary male friendship between Fred and Erik is not persuasively established. When Fred, distraught about Erik's suicide, cries, "He was my best friend," it means almost nothing.

In Warner Bros.'s version of the Fred-Louise-Erik triangle, there is no room for Maugham's idea that the ending gives Louise a freedom from male illusions that she has never had. She is thus a conventional destructive female figure, and in the view of the *New York Times* critic, the story is diminished: "Where 'The Narrow Corner' fails to keep faith is in its insistence on distorting the comparatively slight part of the girl. In a picturesque and tangy chronicle of four interesting men, it is disheartening to find a baby-faced ingénue dwarfing everything down to the size of a South Sea love-story."[25]

The Narrow Corner is also a love story that must have a conventional happy ending, and so Maugham's tale is altered again. Where the novel reveals that Fred left the island disgusted with Louise and then died by falling overboard in suspicious circumstances, the film has him fleeing the authorities, who think that he might have killed Erik. He steals Captain Nichols's ship and, with the aid of three crew members, negotiates his way, in stormy weather, over a treacherous reef and out to sea. Louise, having hidden in the ship's cabin, comes on deck, and the pair sail over a calm moonlit sea to a future together. Perhaps only pedantic moviegoers would wonder how far they will get when Fred is now wanted for Erik's death and the hijacking of a ship.

As far as Warner Bros.'s film wandered from Maugham's novel, it was a model of authenticity compared to its 1936 remake titled *Isle of Fury*. The worst film adaptation of any Maugham work, it seems to have been the product of a team trying to win a quickie film contest. The primary screenwriter, Robert Hardy Andrews, was famous in the profession for speedwriting, once writing scripts for seven daily soap operas and producing one hundred thousand words a week. The studio had given director Frank McDonald a very short shooting schedule and, by working his crews until midnight, he was able to complete the film in sixteen days. This included five days on Catalina Island, where White's Beach stood in for a South Seas shore.

Warner Bros. had intended to have Pat O'Brien play the lead, Val Stevens, and when he backed out, they asked Ian Hunter, who turned down the role three days before shooting began. At the last minute, Humphrey Bogart, who was under contract to the studio, was fingered for the unenviable job. He had appeared on Broadway in *The Mask and the Face*, an Italian comedy translated and adapted by Maugham, and he had just had a film triumph in *The Petrified Forest*. He deserved better roles than that of Val Stevens, he protested to Jack Warner, but he was legally bound. When McDonald commented during filming, "Let's face it, both you and me are hacks turning out shit," Bogart replied, "Why say shit when crap will do?"[26] In later years, he professed to not remember that he had ever made *Isle of Fury*.

The working title of the film was "Three in Eden," but the script appears to have been too tame—even the studio's story department called the material dull—and so it was given a new title to reflect the added melodramatic elements that were supposed to enliven Maugham's story. This included the invention of Val's pearl business and his island divers, played by members of the Los Angeles Mexican community wearing cloth skirts, being frightened to work for fear of a giant "devilfish" on the ocean floor. Bogart, in a diving outfit, is seen fighting a rubber octopus so ridiculous that theater audiences laughed throughout the scene. Having been rescued from the creature's tentacles, Val then must fight off two workers who attempt to rob him of his pearls, and the servant Ah Kay is killed in the process. Finally, Captain Deever, a pale, undeveloped version of Maugham's Captain Nichols, is shot and killed when he threatens Val.

These gratuitous melodramatic episodes overlie a central plot that bears little resemblance to Maugham's novel. The female lead, called Lucille and played by another B movie actress, Margaret Lindsay, bears little resemblance to the coolly beautiful, exotic Louise; and the film begins with her wedding to Val. Like Erik Christessen, he has lived on the island and has been expected to marry Lucille, but he in no way represents pure and idealistic goodness. In fact, he is revealed at the end to be on the run from a murder he committed in the past. The visitor to the island, Eric Blake, is not himself a runaway killer but a police agent sent to arrest Val, but he leaves Val and Lucille on the shore with a promise that he has somehow accumulated enough evidence to exonerate Val.

There was never enough, however, to exonerate the production team that foisted *Isle of Fury* on the public, and Jack Warner, like Bogart, forgot it when he wrote his memoirs.

In 1928 Maugham published *Ashenden or: The British Agent*, a collection of linked short stories based on his experiences as British intelligence agent in Switzerland and Russia in the First World War. It was a book about espionage unlike almost anything that had come before. The pioneers of spy fiction, Erskine Childers, William Le Queux, Edward Philips Oppenheimer,

John Buchan, and others, wrote melodramatic cloak-and-dagger stories of daring and adventurous heroes thwarting enemy spymasters. Their work created a long tradition of romantic treatment of espionage, one that continues with Ian Fleming's James Bond films. Opposed to this is an antithetical view of spying, started by Joseph Conrad's *The Secret Agent* in 1907, the first novel to treat international espionage realistically.

The Secret Agent is a superb piece of fiction, showing how grubby, ineffectual, and tedious the spy's life really is, but it had little influence on espionage literature. *Ashenden*, however, showing much the same kind of world, was, in Eric Ambler's words, "the first fictional work on the subject by a writer of stature with a first-hand knowledge of what he is writing about."[27] It went on to influence many writers—among them Graham Greene, John Le Carré, Len Deighton, and Ambler himself. All of them adopted elements of its central situation: a spy boss recruits an innocent person, often a writer or academic who is a shrewd observer of human nature. This individual accepts the assignment with misgivings and remains an aloof witness to the treacheries and the incompetence of the espionage world. He comes to recognize its moral hollowness.

Maugham's agent is called "Ashenden," a name he used in several works for narrators or characters much like himself. Like his creator, Ashenden is a British writer familiar with Europe and proficient in several languages, and authorship is a perfect cover for someone seemingly idly spending some months in Switzerland. Like Maugham, Ashenden is reserved, shy, very observant of the small details of human behavior, and a shrewd judge of people's motivation and subterfuges. His role is not dramatic: he is an observer, message carrier, and facilitator; and much of his job is monotonous and often futile. Unlike the master spies of earlier fiction, who single-handedly save their nations, Ashenden is a small cog in a large, complex machine. And periodically he discovers that his spymaster back in London has been moving him around like a pawn on a chessboard.

The espionage world of Maugham's novel is not the black-and-white moral landscape of romantic spy fiction; it is a gray world in which both friend and foe engage in unethical conduct in the name of national security. Ashenden not only has qualms about aspects of his missions; he recognizes that enemy agents are doing a job like his and that they experience the same fears and anxieties. Through him the reader is given a sympathetic rendering of the violent ends of foreign spies whom Ashenden reluctantly helps to capture. Thus, when he has been instrumental to sending an English traitor, Grantley Caypor, to his capture and death by firing squad, he cannot help visualizing the dreadful execution scene. And when a mix-up leads to the murder of a completely guiltless Greek businessman at the hands of a hired assassin called the Hairless Mexican, Ashenden's cry is a mixture of frustration with the incompetence and horror over the death of an innocent person. "You bloody fool," he blurts out, "you've killed the wrong man."[28]

Maugham published *Ashenden* in 1928 when, after a decade of hedonism and forgetting, people were prepared to start reading serious examinations of the war that had ravaged Europe. Erich Maria Remarque's *All Quiet on the Western Front* was the best of a host of war novels, and the film industry was quick to put it on the screen in 1930. Studios still saw the espionage story in terms of romantic cloak-and-dagger intrigue, however, and when British International Pictures assigned Alfred Hitchcock to direct an adaptation of *Ashenden* to be called *Secret Agent*, it was on the strength of his major success with John Buchan's thriller *The Thirty-Nine Steps*. Maugham's tales take his agent through various intrigues in Switzerland, Paris, a country identified only as *X*, and then what is clearly Russia, but Hitchcock was not impressed. He chose just two stories out of about fifteen, "The Hairless Mexican" and "The Traitor," as well as elements from an unproduced play adaptation of *Ashenden* by journalist Campbell Dixon. They were Maugham's stories, but in Hitchcock's hands—and those of screenwriters Charles Bennett, Alma Reville, Ian Hay, and Jesse Lasky Jr.—they became almost unrecognizable. "We switched the two stories round," Hitchcock told *Film Weekly*, "made Caypor the innocent victim, turned the Greek into an American, introduced a train smash for dramatic purposes, and obtained the love interest from the play."[29]

Hitchcock wanted Robert Donat, who had starred in *The Thirty-Nine Steps*, for the part of Ashenden, but when the actor's health problems prevented it, he settled for John Gielgud, then one of Britain's leading stage actors but someone with little experience in front of the camera. "I don't know the first thing about film acting,"[30] he told a reporter, and he also could see that the role of Ashenden, complex and fully developed in Maugham's novel, was being reduced to insignificance. Hitchcock had sold the Shakespearian actor on the part by saying that the agent was a modern Hamlet, someone who is reluctant to take action, but the reality was that he saw this as a problem for his film. "You can't cheer for a hero," Hitchcock said, "who doesn't want to be a hero."[31] In the end, he paid lip service to Ashenden's moral qualms rather than offering Gielgud a chance to express deeply felt, nuanced misgivings.

Gielgud worried that, performing with so many actors with strong screen presences, he would not be able to make an impression. Indeed, in his extensively rewritten script, Hitchcock created substantial roles for Madeleine Carroll and Robert Young, both of whom outshone Gielgud. Carroll, who had also played in *The Thirty-Nine Steps*, was a typical Hitchcock heroine: blonde, beautiful, and capable of acting seductively and coolly. In *Secret Agent* she plays the entirely unnecessary part of Elsa, a British agent sent to Switzerland to impersonate Ashenden's wife. She does very little except look beautiful as Hitchcock's filming lingers over her reactions to the events around her. Young, an American actor then in Britain for two films, plays Marvin as his usual character—the wise-cracking, charming ladies man—for much of the film until, going against this type, he is revealed as a ruthless villain. In both guises, he dominates any scene he shares with Gielgud.

Gielgud had the further misfortune of playing many of his sequences opposite one of the greatest scene stealers in film history: Peter Lorre. Called the Hairless Mexican in Maugham's story "because he's hairless and because he's Mexican," he's said in the film to be "neither hairless nor Mexican." Whether of no nationality or a dozen nationalities, Lorre is perfectly cast as *Secret Agent*'s assassin: a sardonic comedian with a touch of Harpo Marx but one who is also a cold-blooded killer. He is, as noted by the reviewer in the *New Republic*, "the assassin as artist. As satyr, humorist and lethal snake, he shows . . . a complete feeling for the juice of situations and the best way of distilling this through voice, carriage, motion. . . . The total is a style, childlike, beautiful, and unfathomably wicked, always hinting at things it would not be good to know."[32] So vivid is Lorre's presence on the screen, suggested one critic, that he seems to be the only character in the room with a body. This is especially true in his scenes with the pale, reserved, and very English Gielgud, the result being that the great classic actor is reduced to serving as a straight man.

Gielgud's performance was met with mixed reviews and different responses from moviegoers. Americans were intrigued to see his entry into filmmaking, but Britons were generally lukewarm about it. C. A. Lejeune, in the *Observer*, wrote that "Mr. Gielgud, cultured, intellectual, and sensitive as he is, will never make what the American magazines are apt to call a 'cinemactor.'"[33] Gielgud himself believed this, and his unhappy experience with *Secret Agent* poisoned him against film roles, except for one wartime propaganda picture, until he did *Julius Caesar* in 1953. He then went on to excel in films and on television, and in 1981 he won an Oscar for Best Supporting Actor.

The fate of the Hairless Mexican in Hitchcock's film presented a problem for the British Board of Film Censors. In Maugham's book, the assassin disappears after killing an innocent man, presumably to carry on his grim trade elsewhere in wartime Europe. In the film, he is with Ashenden, Elsa, and Marvin on a train heading for Constantinople when a British air attack causes it to crash. Hitchcock shot an ending where Marvin is trapped under the wreckage, and when Ashenden cannot bring himself to strangle him, the Hairless Mexican first gives Marvin a flask of water and then shoots him. The reviewer Lejeune, who saw this version in a preview showing, describes what happens next: "Then there comes a terrible and moving shot—the sort of shot that a director only catches very rarely in a whole lifetime of pictures. The spy stops short, with the flask at his mouth—he turns on the Mexican one look of complete surprise and bewilderment—the brandy gushes out of his mouth, and he falls slowly. The Mexican picks up the flask, carefully, so as not to waste any, and drinks, with a satisfied little smile that he has earned his money and the business has been neatly done."[34]

A brilliant ending indeed, but it did not make it into the movie houses. In the days between the preview and the opening night of *Secret Agent*, the British Board of Film Censors demanded an alternate climax. Like the Hays Office rules, the British Board could not permit a murderer, even one killing on behalf of the country, to go unpunished. So as Marvin is dying from the injuries inflicted by the train wreck, the Mexican, either deliberately or accidentally, lays his gun near him, and is shot in the stomach. This allows Lorre to stand up, deliver a flamboyant dying speech, and then collapse. And much of the point of Maugham's story is lost.

Graham Greene, himself the author of superb espionage fiction, gave the best summation of Hitchcock's *Secret Agent*: "His films consist of a series of small 'amusing' melodramatic situations: the murderer's button dropped on the baccarat board; the strangled organist's hands prolonging the notes in the empty church; the fugitives hiding in the bell-tower when the bell begins to swing. Very perfunctorily he builds up to these tricky situations (paying no attention on the way to inconsistencies, loose ends, psychological absurdities) and then drops them: they mean nothing: they lead to nothing. As for Mr. Maugham's *Ashenden*, on which this film is said to be based, nothing is left of that witty and realistic fiction."[35]

Ashenden would eventually be filmed with reasonable fidelity to the wit and perception of Maugham's writing, but it would take fifty-five years and it would be presented on television. In January 1945, it was announced that International Pictures had bought the rights to *Ashenden*, to be written and produced by Nunnaly Johnson. Sixteen months later, the studio reported that the film would be produced by Joseph Sistrom from a script by the eminent screenwriter James Hilton. The pair had consulted with Maugham in New York over an expansion of his stories, including the intriguing promise of "material that could not previously be released."[36] In January 1947, Universal-International advertised *Assigned to Syria*, said to be based on *Ashenden*, but the project was shelved because of a perceived trend away from war films. In 1952 the *New York Times* reported that Universal had assigned screenwriter Robert Buckner to rewrite the script to make it relevant to the problems Britain was then facing in Egypt, but again nothing came of the project.

In November 1991, BBC TV showed a short series of programs based on four of the stories in *Ashenden*, including several that Hitchcock had reworked. The cast included such skillful British actors as Joss Ackland, Ian Bannen, Harriet Walter, Alan Bennett, and Alfred Molina. Alec Jennings, who bore a good resemblance to Maugham, played Ashenden much as he appears on the page, with some added snippets from Maugham's own life. Screenwriter David Pirie heightened the drama of some of the agent's encounters with the enemy but generally made him a thoughtful, morally conflicted man caught in the espionage web. It was a series that satisfied both the viewers looking for a faithful transcription of Maugham and those simply looking for intriguing spy stories.

On the surface Maugham's play *The Tenth Man* is a strange choice of material for a film made in 1936. It was first performed in London in 1910, received lukewarm reviews, and ran for only sixty-five performances. Maugham had burst onto the theater scene two years before in London with four plays running simultaneously on West End stages. They were all light comedies, and Maugham, stung by the dismissive comments of some reviewers, was determined to create some serious works. Aware of the vogue in France for stories of political and financial corruption, he wrote *The Tenth Man*, a drama about an entirely unscrupulous businessman/politician, George Winter.

In a drama of mostly unpleasant characters, Winter is the most unsavory. He is the Radical member of Parliament for Middlepool and a financier who has surreptitiously invested the community's trust funds in a South American gold mine. His scheme is threatened by two developments: an assayer has reported confidentially that the mine is worthless, and his unhappy wife, Catherine, plans to divorce him. To survive, he needs to keep the mining report hidden and he needs to prevent the divorce because it would kill his chance for reelection, which he needs to maintain public confidence in his mining venture. He is supremely confident that he can do both things because, as he says to his wife, people are easily corrupted: "Nine men out of ten are rogues or fools. That's why I make money."

Winter intimidates his wife into abandoning her divorce suit and wins reelection, but he is threatened with exposure over his misuse of the trust funds by James Ford, a North Country farmer and local Middlepool politician. In one way or another, Winter has bought off everyone else, but Ford is the one whose integrity is not for sale. He tells Winter, "You've got through the world by knowing that nine men out of ten are rascals. You've forgotten that the tenth man must cross your path at last."[37] Realizing that he is ruined and facing a prison term for embezzlement, Winter goes to his room, locks the door, and escapes out the window. The play ends with the shocking announcement that a man has been killed on the railway tracks, and ironically, word comes that the mine does contain substantial gold deposits.

Reviewers in London were not impressed by *The Tenth Man*. They found its story too derivative of other well-known political/financial dramas and the play generally boring until the last act, when Winter's scheme unravels at a breathtaking pace. Maugham's dialogue leans heavily on discussion of complicated financial and political practices, and this might well have made the play unsuitable for adaptation in the silent movie era. By 1936—and indeed continuously through the twentieth century to the present day—shady practices in the financial world had increased and become more damaging to the public. Winter, said the *Evening Standard* that year, "is no more unscrupulous than several others who have recently seen the interior of the Old Bailey."[38] British International Pictures thus thought it was time for a film that exposed such wrongdoings, and it hired the Irish director Brian Desmond Hurst to put the story on the screen. A team of four writers produced a screenplay that was faithful to Maugham's plays, despite the story's generally unpleasant characters and cynical outlook. It too ended with Winter's suicide, an act usually disallowed by the Hays Office but permitted here presumably because it was seen as the punishment for a corrupt man's criminal behavior.

Reviews of the film were mixed, with praise for the exposure of asset stripping and other disreputable business and political practices mixed with criticism of the slow pace and the stilted dialogue. Graham Greene commended Hurst's direction and applauded the "humorous and satirical political sequences, and the very fine melodramatic close," but he was scathing about the portrayal of Winter. "Mr. John Lodge," he wrote, "continues to suffer from a kind of lockjaw, an inability to move the tight muscles of his mouth, to do anything but glare with the dumbness and glossiness of an injured seal."[39] This style of acting was not limited to the film's lead, if C. A. Lejeune is to be believed. "The long cast," she said, "includes three of the most fascinating cases of mugging I have ever seen on the screen. Taking them all round, I can hardly remember a more spectacular display of jaw-thrusting, eye-popping, lip-wiggling, and teeth-clenching."[40] Lodge, from a prominent New England political family, quit acting four years after making *The Tenth Man* and went on to a distinguished political career as governor of Connecticut and then served three times as a US ambassador. Presumably jaw thrusting and teeth clenching served him better in politics than it did in films.

As much as the film industry found Maugham's plays and novels a rich source of material, it generally considered his short stories to lack the substance for a feature film. "Rain" and "The Letter" were the exceptions, both with serious plots, deaths (by suicide and murder), and expandable on the screen without the sense of padding. In 1937, however, Charles Laughton and director Erich Pommer, decided to tackle "The Vessel of Wrath," one of Maugham's lighter, somewhat whimsical stories. The pair had just created their own film company, Mayflower Pictures Corporation, with the intention, as the name suggests, of providing movies for the American market. They hoped that their version of Maugham's tale would be an auspicious beginning.

"The Vessel of Wrath," first published in *International Magazine* in April 1931, is in some ways a lighter, more comical look at the world presented in "Rain." Set in the South Seas, on one of the Alas islands in Papua New Guinea, controlled at the time of Maugham's story by the Dutch, it features a notorious protagonist who flouts laws and conventions and who comes up against missionaries attempting to impose their version of morality on the local population. Ginger Ted is a remittance man, sent out from England for unexplained reasons and living as a beachcomber on his two pounds a week and the very occasional bit of work. He is, writes Maugham, "a disgrace to civilization. There was not a single thing to be said in his favour. He cast discredit on the white race. . . . When you saw him in a filthy singlet and a pair of ragged trousers, a battered topi on his head . . . and heard his conversation, coarse, obscene and illiterate, you thought he must be a sailor before the mast who had deserted his ship."[41] Ted spends much of his time drunk, having his way with numerous young local women, and occasionally wreaking destruction in the shops and on the heads of their owners.

Ginger Ted's antagonists are the Reverend Owen Jones, a less fanatical but still determined version of the Reverend Davidson of "Rain," and his unmarried forty-year-old sister Martha, who teaches in the Baptist Mission school and helps her brother in his medical work. Without a sense of humor but resolutely cheerful about life, she seeks out the good in people with "the ferocity of an avenging angel."[42] Tall, thin, flat chested, with a long, thin nose on a sallow face, she seems destined for spinsterhood. Observing this pair and Ginger Ted's antics is the island's Controleur, one of Maugham's many nonjudgmental observers and essentially a spokesman for the author himself. Though the Controleur represents the law, he has an affection for Ginger Ted because his antics break up the monotony of life there.

Ginger Ted's life becomes intertwined with that of the Joneses when circumstances put him on the same small boat as Martha and propeller trouble forces them to spend a night together on a deserted island. Contrary to her "old maid's" fears of assault, he is a perfect gentleman, and she begins to warm to him. When he assists her in dealing with a cholera outbreak on another island, their relationship develops a great deal further, and when the Controleur next sees him, Ginger Ted, now shaven and wearing clean white ducks, announces that he will marry Miss Jones and work with her at the mission. In the words of her brother, "My sister is a very determined woman, Mr. Gruyter. From that night they spent on the island he never had a chance."[43]

For budgetary reasons, Mayflower Pictures shot some of the film in London's Elstree Studios but most of it in the south of France, largely on a semi-abandoned estate called Chateau Robert, where there was a lot of lush, semitropical vegetation to stand in for the South Pacific. Since this was near Cap Ferrat, Laughton and Pommer were able to pay a courtesy call on Maugham at the Villa Mauresque, and they left with his blessings. Bartlett Cormack, who had written the stage version of *The Painted Veil*, wrote the screenplay and was assigned to direct, but when the job drove him to drink and twitching violently in a kind of breakdown, Pommer took over. Among the talented cast was the future acclaimed director Tyrone Guthrie, here doing one of his few on-screen performances as the fussy, fidgety missionary Jones, a performance approaching caricature but fitting the comedy of the story. The world-weary and bored Controleur is played very capably by Robert Newton without the idiosyncrasies and West Country exaggerated speech of *Treasure Island* and other later films. Martha Jones was Elsa Lanchester's first leading role after *The Bride of Frankenstein*, and she plays the termagant spinster with vigor while persuasively conveying her softening toward the rascally beachcomber.

Vessel of Wrath was always intended to be a showcase for Laughton, then considered one of the most skilled screen actors. He had won a Best Actor Oscar for *The Private Life of Henry VIII* in 1933, performed memorably in *Mutiny on the Bounty* in 1935, and starred in *Ruggles of Red Gap* (1935). Given this array, it is hard to accept Laughton's claim that Ginger Ted was his "most significant role to date," and he seemed to have forgotten Ruggles when he complained of being "a little weary of playing heavy, humorless characters."[44] His portrayal of Ted was anything but humorless, and, though Cormack's script adhered closely to the original story, there is far more comedy in the film. Laughton attributed the change to his approach to character and filmmaking, saying that "*Vessel of Wrath* resolved itself into a much broader comedy than we at first intended. I thought, when I started work on the characterization, that the pathos and humour would be fairly divided, but Ginger Ted turned out to be a much funnier character than we anticipated. . . . I have learned never to force a characterization into a specified mould, but allow the character to build itself up from the material. Ginger Ted, I discovered, evoked more laughter than sympathy, so I let him go his own way."[45]

That *Vessel of Wrath* is going to be Laughton's film is signaled in the opening scene, where Ginger Ted awakens face down on the front deck of his shack. Whereas in Maugham's story he does not appear until the seventh page, after the reader has been introduced to the Controleur and Owen and Martha Jones, the viewer follows the beachcomber as he tries in the most rudimentary way to make himself presentable to the world. Laughton, with more than a hint of Oliver Hardy, applies a touch of pomade to his mustache and hair, wipes his hands on his trousers, and, having thus neatened up, puts on a battered straw boater and strolls into town to collect his remittance. Laughton conveys all this with marvelous nonchalance, as if Ginger Ted lives in a world of his own imagining, oblivious to proper behavior and the attitudes of others. We know immediately that he is essentially a decent chap beneath the unkempt exterior because his companion is a dog, a terrier mongrel named "Taffy," who endearingly stretches out on the deck.

Most of the islanders see Ginger Ted as a disagreeable figure—the film's original title was "Give a Dog a Name"—but the Controleur cannot help feeling some affection for him, and Laughton makes sure that the audience feels the same way. In Charles Higham's words, "His portrait of Ted is vivid and affectionate. Shapeless, sweating, unshaven, he appears throughout as a drunken nuisance, a beaten ne'er-do-well whose life is a succession of mishaps; but Charles makes him appealing, good-natured, and hedonistic, so that the audience is on his side from the beginning."[46] Like Shakespeare's Falstaff, Laughton's Ted has the audience with him because he represents hedonistic freedom in combat with the repressive force of the Christian missionaries. Because this is presented as comedy, his drunkenness, violent outbursts, and implied sexual activities with local women raised little concern with filmgoers or censors.

The film nonetheless drew a warning from the Hays Office not to make Rev. Jones a comic figure or a villain, not to include any nudity even with the Natives, and not to use any profanity. Ted's phrase "Aw, nuts in May" was permitted only because in an earlier scene he had heard Miss Jones teaching the schoolchildren to sing, "We are gathering nuts in May, nuts in May." Without that context, it would not have been allowed.[47]

John Grierson shrewdly suggested that one should "see the film as, nearly, in the category of Laurel and Hardy, and you will see *Vessel of Wrath* at its best."[48] For this reason, the least satisfactory part of the film is the final section, where Ted helps Martha minister to the cholera-ridden inhabitants of a distant island. The tone changes and Laughton and Lanchester lose the spark that drove their confrontations, and the story becomes a familiar one of people bravely and indefatigably fighting an epidemic, even, as in the film adaptations of *The Painted Veil*, against the additional threat of hostile villagers. In these circumstances, romance blossoms between them. And as if to deconstruct the characters who have delighted us for most of the film, each apologetically confesses the driving force behind their behavior: he because his father was a straitlaced vicar and she because hers was an alcoholic.

None of this is revealed in the original story, giving the Controleur a shock—and the reader a surprise—when he learns of Ted's plans to marry Martha. And rather than continuing Martha's missionary work in the islands together, the pair are shown happily running the Fox and Rabbit, the pub in England denied him years earlier by his father. Martha, happily selling alcohol, now wears a somewhat low-cut blouse, while Ted, having become a teetotaler, is slightly disapproving of her décolletage. A cuckoo clock appropriately sounds the time as they climb the stairs to bed—followed by the faithful Taffy, who has also made the trip to England.

Released in 1938, *Vessel of Wrath* did well at the box office and critics praised the acting of all the cast, the direction and setting, and the dialogue, much of which was taken directly from Maugham. Looking back years later, the reviewer for the *New York Times* called it a "vigorous comedy and a thing of film beauty,"[49] and Pauline Kael termed it "a charming and neglected comedy."[50] Its success too may have inspired United Artists to film C. S. Forester's *The African Queen* in 1951. Forester's novel, published four years after Maugham's short story, presents enough similarities to suggest that Forester at least borrowed the central situation of a prim missionary woman in conflict with a coarse and rough man. Like Martha, Rose Sayer is the sister of a missionary, and she is forced to work with a hard-drinking Charlie Allnut. And like Martha and Ginger Ted, the pair begin to recognize the attractive qualities in each other and they become lovers. Translated to the screen in the forms of Katharine Hepburn and Humphrey Bogart, they reproduce the tension between Lanchester and Laughton in *Vessel of Wrath*.

The success of *The African Queen* may in turn have inspired London Independent Producers two years later to remake *Vessel of Wrath* under its American title, *The Beachcomber*. For Ginger Ted, now called "Honorable Ted," the studio chose Robert Newton, who, as Long John Silver in *Treasure Island* in 1950, had shown that he could play a character much more colorful than the restrained Controleur of *Vessel of Wrath*. Newton should have been perfect for the part, being, as his castmate Donald Sinden observed, a born beachcomber and heavy drinker. But being a character and acting it convincingly on screen are different things. "When we began *Beachcomber*," recalled Sinden, "he had been on the wagon for three months and a sorry sight he was: gone were the thrown-back head and the fiery eyes; the jerky gestures made by his arms were now limp and seemed to lack purpose. It was tragic to realise that he had now reached a stage when he relied so totally on alcohol to inject spirit into his performance. He was listless and just moped around the studio, hardly talking to anybody. He knew he was not giving his best and this worried him. . . .

Occasionally a low moan escaped his lips. He confided to me that he was not happy with the film."[51]

It is hardly surprising that Newton's beachcomber lacks the energy and joyous unrestrained hedonism of Laughton's. Newton said of his role that "as written by Maugham it's always been rich, colourful and amusing,"[52] but he plays the part too much as a conventional, more thoughtful, and ultimately paler figure. "Honorable Ted" was no doubt meant to be an ironic title but unfortunately it too accurately defines his character in contrast to "Ginger," that is, spirited, Ted. Newton is particularly flat and lifeless in the cholera-fighting scenes, where he seems merely to be an audience for Glynis Johns.

There is a similar diminishment of Martha in Glynis Johns's portrayal, leading reviewers to note how Lanchester's unremitting and irascible pursuer of Ted has become merely schoolmarmish and pert. And Johns is simply too pretty for the role. She had been playing romantic leads in *The Sword and the Rose* and *Rob Roy, the Highland Rogue*, and her Martha is a far cry from the plain spinster of Maugham's story. In an added scene, when she embraces Ted and confesses that "nobody ever kissed me before," she is simply not believable.

Both Sinden as the Controller and Paul Rogers as Martha's missionary brother are capable, but some of the other members of the cast make uncomfortable viewing in the twenty-first century. Donald Pleasence, Michael Hordern, and Ronald Lewis, all fine British actors, appear in brownface and speak with faux Native accents as the Controller's manservant, the headman of a tribe, and the headman's son. The latter two appear in the cholera episode at the end of the film, scenes inflated even beyond those of *Vessel of Wrath*.

The Beachcomber was shot in color in what is now Sri Lanka, and one of its attractions is the lushness and authenticity of the jungle and the beach. As well, the filmmakers were able to make use of many local people to play the tribespeople of the cholera-ridden island. The important roles, those of the headman and his son, were, however, given to Hordern and Lewis, as they lead the tribe to capture and sentence to death Martha and Ted after they fail to save the life of a young woman. The pair are to be killed ceremonially by being trampled by an elephant, but the animal refuses to touch Martha, having recognized her as the person who tended it earlier when it had been wounded in a fight with a crocodile. The tribespeople see this as an exoneration of Ted and Martha, who are free to return home, where they marry and end up working in the mission.

Focusing on the elephant scene, United Artists publicists created a kitschy poster of the beast rearing up and about to trample Martha who in this rendering is a big-breasted beauty in a low-cut dress. "Thundering with New Might and Magnificence," it proclaimed, but most reviewers found the film, at best, a colorful, pleasant diversion and, at worst, a weak reworking of *Vessel of Wrath*. But, concluded Bosley Crowther, "a pale 'Beachcomber' is better than none at all."[53]

Billie Burke in *The Land of Promise*, 1916 (Restoration Graphix)

Pola Negri as Daisy in
East of Suez, 1925
(Restoration Graphix)

An elegant poster for *The Circle*, 1925 (Restoration Graphix)

An Argentinian poster for *The Magician*, 1926 (Restoration Graphix)

The Canadian, with Thomas Meighen as the lead, 1926 (Restoration Graphix)

Lionel Barrymore and Gloria Swanson in *Sadie Thompson*, 1928 (Everett Collection Inc./Alamy)

An inflamed Jeanne Eagels kills her lover (Herbert Marshall) in *The Letter*, 1929 (Photofest)

Joan Crawford assesses the upright Walter Huston in *Rain*, 1932 (Photofest)

Tyrell Davis goes over the top with Violet Kemble-Cooper in *Our Betters*, 1933 (Photofest)

Douglas Fairbanks Jr., Patricia Ellis, and Ralph Bellamy in *The Narrow Corner*, 1933 (Photofest)

Bette Davis tries to seduce Leslie Howard in *Of Human Bondage*, 1934 (Everett Collection Inc./Alamy)

Greta Garbo, clearly the center of *The Painted Veil*, 1934 (Photofest)

Peter Lorre overshadows John Gielgud in *Secret Agent*, 1936 (Photofest)

A very raffish Charles Laughton in *Vessel of Wrath*, 1938 (Everett Collection Inc./Alamy)

Fred MacMurray and Melvyn Douglas vie for Jean Arthur's affections in *Too Many Husbands*, 1940 (Photofest)

Bette Davis dispatches her lover in *The Letter*, 1940 (Photofest)

George Sanders as the painter Charles Strickland in *The Moon and Sixpence*, 1942 (Photofest)

Eleanor Parker and Paul Henreid in *Of Human Bondage*, 1946 (Everett Collection Inc./Alamy)

Tyrone Power, Herbert Marshall, and Clifton Webb in *The Razor's Edge*, 1946 (Photofest)

Somerset Maugham introducing *Trio*, 1950 (Everett Collection Inc./Alamy)

Kim Novak and Laurence Harvey in *Of Human Bondage*, 1964 (Photofest)

Bill Murray seeking enlightenment in *The Razor's Edge*, 1984 (Photofest)

The triumphal Julia (Annette Bening) celebrates in *Being Julia*, 2004 (Photofest)

Edward Norton and Naomi Watts in the stunningly filmed *The Painted Veil*, 2006 (Photofest)

Bette Davis's
Corrosive Mildred

Of Human Bondage

It was inevitable that Hollywood would attempt to put Maugham's *Of Human Bondage* on the screen. Published in 1915, it was the prolific author's magnum opus, a three-hundred-thousand-word book described by American author Theodore Dreiser as the work of a "genius," a "novel or biography or autobiography or social transcript of the utmost importance. . . . The experiences, the dreams, the hopes, the fears, the disillusionments, the ruptures, and the philosophisings of a strangely starved soul, it is a beacon of light by which the wanderer can be guided."[1] Only a decade later, critics declared *Of Human Bondage* a classic, and for several generations anyone considered to be au courant with the most important writing had to have read it. As late as 1990, Gore Vidal observed that "it is very difficult for a writer of my generation, if he is honest, to pretend indifference to the work of Somerset Maugham. He was always so entirely *there*. By seventeen I had read all of Shakespeare; all of Maugham."[2]

Of Human Bondage is a long bildungsroman, or novel of adolescence, a form of literature very popular in the early twentieth century—it was published two years after Lawrence's *Sons and Lovers* and Joyce's *A Portrait of the Artist as a Young Man*. It follows the life and maturation of Philip Carey from his being orphaned in his early youth by the death of his mother to his achieving independence and happiness as a young man. With detailed thoroughness, the novel depicts his tortuous and sometimes tortured journey through adolescence to adulthood. Born with a club foot, which instills self-loathing and feelings of inadequacy in him, he endures a loveless childhood with an aunt and uncle unused to children, suffers through the bullying of an English boarding school, and escapes to a liberating year at the University of Heidelberg. Hoping to become a painter, he joins *la vie de bohème* in an artists' colony in Paris, but when it becomes clear that he does not have the talent to make a decent living from his art, he gives it up and enters medical school in London. By the end of the novel, he has qualified as a general practitioner and is content to settle down in the English countryside and raise a family.

One of the appeals of the bildungsroman is that the protagonist is always more sensitive, more gifted, more sharply perceptive of the world than the average young man—hardly surprising since these books are usually autobiographical accounts by remarkable writers. Their journey to manhood is chronicled in descriptions of the many influences, material surroundings, and people that shape their character. Philip is thus shown absorbing the effect of philosophy lectures in Germany, art discussions in bohemian Paris, and the life-and-death considerations of medical school. He finds several mentors, learns from them, and frequently outgrows their attitudes; and he makes friends, some who remain loyal and some who betray him. He sees various ways that people live, some with purpose and others with futility, and he sees how they die: of suicide from shattered hopes or of a lingering death after a purposeless life. Most important, he wrestles with religious faith, ultimately rejects it, and finds an existential belief by which he can live.

As its title suggests, *Of Human Bondage* is about freedom, a lifelong concern for Maugham, both in his own life and throughout his writing. The deepest and most comprehensive expression of his interest in the freedom of the individual, its theme is the development in Philip of a spiritual independence, a liberation from what the author once called the "strange and ruthless forces that are beyond our control." Although it is a very long novel, there is little in it that is not an integral part of the central theme, each section demonstrating the mistakes, falsehoods, and delusions that Philip must face and escape before he can discover a desirable and feasible pattern for his life. He feels that he is constricted by his club foot, but its internalized effects—self-pity, self-loathing, resentment, vindictiveness, jealousy, and suspicion—are even more inhibiting. Maugham took the title from a chapter heading of *Ethics*, by Spinoza, who wrote that the impotence of people to govern or restrain their emotions constituted bondage.

Philip's greatest bondage, one that eclipses all others for most readers, is his emotional enslavement to an ill-mannered and common Cockney waitress named Mildred Rogers. It is a baffling relationship because, unlike the beautiful or sexually attractive women who fascinate so many of the young men in apprenticeship novels, she is thin, anemic, and has an unappealing, almost greenish, complexion. A snob, she is unintelligent, insensitive, and vulgar; and lacking generosity, cold, and completely selfish, she has few redeeming qualities. Philip is unusual in that he sees Mildred as she is, but he is nonetheless gripped by a destructive obsession with her driven by complex psychological needs arising from deeply rooted feelings of inadequacy.

Mildred is one of three women with whom Philip becomes involved emotionally, but she has the strongest and most long-lasting hold over him. When she breaks off their initial relationship to run off with Emil Miller, an affluent, middle-aged lecher, Philip develops a friendship with Nora Nesbit, a warm and generous woman making her living by writing penny novelettes. This liaison, however, is destroyed when Mildred, pregnant and deserted by Miller, returns tearfully, and Philip abandons Norah to welcome her back. She nevertheless soon leaves him again for his close friend Griffiths, and Philip, twice betrayed, seems to be free of her. However, when he discovers that she has become a prostitute, he cares for her and her baby in his rooms, now moved by pity rather than desire. Eventually, frustrated by his emotional detachment from her, she attempts to seduce him, and when he finally tells her that she disgusts him, she explodes with a torrent of invective:

> She called him every foul name she could think of. She used language so obscene that Philip was astounded; she was always so anxious to be refined, so shocked by coarseness, that it had never occurred to him that she knew the words she used now. . . . She accused him of every mean fault; she said he was stingy, she said he was dull, she said he was vain, selfish; she cast virulent ridicule on everything upon which he was most sensitive. And at last she turned to go. She kept on, with hysterical violence, shouting at him an opprobrious, filthy epithet. She seized the handle of the door and flung

it open. Then she turned round and hurled at him the injury which she
knew was the only one that really touched him. She threw into the word all
the malice and all the venom of which she was capable. She flung it at him
as though it were a blow.

"Cripple!"[3]

When she leaves his rooms next day, Mildred destroys everything she can,
but this does not prevent her from contacting him months later when she
is ill and needs his medical advice. He tells her that she is dying of syphilis,
tries to help her, but is horrified a few evenings later when he sees that she
is still walking the streets.

The third woman with whom Philip becomes involved is Sally Athelny,
the wholesome and loving daughter of a mentor and friend and, ultimately,
his wife. The climactic point of the novel, however, occurs earlier when
Philip's search for a philosophy, a fulfilling pattern which will give meaning to his life, culminates in an epiphany amid the ancient stones of the
British Museum. Remembering a Persian carpet given to him years earlier,
he realizes that the meaning of life is the pattern one makes of it. "There was
one pattern," he thinks, "the most obvious, perfect, and beautiful, in which
a man was born, grew to manhood, married, produced children, toiled for
his bread, and died; but there were others, intricate and wonderful, in which
happiness did not enter and in which success was not attempted; and in
them might be discovered a more troubling grace."[4] Sustained by this belief,
and able to forgive those who have wronged him, Philip is happy.

It was always going to be impossible to make a feature film that would
adequately represent *Of Human Bondage*, just as epics like *War and Peace* or
the *Odyssey* could never be fully presented in a hundred-minute movie. Film
producers, however, were eager to capitalize on the popularity of Maugham
and *Of Human Bondage*, and so they looked to see what slice of the novel
could comprise a movie. All their versions—three feature films and at least
one television adaptation—focused almost entirely on the most sensational
episodes of Philip's story: those around his tortured relationship with Mildred. Several paid lip service to his psychological growth, but almost as
an afterthought, and all offered the moviegoer a twisted love story. RKO
Pictures's 1934 version was advertised as "The Love That Lifted a Man to
Paradise . . . and Hurled Him Down."[5] Maugham's reaction to it was that

"it seemed to me a sketch of my book, a sort of extract. Too much was . . . missing for my taste."[6]

The problem for the film studios was that the Mildred section of *Of Human Bondage* was too indelicate, containing subject matter prohibited by the Production Code. In particular, Mildred's infection with syphilis and her affair with Miller were considered offensive. In May 1933 Joseph Breen wrote to a colleague in the Hays Office that the story would make "the wrong kind of film—the kind of film which constantly gets us into hot water,"[7] and when RKO submitted a script, he warned the studio that it was highly offensive. Producer Pandro Berman and director John Cromwell argued that the novel was a piece of classic literature, and on those grounds Breen agreed to let production go ahead while reserving the right to reject certain material. He required that Mildred be portrayed less slatternly, that she be married to Miller, and that her syphilis become tuberculosis. He rejected some of the drawings of nude female figures that Philip was supposed to have done in Paris, Mildred's comment that "all of it's going on in your head," and a shot of her soliciting in front of a store front. Breen eventually told RKO that, though he did not like the subject matter, he enjoyed the finished film because it was "a serious attempt" to tell "a very serious story."[8]

While *Of Human Bondage* was granted the Production Code's seal of approval, it was vigorously opposed throughout the United States by the influential Catholic Legion of Decency. Daniel Lord, a prominent Catholic priest and one of the drafters of Hollywood's Production Code, condemned Maugham's novel as a "pathological story, . . . morbid, depressing, and unwholesome in the telling."[9] The legion's chapters in Detroit, Chicago, Pittsburg, and Omaha condemned the film for Catholic viewers, and priests picketed outside theaters. Ironically, and unsurprisingly, the protests excited the interest of the public, and theaters in several cities reported attendance records. Even in Chicago, where the legion's campaign had been strongest, the opening week was a sellout and business remained brisk for a month. This did not stop Breen, however, from reexamining the film after its first run and requiring further modifications before being re-released.[10]

When RKO bought the rights to *Of Human Bondage* in 1933, it was to provide a role for the English actor Leslie Howard, who had just won the Best Actor Oscar for *Berkeley Square* and was one of the biggest box office draws of the 1930s. At forty-one he was far too old to play the part of a young medical student, but his ability to portray sensitivity and emotional suffering suited the part of Philip. Casting Mildred was more difficult since most of the established actresses were afraid of losing their public following by playing such a thoroughly unsympathetic character. Benita Hume had been announced for the role, but Cromwell wanted the young Bette Davis, who he knew would have the courage to do it. Davis desperately wanted to do the film because, although she had already appeared in twenty-one movies, "all these pictures and my parts in them," she later said, "seemed to blend into one colorless glob with a few exceptions."[11] The problem was that she would have to be on loan to RKO from Warner Bros., and after telling Cromwell that she would give her life to play Mildred, Davis discovered that Jack Warner would not release her. "It's a terrible role for anybody who wants a career in Hollywood," he told her. "You'll destroy any film following you ever had. You'll never live it down." Undeterred, she harassed Warner for six months until he finally acceded on condition that RKO would loan him Irene Dunne in return. "Go ahead and hang yourself," Warner told Davis.[12]

Howard was given top billing for *Of Human Bondage*, but contrary to Warner's conviction, it was Davis who came out of it with a greatly enhanced reputation. She said that "Mr. Maugham so clearly described Mildred it was like having a textbook to go by,"[13] but she worked very hard on her portrayal. To develop a presentable Cockney accent, she hired an Englishwoman and installed her in her home for eight weeks, listening to, and imitating, the woman's London East End speech. Visually, she persuasively embodies Mildred from the pretty and sexy young teashop waitress at the beginning through the degenerating and increasingly unattractive slattern to the dying wreck at the end. She is very effective at conveying Mildred's initial bored disdain of Philip and her later irritation with his attraction to her. Cromwell uses a great many face-on head shots of both characters, reminiscent of the striking close-ups of Carl Theodore Dreyer's *La Passion de Jeanne d'Arc*, and Davis communicates sullenness, snobbery, and contempt with a raised eyebrow or a sideways movement of the eye. Mildred's cunning and calculating ability to manipulate the besotted Philip is shown by shots of Davis standing behind him or otherwise out of his line of vision.

For much of the film, Davis's performance is disciplined and not exaggerated, befitting Mildred's domination of Philip. This adds force to the climactic—and famous—scene where, having lost control over him after twice betraying him, she realizes that he is entirely indifferent to her. She attempts to seduce him and, when he rejects her by saying that she disgusts him, she explodes with vitriol. Maugham had provided an extraordinarily vivid description of her rage, but the film version gave Davis even more inflammatory lines with which to work (added material in italics):

> *You cad, you dirty swine!* I never cared for you—not once! I was always making a fool of you! You bored me stiff! I hated you! It made me sick when I had to let you kiss me! *I only did it because you begged me. You hounded me, you drove me crazy, and after you kissed me, I always used to wipe my mouth! Wipe my mouth! Well, I made up for it. For every kiss I had a laugh.* We laughed at you, *Miller and me and* Griffiths and me. We laughed at you because you were such a mug! A mug! A mug! *You know what you are, you gimpy-legged monster? You're a cripple, a cripple, a cripple!*

Audiences were stunned by the vehemence of Davis's performance, but they were also shocked by the last sight of her in the film, one in which she is unmoving and silent. Mildred is discovered dying in her rooms, lying expressionless on the floor in a nightgown, her face haggard, her eyes hollow, and her hair disheveled. It was a triumph of cosmetic art, and Davis, as she insisted on doing throughout her career, did her own makeup. She made it clear, she said later, "that Mildred was not going to die of a dread disease looking as if a deb had missed her noon nap. The last stages of consumption, poverty, and neglect are not pretty, and I intended to be convincing-looking. We pulled no punches and Mildred emerged as a reality—as immediate as a newsreel and as starkly real as a pestilence"[14]

Davis said that Maugham's description of Mildred was a "textbook" for an actress, but her portrayal took nastiness and meanness of spirit to another level. Unlike the destructive and unlikeable female characters in other films, Davis's waitress has no redeeming qualities and is seen committing not a single thoughtful or generous act. If there are any moments of sincerity, they are only when she is frightened for herself in the face of poverty or disease. So repulsive is she that it shocked Davis herself when she watched a preview of the film. "I was stunned," said Davis, "I was so much nastier than I had expected. So unforgivably mean. And I looked so ghastly."[15] It may have been a reaction to this viewing that led Davis to turn down another unsympathetic role in George Raft's and Anna May Wong's *Limehouse Blues*. Perhaps as a partial nod to Jack Warner, she told a reporter that she did not want to appear in more such negative parts right away. Still, Mae Tinée, in the *Chicago Tribune*, detected lingering traces of Mildred in Davis's role in *Housewife*. "Like a faint, unpleasant odor, the cheap mannerisms of Mildred cling to her portrayal of the girl in this picture."[16]

If Davis was appalled by her Mildred, she was not alone: audiences so disliked her that when Philip finally voices his disgust with her there was frequently a burst of applause. Despite—or perhaps because of—the Catholic protests, *Of Human Bondage* drew large crowds and played in major cities for months. It was the first film in history to sell out Radio City Music Hall for three weeks. Reviewers, some calling Mildred the most repellant figure ever to appear on the screen, lavished praise on Davis's acting, and there was a public outcry when she was not nominated for an Oscar (won by Claudette Colbert for *It Happened One Night*). Despite the snub, Davis's career took off with the response to her performance, and she told a reporter later that "we have such reverence for the chance this picture gave [me] . . . that everything in our family dates BB (Before *Bondage*) and AB (After *Bondage*)."[17]

Though Howard, too, received some good notices, his performance was less successful than Davis's. For moviegoers with a touch of willing suspension of disbelief, the forty-one-year-old actor looked persuasively like a young man in his early twenties. The problem, though, lay in his acting: he had the mannerisms, gestures, and ambience of a middle-aged man, rather than the energy, excitability, inquisitiveness, and naivete of a young man in the early stage of his life. The film opens with him riding in a Paris taxi, handsome fedora on his head and a pipe in his mouth, looking every bit like an English gentleman going to his club rather than an impoverished art student. The pipe, which remains clenched in his teeth for much of the movie, is probably intended to be a signal that he is a thinker, a philosopher of the human condition. It seems a poor substitute for Philip's lengthy meditations on the world and the meaning of life in the novel.

Philip's club foot is established very early in the film, when the art teacher Foinet asks about other occupations he might pursue, and they both see his lameness as limiting his options. As soon as Philip appears as a medical student at St. Bartholomew's Hospital in London, he is required to display his foot to the other students and patients. And when at times he is shown walking through the streets, it is to the accompaniment of Max Steiner's rhythmic, plodding musical score, reminiscent of "Mickey Mousing," non-diegetic music that suggests the mood and actions of the characters. The problem is that the club foot, and Philip's inferiority complex about it, does not adequately represent the complex psychological state that Maugham describes in the novel.

The club foot is presented as practically the only driving force in Philip's development, and the film shows him undergoing an operation to correct it. Thus made physically whole, he is able to say to Sally at the end, "I had to be free to understand that all those years that I dreamed of escape it was because I was limping through life." The viewer will understand the reference to "limping," but the dream of escape is puzzling because it is the first mention of it. Maugham's protagonist has ambitions of exploring the world, which makes his decision to abandon them to marry Sally all the more meaningful. The film tries, very late in the story, to represent these dreams by Philip's collection of travel brochures, a sheaf that he dramatically tears up as a sacrifice to a life of domesticity with her. His decision is also simplified from that of the novel by the removal of Sally's suspected pregnancy, a device Maugham uses to force Philip to decide what he really wants for his life. When she tells him that she is not pregnant, she frees him to go, but having thought about a future with her, he opts for marriage for the right reason. His decision in the film is a similar affirmation of their relationship, but her remark that "I'm afraid that it's only a noble gesture" seems apropos of nothing.

Considering the acclaim given Bette Davis's performance and the film as a whole, it is somewhat surprising that Warner Bros. decided to remake the story only a decade later. Without new film technology or a new insight into the novel, one can only assume that the studio must have concluded that Maugham's novel was still so popular that filmgoers—even those who had seen the 1934 version—would be attracted by another screen enactment.

Catherine Turney wrote a new script but, except for a few changes, it followed the storyline of its predecessor. Warner Bros. chose the veteran Edmond Goulding, best known for the Oscar-winning *Grand Hotel,* to direct but saddled him with a poorly chosen cast.

Ida Lupino was rumored to be in the running to play Mildred, and like Davis, an actress with a strong screen presence, she might have been excellent. Jack Warner, however, insisted on using Eleanor Parker, little known and then only for playing charming, wholesome characters. Goulding objected to Parker but, after testing her twice, decided to work with her in a Svengali-like manner:

> I worked on her like a psychiatrist. We went from deadly serious to an attitude of "who cares whether you do it or not." I kept this up until she reached the putty stage. She liked the clothes Mildred wore and spent most of the day in them. She came and talked cockney to me. We ran through the scenes together, then she'd go home and work. Actually, I rehearsed with her on the telephone at night. . . . Altogether it took two and a half solid months of work to play around with that girl until she blindly believed in me. We made the test, and I will stake my reputation in the theater and films on the statement that Eleanor Parker is as great and exciting, as thrilling and promising an actress as I've ever directed.[18]

Despite Goulding's commendation and her skill with a Cockney accent, Parker is disappointing as Mildred. Physically, she is too beautiful and healthy looking to be the anemic, underweight young woman of the novel. In attitude, she seems merely petulant and sullen, rather than the calculating, deeply selfish woman of the novel and the earlier film. In simple terms, it is much harder to imagine being obsessed with Parker's waitress than with Davis's. As reviewer Herb Cohn observed, she has "no particular beauty, no wit, no sparkle. She is no grand passion. Not even an introvert, pitying her as much as he pitied himself, could be bowled over by her. She doesn't suit the part."[19]

If Parker was not a good choice for Mildred, the casting of Paul Henreid as Philip was ludicrous. First, he was far too old to play a twenty-three-year-old medical student: he was thirty-eight during the filming and two years on from having played Victor Laszlo in *Casablanca* and Jerry Durrance in *Now, Voyager*, both middle-aged roles. Moreover, born into an Austrian aristocratic family, he had an elegance and sophistication on the screen that made him sought after for some roles but unsuitable for a young middle-class English protagonist. Just as Garbo's accent in *The Painted Veil* is explained by making her character Austrian, Henreid's is accounted for by Philip having an Austrian mother. The Teutonic accent might have been overcome by sensitive and nuanced acting, but Henreid showed little of the internal conflict and suffering of Leslie Howard. According to Bosley Crowther, he performed "in a highly self-conscious and completely unconvincing style. Mr. Henreid gives little indication of the shy and tortured nature of the man in his pompously self-depreciating [*sic*] and emotionally stiff attitudes. . . . Where Mr. Howard and Miss Davis created a subtle suggestion of a physically noxious bond, [Henreid and Parker] act a thoroughly unmoving and peculiarly queasy charade."[20]

Some of the problems of the film can be attributed to Turney's screenplay. If the 1934 adaptation overplayed the importance of Philip's club foot, this remake barely acknowledges it, and thus there is little justification for Philip's antagonistic response to Mildred's initial indifference to him. Rather than being stung by her behavior on their first meeting, a response sparked by a feeling of inferiority, he seems merely intrigued by her and mildly interested in becoming more familiar with her. The audience is told through a voiceover of his growing obsession with her, but the reasons for its grip on him is never clear. At the film's end, Philip mentions his impediment, but by this time the audience has pretty much forgotten it.

Turney's other departure from the 1934 script is a positive one, an exchange between Philip and Thorpe Athelny that incorporates some of the philosophical elements that are central to the novel:

PHILIP: I had so many hours to think since I saw you last. I can tell you the history of a man in one line: he's born, he suffers, and he dies. . . . It's all part of a design, one of a set of patterns.

ATHELNY: The most obvious pattern and the most beautiful one to me is that man is born. He grows into manhood. I mean manhood. He marries, produces children, toils for his bread, and then he dies.

PHILIP: Well, I feel that in giving up my desire for happiness I'm throwing away the last of my illusions.

ATHELNY: Everyone suffers from some defect of body or mind. You can say that the whole world is like a sickhouse with no rhyme or reason for it. . . . The only reasonable thing you can do is to accept the good in men and be patient with their faults. Remember the dying god once said, "Forgive them. They know not what they do."

Turney has extracted these ideas from several lengthy passages late in the novel where Philip experiences epiphanies and has woven them plausibly into a dialogue between two thoughtful characters. On one level it provides a justification for the acceptance of life at which Philip has arrived, but it comes across as more of an afterword than the culmination of a belief system the protagonist has been shown working toward. In the novel, for example, the idea of a pattern for one's life is sown early when Philip is given the Persian carpet, and it recurs when, in moments of doubt, he looks to it to decipher its meaning. And the concept of Christlike forgiveness carries a great deal more weight because it can extend to a great many more people Philip has known than just Mildred and Griffiths.

For whatever reason—Goulding's direction, Turney's script, or the acting of the principals—this production of *Of Human Bondage* was troubled, and a disastrous preview showing caused it to be shelved for nearly two years. A death scene of Mildred proved to be too grim and was cut, but the problems seemed engrained in the filming of every scene. According to Henreid, the script was excellent, but Goulding insisted on rewriting it along the way until it was more his work than Turney's. Moreover, the director was fond of very long takes, with few changes of camera angles and few close-ups, and this robbed the film of much dynamism. Producer Henry Blanke, said Henreid, believed it was an irretrievable disaster. "The screening of the first print," he said, "depressed all of us, and that night, at Romanoff's, Lew [Wasserman], Blanke and I sat around the table with our wives as if at a wake. Finally, with a sigh, Blanke said, 'Lew, Paul, the picture is a complete disaster. . . . You can think all about it all you like, but I don't think anything you can come up with will save our skin.'" Henreid, though, went home and, working from his memory of the showing, wrote notes about how the film could be recut using more close-ups, and, said Henreid, "the extra-long scenes and repetitions that made the print so boring were eliminated." Blanke was persuaded to use the new version, and, in Henreid's opinion, "We ended up with a good film; in fact, except for Leslie Howard's brilliant performance, I felt it was better than the 1934 version."[21] Unfortunately, neither critics nor filmgoers agreed with Henreid's high estimation of his work.

Commenting on the 1946 version of *Of Human Bondage*, critic Philip K. Scheuer observed, "I doubt if anybody will ever do justice to this book—unless, mayhap, the British tackle it themselves."[22] In 1964 the Seven Arts Productions put together a team comprising almost entirely British artists for a version shot in Ireland: the director Ken Hughes (who replaced Henry Hathaway during the shooting), screenwriter Bryan Forbes, and a cast made up of such notable actors as Robert Morley, Siobhán McKenna, Jack Hedley, and Roger Livesey. For Philip Carey, they chose British actor Laurence Harvey, who had burst into prominence as the caddish Joe Lampton in *Room at the Top* in 1959 and as a zombielike, brainwashed soldier in *The Manchurian Candidate* in 1962. The only American in a significant role was the actress who played Mildred, Kim Novak, a selection that caused Dorothy Kilgallen to call it "the most ridiculous bit of casting ever."[23]

It could, though, have been even more ridiculous. The director initially assigned to the film, Henry Hathaway, wanted Marilyn Monroe, believing that she would excel in the part. He was not the only one who thought Monroe capable of doing it: three years earlier Lee Strasberg had learned that 20th Century Fox had taken out an option on *Of Human Bondage* and was about to commission a screenplay. Monroe, thought Strasberg, might be interested in the part. Joe Moskowitz, vice president of Fox, added that Marlon Brando (then thirty-seven!) might well want to play Philip in the picture with her and, if he was unavailable, Paul Scofield (thirty-nine years old) would be an "interesting co-star." They could be directed by José Ferrer.[24] Nothing came of this proposal, however, and when Hathaway's second and third choices, Elizabeth Taylor and Natalie Wood, declined, Novak got the job. What ensued was a rancorous and chaotic film shoot, what Harvey described in a letter to his parents as "without exception, the most horrifying experience I have ever had in my entire theatrical career."[25]

Monroe was a talented actress, more skilled than she is often given credit for, and perhaps she could have made something of Mildred, but she was too beautiful, too voluptuous to suit the part of the anemic, androgynous Cockney waitress. Novak, whom Columbia Pictures had promoted in the hope that she would be another Monroe, presented the same problem: she simply was too gorgeously full bodied. Her screen presence had served her well in the two roles she played in Hitchcock's *Vertigo* and in *Bell, Book and Candle* opposite James Stewart, but it was not appropriate for Maugham's Mildred. Moreover, on her arrival in Ireland Novak admitted to the press that she was having trouble mastering the Cockney accent that Hathaway thought essential to the period and place in which the film would be set. Hathaway assigned a Cockney chauffeur and a Cockney maid to her, but none of their East End dialect rubbed off on the actress. The result, as presented in the finished picture, was a disaster, an accent unidentifiable with any setting.

Hathaway was a veteran of eighty films but, frustrated with Novak's linguistic deficiency and the growing enmity between her and Harvey, he quit the production in the middle of a scene. As he left, he told Bryan Forbes that "this picture was lost before it even began—didn't you know that? Why do you want to sit around and watch the disintegration of your script?"[26] Forbes, however, was assigned to replace him temporarily until Ken Hughes could take over. On Hathaway's departure, Novak disappeared for four days, and Hughes pleaded with Elizabeth Taylor to replace her, but Taylor shrewdly asked for much more than the studio would accept.

Harvey, meanwhile, wanted to leave the production, but he could not afford the $750,000 to buy out his contract with Seven Arts. He was desperate enough even go to what he thought was the highest authority: the author himself. Earlier, on Easter weekend, he had flown to the south of France to Maugham's villa at Cap Ferrat to consult with Maugham about how to play Philip. The author, however, was then eighty-eight years old and deep into senility, and though pleasant and civil, all he could do was wish the actor the best of luck. When turmoil engulfed the *Of Human Bondage* production, Harvey telephoned Maugham to urge him to recall the rights to the story, but Maugham probably still knew enough to realize that he could not legally break his contract with Seven Arts. He refused to intervene, mischievously asking Harvey, "Has my little book really caused so much trouble?"[27]

With two leading actors who hated each other and a frustrated replacement director, the production limped to its conclusion, going far over budget and ending up with a poor film. The main problem was that Novak had no more understanding of Maugham's Mildred or even of Forbes's screenplay than she had a facility with Cockney dialect. "Mildred," she told reporters at the start of the shoot, "with all her faults, was an honest person who never put on airs. She was simply herself no matter how hard it was on those around her."[28] Aside from the fact that Mildred is deeply snobbish and is repeatedly dishonest with Philip, she is much more than simply a free spirit going her own way. Novak, however, blandly plays her as a tease, rather than a tormentor, like the high school beauty who accepts the worship of a lovesick nerd but never sees him as a serious suitor. The result is a common story of unrequited love between a man and a woman rather than an exploration of a damaging obsession of a young man for an unattractive and very unworthy object.

Harvey's performance is slightly better than Novak's, but he contributes to the failure. At thirty-five years, he was perhaps too old for the part, and his screen persona of the stylish, pin-striped cad or the aristocratic figure such as Colonel Travis in *The Alamo* was not easily transformed into that of an insecure, vulnerable young medical student. As Paul Gardner remarked, "Laurence Harvey will be remembered as the screen's fastidious playboy who most mothers feared their daughters might marry—or be ruined by—during an afternoon in the country."[29] In *Of Human Bondage*, his performance is simply superficial and uninspired, and he never persuades the viewer that Philip is deeply obsessed and tormented by Mildred. Nowhere is this more pronounced than in her rejection of him. "It is," commented the *New York Times* reviewer A. H. Weiler, "simply projected as a placid parting of the ways rather than the pained, soul-searching wrench of an intelligent, sensitive man arriving at the threshold of emotional maturity. . . . He appears to be more distracted than heartsick or emotionally undone."[30]

In the end this rendering turned out to be the weakest of the three film adaptations of *Of Human Bondage*. Given the limits of the feature film, of course, none comes anywhere near re-creating the novel's lengthy and complex emotional and philosophical exploration that takes Philip from childhood to young manhood. Technology, however, has caught up to the very long novel, and the twenty-first century innovation of serial programs offered over several seasons on cable television and internet streaming services is admirably suited to showing the many stages of Philip Carey's life. Perhaps an enterprising film company will use the new media to do justice to Maugham's magnum opus.

CHAPTER 6

Garbo Speaks Maugham

The Painted Veil

The Painted Veil, a novel published in 1925, is one of many of Maugham's studies of women trapped in ill-chosen and empty marriages. *Mrs. Craddock* was for its time (1902) a rather daring narrative about a woman whose passionate nature leads her to marry unwisely, discover that her husband is dull and unresponsive, and finally achieve freedom through his death. This pattern of regrettable marriage was repeated in 1937 in *Theatre*, where Julia, in a marriage that is more like a business partnership, finds liberation in the creativity of her acting; and it is the implied reason for Leslie's infidelity in "The Letter." In *The Painted Veil*, Kitty is pressured by the social custom of her upper-middle class into a loveless marriage to a reserved, undemonstrative man. Her husband's death eventually frees her from marital confinement, but this happens only after she has undergone a spiritual and moral regeneration.

At the beginning of *The Painted Veil*, Kitty Garstin is a superficial and silly young woman, a product of her class and her mother's shallow pretensions. Ambitious for social success, Mrs. Garstin has assimilated all the trappings of convention and decorum, and she is constantly scrutinizing and evaluating everything around her in light of advancement in status. Kitty has absorbed her mother's ambitions, and she accepts that she is expected to make a brilliant marriage, regardless of whether it is a satisfying one. When her younger sister becomes engaged, Kitty is mortified at the humiliation this will elicit in social circles, and to escape her mother's caustic tongue she marries Walter Fane, a bacteriologist working in Hong Kong.

The marriage fails because, while Kitty is lively, exuberant, and passionate, Walter is restrained, cold, and controlled, a man ill at ease in groups and unable to respond to his wife's emotional demands. Kitty soon reaches a state of resignation where she neither loves nor hates her husband but merely reacts to him with indifference. Settled in Hong Kong, she, like Leslie in "The Letter," inevitably has an affair with a man who is the antithesis of Walter, the handsome, virile, and popular Charles Townsend. Not recognizing the real nature of Townsend's interest in her, she imagines that everything would be perfect if she could leave her husband and marry him. When Walter discovers the affair, however, Townsend turns his back on her, and Walter forces her to accompany him to a cholera-stricken outpost, Mei-tan-fu. He expects that she will contract the disease there and die.

At this point Kitty is not much different from many of Maugham's English characters living in British colonies: privileged, snobbish, and shallow. Mei-tan-fu, however, provides her with a spiritual experience, and the rest of the novel recounts her transformation to a woman determined to give her life depth and meaning. Maugham had made an extensive trip to China in 1922, and though he was an atheist, he was fascinated by both the mysticism of the East and the religious dedication of the Catholic nuns who devoted their lives to service in an alien country. Volunteering to work at an orphanage, Kitty sees that the nuns, particularly the Mother Superior, live in simplicity, love, and faith. As well, she is influenced by the company of the deputy customs commissioner, Waddington, a man who drinks too much but who tells her about Chinese history and culture and the Tao. She meets his Manchu wife as well, a woman whose elegance and self-possession suggests a spiritualism and depth far beyond what she has known: "Here was the East, immemorial, dark, and inscrutable. The beliefs and ideals of the West seemed crude beside ideals and beliefs of which in this exquisite creature she seemed to catch a fugitive glimpse."[1]

While Kitty is undergoing spiritual growth in the remote outpost, she discovers that she is pregnant and, when Walter dies of cholera, she returns to Hong Kong on her way to rejoin her family in England. Townsend is undoubtedly the father of her child, but she has come to recognize him for the philanderer that he is, and after briefly succumbing to him again, she leaves for home determined to live a more honest and consequential life. It is an ambition made easier by the convenient death of her mother, an event that facilitates another of her goals. Convinced that her child will be a girl, she is determined to bring her up to avoid the traps of pretension and social custom that had shaped her own life. "I'm going to bring up my daughter," she says, "so that she's free and can stand on her own feet. I'm not going to bring a child into the world, and love her, and bring her up, just so that some man may want to sleep with her so much that he's willing to provide her with room and board and lodging for the rest of her life. . . . I want her to be fearless and frank. I want her to be a person independent of others because she is possessed of herself, and I want her to take life like a free man and make a better job of it than I have."[2]

The Painted Veil is a good novel, and its story of a shallow woman growing into a thoughtful, independent, and self-possessed one in the early twentieth century should have provided rich possibilities for an actress. Metro-Goldwyn-Mayer (MGM) thought so and tried to buy the rights in 1932 with the intention of filming it with Joan Crawford. When Crawford and then Joan Bennett were dropped, Richard Boleslawksi, the Russian-born, Stanislavski-trained director urged Greta Garbo to read the novel. She did and, surprisingly, found it "overpolished and cynical. . . . What upset me most was the shallowness of Maugham's characters and the emptiness of their lives. They were two-dimensional and purposeless."[3] When she rejected the role, three screenwriters—John Meehan, Edith Fitzgerald, and Salka Viertel—were employed to produce a script that finally persuaded her. Ironically, their adaptation eliminated any depth that Maugham's novel did have and made for a poor film.

As its advertisement in a trade journal indicated, MGM clearly gave the presence of Garbo, then the screen's most charismatic actress, precedence over Maugham's story. "Somewhere in the literature of the world," it proclaimed, "there is a story that flames with the fire that Garbo can portray. Somewhere lurks a narrative of power that Garbo can tell to your audience, of smoldering love, of high adventure and tenderness that yields tears. Metro-Goldwyn-Mayer has found that story. It is Somerset Maugham's *The Painted Veil*, destined to pack theatres throughout the world, to enthrall love-hungry hearts with its romance portrayed immortally by the one and only Garbo."[4]

Indeed, the first thing that audiences saw was "GARBO" spread across the screen, and it remained in the background throughout the rest of the credits. French film critic André Bazin called her a "socioreligious phenomenon,"[5] and the effect of her name was described in *Vanity Fair* by Helen

Brown Norden: "The moment those five letters are flashed on the screen, something tenses in the audience reaction, and you feel that a magic all too rare has somehow entered the room." It makes, she said, "reverent fanatics out of those who otherwise deem themselves but sane and simple folks."[6]

In this version, adapted for Garbo, Kitty becomes Katrin, the daughter of a professor at an Austrian university, a change presumably made to account for her accent, but this change in origin entirely removes the class background that made Kitty shallow and frivolous. Part of the problem is that Garbo may have known that her powerful, glamorous on-screen presence would make it impossible for her audiences to see her as superficial and vapid. Katrin, in fact, has an adventurous spirit, and she accepts Walter's proposal not to avoid the social humiliation of still being unmarried but as a way to travel to the other side of the world. The courtship is composed of a few perfunctory scenes in the family kitchen, and the couple is soon seen, courtesy of some footage shot in Asia (material that would be recycled in *The Good Earth* in 1937), entering Hong Kong harbor. Waiting for them is Jack Townsend, played by George Brent, an Irish actor whose slick good looks and lightweight acting were perfectly suited for the part of the glib and smooth ladies' man.

Maugham does not spend a lot of time describing the development of Kitty's affair with Townsend because infidelity is not the primary interest of the novel. It is only the catalyst for the evolution of her emotional growth. Almost half the film, however, deals with Townsend's seduction of her, making it top-heavy with the matter of adultery. Surprisingly, the original cut was even longer and, after complaints from preview audiences, MGM ordered three days of retakes, which were directed by W. S. Van Dyke because Boleslawski had already moved on to his next picture. The studio, however, was reluctant to excise a protracted Chinese fantasy sequence it had commissioned from Hubert Stowitts, the dancer who had mounted the faun sequence in *The Magician*. An elaborate enactment of a Chinese myth of the rescuing of a maiden (the moon) by the Sun God so that the pair can rule the heavens forever, this Asian Busby Berkeley number is supposed to assist Townsend's winning of Katrin. Together with a visit to a fortune teller, it is the only contact Katrin has with local culture and beliefs.

In Mei-tan-fu, Katrin learns nothing about Eastern mysticism or spiritual values—or indeed anything of value—from Waddington. Gone is the *raisonneur* of the novel, to be replaced by a clownish character played by comic actor Forrest Harvey. There is no Manchu wife who might open Katrin's eyes to a world of the mind and spirit beyond, and there is none of the interaction between Kitty and the Mother Superior or any other nuns. Thus the transformation in her is reduced simply to an adjustment in their marriage: her growing recognition of the admirable qualities of her husband and his realization that he overreacted to the affair in Hong Kong. In a defense of marriage more likely aimed at the film's audience than at Katrin, Walter says, "But if all the men who were hurt simply quit, . . . bad business."

Garbo had wanted Frederic March to play Katrin's husband, but the studio chose Herbert Marshall, who was becoming very adept at playing wronged, suffering husbands. While this made him perfect for the role of Robert Crosbie in *The Letter*, his Walter Fane is far from Maugham's embittered and unforgiving character. His screen manner effectively conveys decency and wisdom in his forgiveness of, and reconciliation with, Katrin. The film, though, stretches credibility in the magnanimity he displays when, in a line more appropriate to *The Letter*, he asks her if she still loves Townsend. Though Maugham's Kitty has outgrown her lover, recognizing him for the rake he is, Katrin does not reply, indicating that she is still infatuated. Walter recognizes this and, instead of being angry or hurt, he goes over to her, strokes her hair, and says, "I'm so sorry."

All of this happens far too quickly, sped along by scenes of Walter working tirelessly among the cholera victims and ordering necessary but unpopular measures such as burning down an infected village. In the novel, he spends long, hard hours at the hospital, and he eventually contracts the disease and dies. Though he has softened somewhat toward Kitty, he has not rediscovered love; and for her part, she is anxious for him to forgive her, not for her sake but for the tranquility of his own soul. All she can elicit from his dying lips, however, is the final line—"The dog it was that died"—of Oliver Goldsmith's poem "An Elegy on the Death of a Mad Dog." His point is that indeed he had brought her to Mei-tan-fu so that she would die but, ironically, he was the one to be struck down. Kitty sees him buried, goes to Hong Kong, has a brief encounter with a still rakish Townsend, and sails to England to rebuild her life with her father and her unborn child.

In the Garbo film, Katrin does not become pregnant and Walter does not succumb to cholera. He is, however, stabbed in the civil unrest caused by his orders to burn a village, and she is distraught by the possibility that he will die. Meanwhile, in a scene seemingly tacked on, Townsend arrives unannounced in Mei-tan-fu, having decided to leave his wife and marry his lover. When the agitated Katrin tells him that she loves only Walter, he chivalrously backs away, thus signaling his entry into the ranks of the good and enlightened—and no doubt placating the Hays Office. Katrin is then free to turn to Walter, who is recovering from his wounds, and she embraces him, exclaiming: "Don't leave me. I love you." The opening credits had promised lots of Garbo and at the end the camera lingers on her as, dressed in a nun's/nurse's outfit, she leans over Marshall like a rescuing angel.

Boleslawski and Garbo succeed in reducing Maugham's story of spiritual and emotional growth simply to one about infidelity and the eternal triangle. As such, many reviewers pointed out, it added very little to a well-worn subject. "The drama," said the London *Observer*, "apparently presupposes a cinema in which no one has ever heard of adultery before,"[7] and *Film Daily* referred to "the theme's triteness, . . . the old triangle situation in a fever-ridden far-off place."[8] Mae Tinée, in the *Chicago Tribune*, called the film "a rather ponderous affair, moving slowly along the tracks of the eternal triangle. It is completely uneffervescent and is clotted with close-ups of the heroine."[9] But perhaps, as film critic Richard Schickel, observed, the story did not really matter to moviegoers and reviewers: "More often than not, in reading the typical review of a Garbo film, one is left in the dark as to what, precisely, its story might have been. But about the actress herself there are always several paragraphs of dubious generalities."[10] Maugham, however, may have heard enough about what had been done to his narrative. He wrote to a friend: "I cannot *imagine* that anything is likely to take me to see the film. I cannot bear seeing my works when they are made into pictures."[11] He had, however, not balked at attending showings of *Sadie Thompson*, *The Letter*, *Of Human Bondage*, and other screen adaptations.

The Painted Veil did no better at the box office than it had done among the critics, but in 1955 MGM announced that it would remake it with Ava Gardner and that location sequences had already been shot in Pakistan. When the film appeared in 1957, retitled *The Seventh Sin*, it was Eleanor Parker who played the lead (here called Carol Carwin), with Bill Travers as her husband, and Jean Pierre Aumont as the lover. The screenplay by Karl Tunberg followed Maugham's novel much more closely than the Garbo film—many of the lines are, with the occasional modernization, repeated verbatim—but there are still some significant deviations. Maugham's title was taken from Percy Bysshe Shelley's sonnet, which begins "Lift not the painted veil which those who live call life," and it suggests a philosophical search for some reality beyond illusion. "*The Seventh Sin*" clearly identifies the theme as the much more common one of adultery, and like the earlier film, its center is the marriage of Carol and Walter Carwin.

The Seventh Sin, now set in Hong Kong in 1949 and beginning with Walter's discovery of his wife's affair, provides no flashback to establish the superficial nature of Carol. The history of her relationship with Walter is instead briefly conveyed by him in an angry outburst where he claims that she married him out of embarrassment with a younger sister's wedding. He goes on to describe her as "shallow and frivolous and vain, but I loved you. I knew your sense of humor was cheap and the people you enjoyed were second-rate, but I loved you." Parker is neither a good enough actress to confirm the truth of what he is saying, nor is she given much with which to work. When at the film's close she sums up her spiritual growth by saying that "for the first time I'm beginning to like myself, and I want to go on liking myself," it does not seem that much has been accomplished.

The acting in *The Seventh Sin* is capable, but both Travers and George Sanders (Waddington) are badly miscast. Maugham's Walter, a supercilious, cold, and self-controlled scientist, is hard to recognize in the six-foot, four-inch ruggedly handsome Travers, who a year earlier in *Wee Geordie* had played the part of the strongest man in the world. And few female moviegoers would believe Carol when she shrieks at him that she never found him physically attractive. As one reviewer observed, "Travers glowers through the husband role without penetrating it."[12] Sanders, with his smooth baritone voice and suave delivery, is a far cry from the short, affable, philosophical Waddington of the novel. The viewer does get to see his Manchu wife, whom he clearly loves, in one of the film's most effective scenes, but Sanders plays him as a bit of a rake with an eye for Carol's beauty, and his wolf whistle as she leaves the harbor is disconcerting.

The Seventh Sin adheres to Maugham's story by having Walter die from cholera, without having forgiven Carol and with Goldsmith's "the dog it was that died" on his lips. The filmmakers, however, manage to soften the author's bleak view of the marriage by some verbal gimmickry in the form of an idiosyncratic explication of the poem by the Mother Superior (excellently played by Françoise Rosay). "It is about a dog," she tells Carol, "that went mad and bit the *one he loved most*," and the last line of the poem is "the dog it was who died—*of remorse*" (embellishments in italics). Maugham expected his readers to be literate and familiar with Goldsmith's poem; the producers of the film, however, obviously thought they could mislead their less knowledgeable viewers. It was nevertheless enough to allow Carol to see her marriage more positively and to end the film with a declaration of its value: "I know Walter and I had an awful time. By all ordinary standards our marriage was a failure. But it wasn't a complete failure, not in the end for all sorts of reasons that I really don't understand yet." It was the last of what one reviewer called a "hollow string of superficialities,"[13] and it led another to conclude that Carol's "transformation, through sacrificial sweat, is not nearly as effective as the author intended."[14] It did not do well at the box office.

It took thirty-nine years for the third, and best, film to be made from *The Painted Veil*. In the mid-1990s film producer Sara Colleton was working with writer Ron Nyswaner to create a satisfactory screenplay for a twenty-first-century audience, and among the many drafts were some that wandered far from the novel and one that gave Maugham's story a feminist interpretation. Nyswaner also wrote a version that was extremely close to the original, but Edward Norton, who joined the project in 1999, felt that it was too bleak for anyone to back it. "The novel is almost unremittingly bleak. And the reason is I think Maugham had a pretty dim view of British colonials to change. But I went on the assumption that if you were willing to allow Walter and Kitty to grow, then you had the potential for a love story that was both tragic and meaningful."[15]

Norton, who, as both producer and leading man had a strong influence on the production, read the novel as an account of a couple who marry blindly and in haste and have to learn each other's strengths and thus fall in love with the real person. "The painted veil," he believed, referred to the illusions that mask the reality of people and situations, and Maugham's story is about what happens when those illusions are torn away. "Sometimes the greatest journey is the distance between two people," the tagline that became popular even among those who never saw the film, indicates that the tale is a two-hander rather than the story of a woman's growth. At Norton's instigation, the role of Walter was thus expanded over that in the novel or in the earlier film versions. Rather than the resentful and priggish betrayed husband who carries his bitterness to his grave, this Walter is transformed as he softens toward Kitty and recognizes the deepening of her character in the devastation of the cholera. Norton is much better suited to the role than Herbert Marshall or Bill Travers, able to portray the pinched, socially awkward scientist but also the vulnerable man who has been deeply wounded but can learn to love his wife again.

Nyswaner claims that *The Painted Veil* differs from other relationship movies because it is the male who suffers the heartbreak. Certainly, Norton is convincing in the early scenes where Walter becomes attracted to Kitty and conducts an awkward and hasty courtship. It is not hard to believe that he is smitten by her beauty and charm and thinks that her upper-middle-class attitudes will not be an impediment to a satisfactory marriage. Similarly, when Walter discovers Kitty's affair, Norton provides a very credible portrayal of male wounding by underplaying his response. Walter coldly and clinically lays out his plan for them both to travel to the cholera center, having accurately diagnosed Townsend's insincerity, but clearly he is seething inside. This attitude continues in Mei-tan-fu, and both Norton and Naomi Watts, as Kitty, convey the marital chill and hostility very well.

This version of *The Painted Veil* sketches Kitty's class background, the courtship, and even the affair with Townsend, played persuasively but with restraint by Liev Schreiber, with admirable economy. The largest part of the film is set in China, and it is here that the script differs considerably from the original novel. Walter sees Kitty caring for the children of the Catholic orphanage, messy and dangerous work, and begins to recognize a depth in her that she did not have when they first met. As he becomes emotionally closer to her, he says, "It was silly of us to look for qualities in each other that we never had." While this is true of him, Kitty never had any illusions about what kind of man she was marrying, responding to his proposal by telling him, "I don't know you at all." What she learns about him in Mei-tan-fu is his dedication to his work, especially his concern for the local people suffering from the ravages of cholera. Unlike Maugham's Kitty, she is particularly touched to hear from the nuns that he is affectionate with the children, a trait the film reinforces with a scene showing him handing out candy.

Admiration for someone's moral qualities does not, however, ensure love. Intrigued by the bond between Waddington and his Manchu mistress, Kitty asks her why she loves him, and she replies that it is because he is a good man. Kitty's response, "As if a woman ever loved a man for his virtue," is worthy of Maugham, but it is ambiguous in the context in which it is delivered. After seeing Waddington and his mistress in a passionate embrace, the Fanes go home and make love for the first time in months. They wake in the morning, hung over but wearing slightly embarrassed, happy grins, and for the remainder of the film they draw closer to real intimacy and understanding. This newfound love withstands even Kitty's pregnancy, to which, when she confesses that the father might be Townsend, Walter reacts with equanimity: "Well, it doesn't matter now, does it?"

The film thus moves far from the novel, in which there is little thawing in Walter's attitude to Kitty and no birth of any love, physical or emotional, between them. Though she recognizes his admirable qualities, Maugham's Kitty realizes that "it had been so impossible for her to love him. It was a relief that she need never again submit to his caresses."[16] When Walter is dying of cholera, she is not overcome with grief, only regret that she fails to elicit the sign of forgiveness of her from him that she thinks will let him die at peace. The film, despite the growth of the Fanes' relationship, resists the temptation to follow the Garbo version by having Walter recover, instead following the novel by having him die. There is forgiveness at his deathbed, but it is the reverse of that of Maugham's story: Walter's dying words are "forgive me," to which Kitty replies: "There is nothing to forgive."

With the reconfiguration of *The Painted Veil* as love story rather than a tale of Kitty's spiritual development, Watts's role becomes smaller than that in the novel or previous film adaptations. In the early scenes, meant to establish Kitty's shallow family and social background, she is given little to work with but conveys much with a simple gesture, such as the forced grimace of a smile she gives guests at a family house party. With similar economy, the gulf between the English counties and rural China is beautifully indicated by a shot of her fashionable shoes begrimed in the Asian mud. As time goes on in Mei-tan-fu, she becomes accustomed to the messy, uncomfortable business of caring for the Chinese orphans just as Walter is engaged in the awkward business of trying to save the villagers from cholera.

The two major instruments of Kitty's growth in the novel, Tim Waddington and the Mother Superior, are important but reduced figures in the film. Toby Jones is excellently cast as Waddington, physically matching the character delineated by Maugham and providing a gentle and wry commentary on the Fanes' marriage, the Catholic nuns, and the Chinese milieu. Moreover, unlike the British colony in Shanghai, which is earlier shown watching a Chinese theatrical performance without understanding a single word of it, Waddington has lived in Southeast Asia for a long time and has adopted some of its ways. Kitty and Walter inadvertently discover him with his Manchu wife, smoking opium pipes and then engaging in some tender lovemaking. Maugham's presentation of the Chinese wife as a catalyst for spiritual birth is probably impossible to embody on the screen, but the scene shows the Fanes that love can cross the great gulf of cultural differences.

Diana Rigg plays the Mother Superior superbly, but her role is largely to introduce Kitty to the efforts of the nuns and to provide perspectives on Walter's work and on their marriage. There is little of the novel's sense of mystery, of otherworldliness, about her that inspires Kitty to look for values beyond the temporal. In fact, instead of her explanation of her dedication to a religious life, the film shows the Mother Superior explaining that her relationship with God has long ago settled into that of a complacent marriage: she and the Deity coexist but without much communication between them. Such a life, she says, is her duty, and the implication is that Kitty has her own marital duty. The sacrifices of the nuns and the spiritual example they may be for Kitty is further depreciated when Walter argues that the nuns are simply religious colonialists, taking in the children to the orphanage simply to turn them into little Catholics. "None of us," he says, "are in China without a reason."

When Norton first considered filming *The Painted Veil*, he saw the story playing out on an expansive, spectacular setting like the panoramic vistas of *Out of Africa*, the evocative desert of *The English Patient*, or the backgrounds to any David Lean film. Nyswaner and the director, John Curran, agreed that Maugham's story should be opened out and that it should be shot in China, where no major Western movie had been made for decades.

Despite the inevitable difficulties with Chinese government bureaucracy, they chose to locate in Guanxi Huang Yao Ancient Town, in Guanxi Province, in the southern part of the country. Largely untouched by modern civilization and technology, the town perfectly represented the cholera-ridden Mei-tan-fu, and the local population provided hundreds of extras with an authenticity that would never have been found in Hollywood or London. Situated on the Li River, the town is surrounded by steep mountains covered by lush vegetation, and captured in the morning mists, they are stunningly evocative. The film lacks the novel's emphasis on Chinese culture and mysticism, but the dreamy, almost opaque, scenery is suggestive. At the least, it creates a mystical atmosphere, one in which such matters as social stature, infidelity, and egocentricity can be properly rated and overcome. This effect is enhanced by the Golden Globe–winning musical score of Alexandre Desplat and the piano playing of Lang Lang. The soundtrack is particularly effective when Kitty is seen and heard playing Erik Satie's haunting and poignant "Gnossienne No.1" both in her English parlor and then more movingly in the orphanage.

Together with the visual opening out of the Chinese setting of Maugham's novel, the film team determined that the rebirth of the Fanes' marriage would be more dramatic if it took place against important historical events. The action is thus set in 1925 and moved from Hong Kong to Shanghai, where eleven local workers were killed by the occupying British troops during a labor demonstration. Throughout the Mei-tan-fu scenes, the nationalist army lurks in the background, and a local warlord must be placated before work can be done. Moreover, the army's Colonel Yu is given a conversation with Walter in which he articulates the resentment of being an occupied country, an obvious reference to the twenty-first-century Western occupations of Iraq and Afghanistan. "How can you not see the resonances for now?" observed Norton. "China was this anarchic, warlord-ruled place, Westerners are there exploiting it, and the Chinese are getting sick of that intervention."[17] One of the interveners, of course, is Walter, and Norton explained that he was intended to be "the proxy for the arrogance of Western rationalism."[18] The problem here, though, is that at the same time the film presents Walter as being the most effective force in mobilizing and orchestrating the fight against cholera. He is the one who inveighs against burials of the dead close to the river, and he is the one who devises a scheme to redirect fresh drinking water into the village. And he is shown, with dramatic virility, riding horseback across the valley to try to prevent the incursion of cholera-infected people from a neighboring village. The result is that it is hard to see him both as a heroic positive figure and as a colonial exploiter.

This version of *The Painted Veil* is a product of its time, and it takes liberties with Maugham's story, but it is by far the most satisfying of the film adaptations. Visually stunning and excellently acted, it provides an affecting account of an unsuitable marriage transformed, albeit too late, into a good one. Still, it is interesting to speculate about what might have been created from the feminist script, perhaps filmed by a female director such as Jane Campion, one that retained the novel's focus on Kitty's spiritual growth. The Norton version essentially ends with the death of Walter, eliminating Maugham's account of Kitty's encounter with Townsend in Hong Kong and her return to Britain determined to raise her daughter-to-be as an independent woman. Instead, the last scene is a perfunctory one showing Kitty in a London street with her five-year-old son, a boy who looks as if he could be Edward Norton's or Liv Schreiber's offspring but is significantly named "Walter." They encounter Townsend, who, clearly intending to rekindle his romance with Kitty, suggests getting together with her. She firmly declines and, when her son asks who the man is, she replies: "No one important, darling."

This last line is intended to convey that Kitty is free of a passion for a former lover, but it does not convey much of a sense that she has gone through a significant personal growth. In film reviewer Liam Lacey's words, "From the story's start to its ending back in London, Kitty goes through hell and transforms from shallow to plucky. That seems a long way to go to not get very far."[19]

CHAPTER 7

Fascism, Bigamy, and the Creative Spirit

The 1940s

Of all Maugham's light drawing-room comic plays, none is as insubstantial and frothy as *Home and Beauty*. Written in late 1918 while he was recovering from tuberculosis in a sanatorium in Scotland, it was, as he said, a farce that "pretends to be no more. . . . It was written in the highest possible spirits. It was intended to amuse."[1] Seeing its first performance, as *Too Many Husbands*, in the United States in 1919, Alexander Woollcott said, "It is a play so fragile, so light of touch, and so thoroughly and untranslatably English. . . . The result is an evening of unalloyed amusement." Anticipating the charge that the play is "slight," Woollcott responded by writing: "It certainly is. It is almost as slight as *The Importance of Being Earnest*."[2]

In *Home and Beauty*, Maugham borrows a situation made famous in the poem "Enoch Arden" by Alfred, Lord Tennyson: a man shipwrecked and missing for years returns home to find that, having assumed that he is dead, his wife has remarried and has a child. But whereas Tennyson's tale is serious and Enoch suffers in silence without revealing himself to his wife, Maugham turns the plot upside down to splendid comic effect. His intentions are obvious in the cast list: "Victoria, a dear little thing"; "William, a hero"; and "Frederick, another [hero]"; "Mr. Leicester Paton, wrangler [cheater]." William Cardew is the husband who, presumed killed in the war, returns to find that his wife, Victoria, has married his best friend, Frederick Lowndes. In Maugham's rendering, the situation is richly farcical, with numerous witty, epigrammatic lines, but when the expected battle between the men for their wife's hand is about to take place, the audience

160

is given a surprise. Both men are eager to yield to the other, having found that marriage to the attractive but self-centered and pampered Victoria is exasperating and burdensome, and they offer a litany of grievances:

> FREDERICK: I confess that sometimes I've thought it hard that when I wanted a thing it was selfishness, but when she wanted it, it was only her due.
>
> WILLIAM: I don't mind admitting that sometimes I used to wonder why it was only natural of me to sacrifice my inclinations, but in her the proof of a beautiful nature.
>
> FREDERICK: It has tried me now and then that in every difference of opinion I should always be wrong and she should always be right.
>
> WILLIAM: Sometimes I couldn't quite understand why my engagements were made to be broken, while nothing in the world must interfere with hers.
>
> FREDERICK: I have asked myself occasionally why my time was of no importance while hers was so precious.
>
> WILLIAM: I did sometimes wish that I could call my soul my own.[3]

Frederick insists that it is time for William to take up "the white man's burden." The solution, however, comes in the form of a third husband, Mr. Leicester Paton, whose chief attraction is that he owns a Rolls-Royce. After a comic scene—ironically containing the only serious commentary in the play, a critique of the absurd and rigid British divorce laws—a shrewd lawyer devises a way for Victoria to divorce two husbands. This involves the use of two professional co-respondents, women who spend the evening with the men in a hotel, thus enabling Victoria to divorce both on the grounds of infidelity. The play ends with William and Frederick toasting Paton and adding: "And for us—Liberty."[4]

When Columbia pictures decided to make a film adaptation of *Home and Beauty* in 1939, it immediately ran into opposition from the Hays Office. The planned movie, it said, violated the Production Code because of its "apparent lack of any respect for the sanctity of marriage; its farcical treatment of the subject of bigamy; and its very frank and detailed discussion of the unsavory subject of divorce by collusion."[5] The discussion of divorce collusion, the subject of a good deal of humor in Maugham's play, was eliminated entirely from the film. Victoria rids herself of the extra husband and avoids a charge of bigamy through a straightforward legal ruling from a judge, though at the end, the studio gets away with the suggestion that she will be maintaining a close relationship with each man.

In addition to adapting its screenplay to meet the Hays Office requirements, Columbia agreed with Woollcott that the play was "untranslatably English." Claude Binyon's script necessarily expunged the dated references to the war, rationing of foodstuffs and coal, and the shortage of household staff. Ironically, these frustrations of wartime life familiar to English audiences in 1919 would become common to many Americans after Pearl Harbor. Working two years before that, however, Binyon reset Maugham's story to the eastern United States, removing any references to war and making the two male leads partners in a publishing firm. Furthermore, he went far beyond this to nearly completely rewriting Maugham's story, leaving his adaptation to resemble the original only in the basic situation of a woman finding herself married to two men. Indeed, so little remains of *Home and Beauty* that one might wonder why Maugham's name was attached to the production, except of course that it would attract many filmgoers looking for the wit and storytelling of the noted English playwright.

Wesley Ruggles directed what was called *Too Many Husbands* (*My Two Husbands* in the UK), and the principals were well-known actors: Jean Arthur (Vicky), Fred MacMurray (Bill Cardew), and Melvyn Douglas (Henry Lowndes). Arthur worried that she was not beautiful enough to make a credible object of rivalry between two husbands, and she was not happy when MacMurray playfully suggested that they could shoot her with an Indian blanket over her head. The trio played the scenes as farce, but a much broader, more physical comedy than that of Maugham's play. Henry, for example, faints on hearing the news that Bill, supposedly shipwrecked and dead, is alive and returning, MacMurray and Douglas frequently go nose to nose glaring at each other, they try to prove their athleticism to Vicky by jumping over furniture (and, of course, falling on their faces), and they engage in an exaggerated competition in a dance hall. Gone are all the epigrammatic witty lines that made Maugham's play a delight of gossamer humor.

The most striking alteration to *Home and Beauty*, however, is the reversal of the husbands' attitudes toward their shared wife: rather than being eager to yield their rights to her, which was the foundation of the humor in Maugham's play, they spend all their time competing to win her. To fit this scenario, Binyon makes Vicky not a snobbish, pampered woman of leisure but a woman suddenly very pleased with having two men paying inordinate attention to her wishes and feelings. The competitive claims of the men are resolved not by a third party and arranged divorces but by a threat of bigamy charges against Vicky and a judge's decision that she is legally married to Bill. That appears to settle matters except that Vicky explains that Henry is now part of the family, whereupon the three of them go out to a dinner and dance together. The film ends with the trio dancing together and Vicky saying, "We'll have to do this often," suggesting that Henry will not disappear and will wait for an opportunity to win her again.

Film reviewers complained of the thinness of the plot of *Too Many Husbands*, particularly the seemingly endless indecision of Vicky about the men, and Ruggles and the studio itself seem to have been unsure about how to end their story. In a well-publicized event, they brought in twenty-four Los Angeles college women to indicate which of two endings they preferred; the vote was indecisive, Ruggles told reporters, and in any case the ending had already been chosen. There are indications, as well, that Binyon and Ruggles had intended the losing husband to end up with their company's secretary, Gertrude Houlihan, as a consolation prize. How else to explain the early scene in which Gertrude, played by the attractive Dorothy Peterson, confesses at length to Vicky that she has been in love with both Bill and Henry and has even imagined honeymooning with each one. If this exchange was not intended to set her up as an eventual partner for one of the men, it was entirely superfluous.

Columbia had paid lip service to *Home and Beauty*, but in 1955 it offered an adaptation that did not even do that. Harry Cohn commissioned a screenplay called "The Pleasure Is All Mine" for Rita Hayworth, but when she became unavailable, he offered it to Betty Grable, who would be on loan from Darryl Zanuck at 20th Century Fox. It was Columbia's first 3-D musical, and Grable would be performing with William Holden and Henry Fonda. In the end, the two husbands were played by the lesser-known Jack Lemmon, who was, however, coming off his first major success in the Judy Holliday comedy *It Should Happen to You*, and the dancer-choreographer

Gower Champion. Grable's career was on the decline, and she hoped that the musical, ultimately called *Three for the Show*, would give it new life.

By 1955 the story of two people married to the same person had been filmed a number of times, leading John L. Scott to observe that the story line of *Three for the Show* "must be one of the oldest plots in recorded history."[6] Clichéd as it was, it bore little relation to *Home and Beauty* beyond the central idea of a missing and presumed dead husband unexpectedly returning and discovering that his wife has remarried. Here Lemmon's Marty Stewart is a Broadway songwriter missing in action in Korea who returns to discover that his show business partner and dancer, Vernon Lowndes (Champion), has married his song-and-dance star wife, Julie (Grable). Julie likes the idea of having two husbands, a situation that met with the disapproval of the Hays Office and the Catholic Legion of Decency, but she soon parts company with both men. The film then becomes a different movie: a clichéd story of backstage attempts to put on a successful musical show. Marty and Julie become reunited and Vernon falls for Gwen (Marge Champion), a friend and a dancer in the show.

Though *Three for the Show* did well at the box office, reviews were generally negative. Critics noted the triteness of the Enoch Arden plot—and one of the great ironies of this criticism is that Maugham's play was the only version that ever turned it upside down. Reviewers were also lukewarm about yet another backstage showbiz story, and many concluded that the brilliance of the Champions' dance sequences and Gershwin songs did not compensate for the lack of witty and interesting dialogue. Lemmon, who later admitted that he had not been interested in the story or his part, was dismissive of the film, saying, "There's not much to say about it. It was a Hollywood musical."[7] Grable had hoped that the picture would revitalize her film career, but in fact she made only one movie after it. Looking back, Marge Champion joked, "We finished off Esther Williams and Betty Grable."[8] Most likely, though, nobody was to blame, least of all Somerset Maugham; he was nowhere near the production.

When Maugham wrote *The Moon and Sixpence*, a novel published in 1919, he was focusing on a type of figure that had begun to fascinate authors and would come to intrigue filmmakers: the artist. The early years of the twentieth century saw a proliferation of the *kunstlerroman* or artistic novel, fictional accounts of creative characters and the artistic process, among them George Gissing's *The Private Papers of Henry Ryecroft*, D. H. Lawrence's *Sons and Lovers*, James Joyce's *A Portrait of the Artist as a Young Man*, and Theodore Dreiser's *The Genius*.

This growth of the *kunstlerroman* was largely a response to the concerns, anxieties, and tedium of the modern age; and many people looked back with fascination to the generation of antisocial artists who came to prominence at the turn of the century. In Paul Verlaine, Richard Wagner, Vincent van Gogh, Arthur Rimbaud, and Paul Gauguin, they saw men who had defiantly rejected conventional morality and orthodox social attitudes. This interest in individuality, creativity, and rebellion was a form of romanticism engendered by the widespread disillusionment with the waste and futility of the First World War and by a growing feeling that increased mechanization and industrialization were destroying people's instinctual qualities. Many occupations had become so specialized or routine that the creative sense was lost, and so the artist, said Van Wyck Brooks, had come to represent someone whose essential humanity had not been ground down by mechanization. "No wonder," he wrote, "the artist has come to be the lodestone of so many wishes. He alone seems to be able to keep open the human right of way, to test and explore the possibilities of life."[9] For Maugham, who pursued freedom of action and thought all his life, the artist was an attractive figure because he was one of the very few types of people who seemed to be able to carve his own path in the world. "The artist can within certain limits," he said, "make whatever he likes of his life. In other callings, in medicine for instance or the law, you are free to choose whether you will adopt them or not, but having chosen, you are free no longer. You are bound by the rules of your profession; a standard of conduct is imposed on you. The pattern is predetermined. It is only the artist, and maybe the criminal, who can make his own."[10]

For the artist Charles Strickland in *The Moon and Sixpence*, Maugham used the postimpressionist painter, Paul Gauguin, with whom he had some familiarity. During a year among the artistic community in Montparnasse in 1905, he had been told about a mysterious, talented, and antisocial painter living in Brittany, and he wrote briefly about him in *Of Human Bondage*: "He's behaved like a perfect cad to his wife and children, he's always behaving like a perfect cad; the way he treats the people who've helped him—and sometimes he's been saved from starvation merely by the kindness of his friends—is simply beastly. He just happens to be a great artist."[11]

The Moon and Sixpence fleshed out the basic Gauguin story into a full novel, but it was not a biography. "I took a famous painter, Paul Gauguin," Maugham wrote in 1943, "and, using the novelist's privilege, devised a number of incidents to illustrate the character I had created on the suggestions afforded me by the scanty facts I knew about the French artist."[12] The "scanty facts" were, in fact, the myths that had grown around Gauguin: his instantaneous conversion from business to art, his abandonment of family, his ruthlessness, his idyllic life in Tahiti, and his death from leprosy. The reality of the painter was so different that his wife commented that she could not find a single trait that he shared with Maugham's Strickland.

At the beginning of *The Moon and Sixpence*, Strickland is an ordinary, conventional London stockbroker with a wife and two children. The narrator, unnamed but an author much like Maugham, meets him through artistic gatherings arranged by the equally conventional Mrs. Strickland. One day the narrator is summoned to the Strickland home because Charles, without explanation, has suddenly absconded to Paris. It turns out that he has not, as expected, run off with a woman but gone to the City of Light to take up—in middle age—a career in painting. Having permanently left his family, his job, and his life in London behind, he scrapes out a living obsessed by the need to express his deepest impulses on canvas. He is befriended by a congenial but unimaginative painter, Dirk Stroeve, and when he falls gravely ill, Stroeve takes him into his apartment to recover. Strickland callously rewards this generosity by stealing the affections of his benefactor's wife, using her as a model, and then abandoning her. She kills herself, and Stroeve, shattered by the betrayals, retreats from Paris to his native Holland.

After the passage of some years, the narrator comes across word of Strickland when stopping off at Tahiti. From various witnesses, he learns that the painter had left France and ended up in Polynesia, where he could live practically as a beachcomber. He was given a young woman, Ata, as a mistress, fathered several children, and lived in isolation away from the general population. Compelled by some inner demon, he was interested in little other than painting, selling his creations for very little or giving them away. When he learned that he was dying of leprosy, he created his great masterpiece on the walls of his rudimentary house and gave orders that it should be burned on his death. Many of his other canvases survived, however, and were recognized as works of genius, giving him a posthumous reputation as a great artist.

Like Daniel Defoe in *Robinson Crusoe*, Maugham adopts the pretense that the *Moon and Sixpence* is not a novel but a memoir of a real and famous painter, and with mock gravity he comments on various scholarly studies of Strickland. These range from early critical articles, books of "notes" about his works, a family apologia, and the inevitable caustic academic dissection, all of which miss his essential genius. The novel ends back in London, the milieu from which Strickland had fled, where his wife and children are basking in his fame and where yet another sanitized version of his life is being written by a distinguished American critic. Everyone—widow, family, friends, and critics—has vested interests in advancing his or her own versions of the man, but they all misunderstand and misrepresent him. Through the viewpoint of someone who had a unique knowledge of the artist—the narrator—the reader is supposed to see the real Strickland and the source of his passion and genius.

Throughout his life and his career, Maugham was convinced that creativity could not exist without freedom. In a short story published three years after *The Moon and Sixpence*, "The Princess and the Nightingale," a caged bird explains that "I cannot sing unless I'm free, and if I cannot sing I die."[13] This perfectly describes Strickland, a man possessed by an aesthetic sensibility from which he can be liberated only through the medium of paint, and the novel shows him breaking away from physical and emotional restrictions in order to find that creative freedom. His bolting to Paris is a bid for freedom from tedious, repetitive stockbroking, family obligations, and an artificial and superficial salon life adopted by his wife. His shuffling off any sense of morality makes this abandonment easier, and it allows him to exploit Stroeve and his wife, and to drive her to suicide without any feeling of guilt. Maugham here is posing a fundamental question: how much reprehensible behavior should society tolerate from artists for the sake of enjoying their great art? George Bernard Shaw had dramatized the issue in *The Doctor's Dilemma*, forcing his audience to weigh the relative value of goodness and art, and it has continued to perplex the public as it witnesses the antisocial behavior of many of its admired musicians, actors, and other creative geniuses.

Maugham in *The Moon and Sixpence* is also attempting to go much deeper than Strickland's rejection of conventional social life to get to the heart of his creativity. We are told that his paintings are monumental and unique, but Maugham, like every author who has written about works of art, cannot do the impossible: make the reader feel the power of color, shape, movement, and sound through words on the page. If a great poem cannot be adequately replicated in prose, how much more difficult it is to give a powerful and complete literary rendering of the effect of a painting or a sonata. Maugham adopts the strategy of providing the testimonies of a number of witnesses to his painter's greatness, most notably Dr. Coutras's lengthy evocation of Strickland's final and greatest work in Tahiti. In the end, the reader must trust that his paintings are the work of a genius.

Some critics have complained that, beyond Strickland's paintings, the reader does not see much of the inner workings of the painter's mind. If there is an opaqueness around his thoughts, it can be attributed to Maugham's use of a narrator for the first time since *The Making of a Saint* (1898), a device that always distances readers from the characters and the experiences being described. Moreover, the storyteller in *The Moon and Sixpence* is far more intrusive and prominent than the usual chronicler; and his comment that in Strickland he found "a Roland for my Oliver" suggests that he should be considered an important character in his own right. In the twelfth-century epic poem *Chanson de Roland*, Oliver is the prudent, wise figure and a foil to the hero, the boldly and recklessly courageous Roland. In Maugham's novel, the young, somewhat priggish, and pretentious narrator has a limited experience of the world, thus making him a foil for the impulsive, passionate, and amoral Strickland.

While it is always risky to associate a fictional narrator or a character with his creator, it is not difficult to see aspects of Maugham in both his storyteller and in Strickland. In *Of Human Bondage*, published four years before *The Moon and Sixpence*, the autobiographical Philip Carey settled for a modest, conventional life as a married doctor living in the country. Maugham later admitted that in 1913 it was the kind of life he thought he would like to have, but there was still a part of him that wanted travel, adventure, creativity, and even perhaps a touch of danger. In *The Moon and Sixpence*, he expresses that restless side of him in Strickland, but he hedges his bets by grounding the story on the observations of a character who can admire but dare not emulate him.

Soon after *The Moon and Sixpence* was published to critical acclaim and a wide readership in 1919, it attracted the attention of Hollywood movie studios. The film industry would eventually make hundreds of pictures about artists—Van Gogh, Frida Kahlo, Pablo Picasso, Ludwig van Beethoven, Wolfgang Amadeus Mozart, Auguste Rodin, Jackson Pollock, and countless others—as well as biopics of just about every popular musician and actor. It was not until 1936, however, when Charles Laughton played the lead in *Rembrandt*, that moviegoers were treated to a serious study of a creative genius. Before then, Hollywood was more interested in cowboys, swashbucklers, melodramas and comedies, but it could not ignore the attraction of filming a best-selling novel by someone with Maugham's name. Of all the film adaptations of his work, though, *The Moon and Sixpence* had the most complicated history, and it was not until twenty years later that it finally appeared on screen.

In October 1942 the dramatic agent John W. Rumsey surveyed the files of the American Play Company for the *New York Times* and reported that in June 1921, the International Film Company bought the rights to *The Moon and Sixpence*, but the studio folded a decade later without the picture being made.[14] A stage version written by Edith Ellis was mounted in London in 1925, prompting Joseph M. Schenck and Jesse Lasky to consider putting it on the screen, but nothing was done. Warner Bros. and Famous Players looked at the script and backed off, but Metro-Goldwyn-Mayer, on the advice of screenwriter and executive June Mathis, took out an option. Rex Ingram was eager to direct it, but his quarrel with Louis B. Mayer stood in the way of that, and eventually the option expired. In 1932 RKO bought the rights and took out an advertisement in *Variety* for an adaptation to be written by Gene Fowler and Rowland Brown and directed by E. H. Griffith. The story of the memorable painter, it said, was perfect for its star, John Barrymore: "A Barrymore role so fitted to him that Maugham could well have had Barrymore in mind when he penned this romantic story that sweeps from society's drawing rooms to the lazy glamor of the South Seas with its starry nights and one woman to make a man forget memories he thought could not be erased."[15] It is intriguing to think about what Barrymore might have done with the part of Strickland, but the film was never made.

In 1933 Ellis got Maugham's permission to put her play adaptation on at the Pasadena Playhouse, convinced that a performance there would attract the attention of the film studios. Charles Laughton saw the highly praised production, but Paramount, though interested, did not pursue the matter, and Laughton became Rembrandt instead. As the 1930s went on, MGM showed renewed interest, as did Darryl Zanuck, Columbia, Reliance, and Universal, and in 1939 Warner Bros. finally bought the rights with the intention of featuring Edward G. Robinson. His being an art collector, it was speculated, would give him special insight into the eccentricities of the creative genius. Once again, the project hit a roadblock and stagnated, and the rights were transferred to MGM. The word in Hollywood was that *The Moon and Sixpence* was unfilmable, dismissed as, in the words of one producer, "the story of a disagreeable character, a painter whose paintings are burned and who dies of leprosy—this is entertainment?"[16]

With all the major studios backing away from *The Moon and Sixpence*, the rights were bought by a small independent production company recently formed by producer David Loew, writer Albert Lewin, and the young associate producer Stanley Kramer. Loew-Lewin paid $25,000 for the option and, in 1942, shot it in only thirty-two days at a relatively low cost of $401,000, saving money by having Lewin write the script and direct the film and by using a cast without major stars. Despite the lack of a big name on the marquee, said Lewin, "the subject matter, Maugham's name, and the title sold that film,"[17] and, distributed by United Artists, it did very well in the theaters and subsequent television showings.

While *The Moon and Sixpence* may not have featured major leading actors, it had some excellent performances. Herbert Marshall, playing the narrator (with the name "Geoffrey Wolfe"), had by then a solid reputation as a supporting actor to a series of leading ladies, and he was appearing in his fourth Maugham film. As in *The Razor's Edge*, he was the perfect observer and commentator on the central action of the story: reserved, understated, gentlemanly, curious, and sympathetic. Very much like Maugham himself, he is a foil to the passionate, antisocial, amoral Strickland, played by George Sanders in his first leading role in a major film. Sanders is good, but his characteristic suavity and whiskey-smooth voice, excellent in the early, London scenes, is hard to disguise in the later episodes where his character has become the fiercely dedicated and satyrlike artist. Equally as proficient as Marshall and Sanders, the Hungarian American Steven Geray is memorable as Dirk Stroeve, his short plump physique and earnest, spectacled face perfectly making him both comic and pathetic. None of the remainder of the cast were well known.

Why did Lewin and Loew succeed in making the film when so many other studios failed? Lewin claimed that earlier attempts were stymied because much of Maugham's novel is told in the first person by a narrator who is frequently involved in the action, and no screenwriter had figured out how to move smoothly and easily back and forth from narration to direct action. Voice-over narration, it is true, had hardly ever been used in the early years of sound pictures, as filmmakers were proud simply to show figures talking on the screen. It was not until 1939 that voice-over became a common device, used in a quartet of movies: *Juarez*, *The Roaring Twenties*, *Wuthering Heights*, and *Confessions of a Nazi Spy*. Lewin must have been aware of these pictures, but he later said that he borrowed a technique from Sacha Guitry's 1936 film *Le Roman d'un Tricheur* to solve the narration problem. "He told his story," Lewin explained, "in the first person, the action carried it along, and at intervals, when necessary, he talked again."[18]

The influence of Guitry is immediately apparent in the opening scene of *The Moon and Sixpence*, where Wolfe, in his London apartment with his oblivious manservant, turns to the camera and breaks the fourth wall to address the film's audience. He continues to talk of Strickland in his bathtub, as he dresses, and finally at his writing desk, where he begins to pen his account of the painter. Lewin further blends the narrator's commentary with the film's action by taking some of the comments directed to the reader in the novel and weaving them into the narrator's dialogue with other characters. According to Lewin, Maugham read the script before production began and wrote very positively to him about it: "I consider it a brilliant piece of work," said the author. "Your treatment seems to me not only ingenious but highly original and if it results in a successful picture I believe you will achieve something very like a revolution in the picture industry. You have produced a highly adult piece of work and adhered very honestly to the theme of the story. I cannot imagine that a movie could be adapted in a better way."[19]

As much as the intrusive presence of the narrator might have presented a problem for film adapters, there were other features of *The Moon and Sixpence* that were major stumbling blocks for the studios. To be a truly persuasive portrait of an artistic genius, the audience needed to see Strickland in the act of creation and to see the acclaimed results of his imagination. The novel never describes the painter putting his visions on canvas, but it does provide a long verbal evocation of Strickland's final great painting on the walls of his Tahitian house. This comes from the testimony of Dr. Coutras, who tells the narrator about a final visit to the dying man, and it is only partially successful in letting the reader feel the full impact of the stunning work. Being itself a visual medium, however, a film can let the viewer see both the creating and the creation.

For *Rembrandt*, Laughton had learned how to stand at an easel, hold a brush to simulate painting without the audience ever seeing his stroke touch the canvas. Many of the finished pictures, familiar because of Rembrandt's fame, are displayed to viewers within the film and those in the movie theaters. In *The Moon and Sixpence*, however, Strickland is never shown at work and none of his paintings, including the key one of Blanche Stroeve, are seen until the climactic, revelatory vision of Dr. Coutras at the end. The impact of this exposure of the painter's tormented imagination is meant to be intensified by several shifts in cinematography. Most of the film— the London and Paris scenes—is shot in black-and-white, but this changes abruptly to sepia when the action shifts to Tahiti. This, one assumes, is supposed to heighten the feeling of warmth and softness in Polynesia and to signal a dramatic change in Strickland's life and artistry. Then, as when Dorothy dreams of the fantastic land in *The Wizard of Oz*, when Dr. Coutras sees his last great work, the film suddenly changes from sepia to vivid color. This shift was intended to astonish the theater audience and to suggest that in a world of modest tones, the mind of the blind Strickland could envisage wondrous brilliance.

Unfortunately, Strickland's magnum opus failed to impress filmgoers. The producers of *Rembrandt* had the good fortune of being able to use the Dutch master's paintings, notably his magnificent "The Night Watch," but

Lewin was unable to utilize a similar great work. He secured the permission of the Boston Museum of Fine Arts to reproduce Gauguin's masterpiece "Where Do We Come From? What Are We? Where Are We Going?" but the painter's son, not wanting his father to be linked to Strickland, threatened to sue if the piece was used. Lewin then had two classical paintings, Botticelli's *Spring* and Bernadino Luini's *Bath of the Nymphs*, enlarged to the size of a wall and employed a young Russian American artist, Dolya Goutman, to paint over all the figures and objects. The mythical figures were converted to Tahitian girls and the cypress trees to palms, but the result looked little more than the work of a clumsy amateur and a far cry from the artistry of Gauguin.

Lewin, however, did manage to suggest Gauguin in Polynesia, albeit in a secondhand way. The novel has a brief reference to Strickland being haunted by the image of an island, green and sunny, surrounded by vivid blue water, where he can paint in peace and without distractions. In the film, as he voices this longing it is also represented visually by a small carved idol of a Tahitian goddess he has acquired in Paris. This piece was commissioned from an Icelandic sculptress, Nina Saemundson, who worked from a Gauguin print.

The makers of *Rembrandt* did more than just liberally use the painter's real works; the film was shot and printed with a chiaroscuro effect—the shading of light and dark—as if the viewer is seeing the action through Rembrandt's creative vision. Gauguin's postimpressionistic style, however, was much less realistic than that of the Dutch artist's, and it would have been difficult to reproduce it through a film camera lens. Lewin nonetheless shot a number of Tahiti family scenes, particularly those focusing on Ata and her child, that mirrored Gauguin paintings, but it is doubtful that many filmgoers were knowledgeable enough to spot the resemblance.

In making *The Moon and Sixpence*, Loew and Lewin faced another, more difficult problem that had thwarted studios over the years. From the beginning, the Hays Office had disliked a story of a ruthless, amoral man who abandons his wife and children, has an affair with another man's wife, and ends his days living illicitly with a young Polynesian woman. When the Catholic Legion of Decency was formed in the mid-1930s, it soon added its considerable voice to the Hollywood censors. This forced Loew and Lewin to change their script so that Strickland is divorced by his wife and thus able to marry Ata, giving the filmmakers the opportunity to add a completely gratuitous and lengthy wedding scene, complete with Javanese dancers and drummers. One of the film's posters trumpeted these modifications by announcing, "FOUND! A way to film the story they called too frank, too revealing for the screen."

The film, however, does much more than simply legitimize the relationship between Strickland and Ata, and it goes well beyond Maugham's characterization of their life together. The novel, with its focus on the creativity of the man and on women as impediments to that creativity, is necessarily misogynistic. Mrs. Strickland is abandoned, Blanche Stroeve is exploited and discarded, and Ata is simply a submissive mistress, cook, and model. When someone asks him if he is happy with her, Strickland replies: "She leaves me alone. . . . She cooks my food and looks after her babies. She does what I tell her. She gives me what I want from a woman."[20]

In the film, however, when the earth-mother figure Tiaré asks him about life with Ata, Strickland says, "I'm very happy. I feel differently about Ata somehow." Tiaré then amplifies the painter's thoughts by saying, "If you ask me, he was in love with her and didn't know it." This possibility is confirmed when Ata is hit by a rock thrown by angry villagers, and Strickland, revealing a tenderness not seen in the novel or earlier in the picture, gently takes care of her wound. With her on her knees, he struggles to find some words: "There's something I've wanted to say to you, Ata, but I can't seem to find the right word." Ata, of course, knows the word and says, "Love," and Strickland repeats, "Love." This softens the misogynism of the novel by implying that the amoral, unsociable painter has mellowed and matured and at last found happiness with a woman in Tahiti. It makes the story much more palatable to filmgoers looking for a conventional male-female relationship and for a form of happy ending.

Lewin's adaptation satisfied the Hays Office. He had legitimized Strickland's relationship with Ata and had softened the artist's contempt for women, and he had not shown any scenes of sexual contact between the painter and Blanche Stroeve or Ata. He had not even given moviegoers a glimpse of the nude painting of Blanche, which plays such an important part in the novel; and perhaps mindful of their sensibilities or remembering the Hays Office proscription of "gruesomeness," he gave Sanders's face only a hint of the ravages of leprosy. None of this satisfied the Catholic

Legion of Decency, however, which insisted on a disavowal of Strickland immediately at the beginning of the film. "This is the story of Charles Strickland, the painter," it proclaimed, "whose career has created so much discussion. It is not our purpose to defend him." Then, after eighty-nine minutes of being captivated by a creative genius, the audience is, in effect, again exhorted not to imitate him: "Such was Strickland. He trod rough-shod over his obligations as husband and father, over the rights and sensibilities of those who befriended him. Neither the skill of his brush nor the beauty of his canvas could hide the ugliness of his life, an ugliness which finally destroyed him." Lewin objected to these editorial comments, which in fact contradicted almost everything he had put on the screen, and he later claimed, incorrectly, that they soon were omitted.

Maugham, not surprisingly, hated these disclaimers, but he liked the film itself and he made several live appearances, at no cost to the producers, at showings in the United States. This included a gala premiere attended by several celebrities at Edgartown on Martha's Vineyard. For the rest of his life he would say that it was the most satisfactory of the cinema adaptations of his works. But how satisfactory? Following a private screening before the premiere, he told reporters that "it is a good film—but I seem to be able to recall the book only vaguely."[21]

The Loew-Lewin film version of *The Moon and Sixpence* was the only one ever made for theatrical release, but at least one of the television adaptations deserves mention. In April 1951, an episode of "The Somerset Maugham Theatre" featured Lee J. Cobb as Strickland, and in November 1967, the BBC presented a version with the English actor Charles Gray in the lead. The most acclaimed adaptation was presented on NBC in October 1959, when David Susskind assembled a cast of some of the finest actors in America. It included Geraldine Fitzgerald (Amy Strickland), Hume Cronyn (Dirk Stroeve), Jessica Tandy (Blanche Stroeve), Denholm Elliott (narrator/author), and Cyril Cusack (Dr. Coutras). Though unsettling to twenty-first-century viewers, the great classical actress Judith Anderson was capable as Tiaré Johnson, and a young Jean Marsh captured the innocence and devotion of Ata. At the heart of the production, however, was Laurence Olivier, whose performance as Strickland was his first appearance on American television. The opportunity to see the man considered by many people the greatest actor of the twentieth century led at least one journalist to call the event "the most eagerly-awaited single program in television history."[22]

The ninety-minute script, after two adaptations proved unsatisfactory, was written in seven exhausting days by screenwriter S. Lee Pogostin and director Robert Mulligan. The result was an excellent treatment of the novel, faithful to Maugham's ideas despite a tightening of the plot (it is Amy Strickland rather than the narrator, for example, who confronts her runaway husband in Paris) and the fabrication of new scenes (for example, a conversation about art between Strickland and Ata). Like the earlier film, there was only the briefest shot of Strickland painting, but by 1959 the Gauguin estate raised no objection, and they were able represent his work with the French painter's early Tahitian painting *La Orana Maria* (*Hail Mary*).

It is, though, Olivier's performance that distinguishes this production and that, despite the dated studio sets, makes it worth watching six decades later. His great achievement, as critic John Crosby pointed out, is to inhabit Strickland and embody his transformation from conventional man of business to creative genius. "Sir Laurence Olivier," he wrote, "plays the possessed painter with a brilliance and sureness of touch and shattering power that the role absolutely requires if it is going to work at all. . . . Olivier's Strickland changes from a timorous stockbroker to a rude, almost bestial artist in Paris, finally achieving a nobility and grandeur in the last phase of his life in Tahiti. . . . The character grows and grows on you at the end and he is a truly monumental figure. This is a very great achievement for a character in a television drama. In fact, Olivier may be the only one I ever saw do that on TV."[23]

Olivier famously worked on characters from the outside in, and he quipped that in *The Moon and Sixpence* the heavy leprosy makeup in the final scene did the acting for him. And even before that, the bushier eyebrows and the full, seemingly untrimmed moustache and beard of the Paris scenes signaled a change from the well-turned-out gentleman at his wife's party. But the most powerful effects come from within Olivier, a growing energy seen in the eyes and heard in guffaws of laughter as if a satyr or demon was taking possession of him. At the same time, when he describes his desire—his need, actually—to paint or to find some green secluded part of the earth, there is a wistfulness in the eyes and in the voice. It truly lifts Maugham's possessed artist off the printed page.

Led by Olivier, *The Moon and Sixpence* won a number of television awards. He was given an Emmy and a Sylvania Award, Mulligan won a Best Director Emmy, and Pogostin received a Sylvania Award for Best Television Adaptation. The production was recognized with Sylvania Awards for Outstanding Telecast of the Year and Best Dramatic Program, and David Susskind received a Peabody Award for producing "a drama of style and substance, directed with imagination, and featuring a distinguished performance by Sir Laurence Olivier."

The novel *The Hour Before the Dawn*, published in the United States in 1942, is one of the worst things that Maugham ever wrote, so bad in fact that he never allowed it to be issued in Great Britain. Behind his apologetic epigraph, Alexander Pope's "In every work regard the writer's end / Since none can compass more than they intend," lies an interesting publishing history. Maugham had been in the United States since October 1940 working on behalf of the British government to counter German propaganda and present the British case and to bring the Americans into the war. In early 1941, at the urging of the British Ministry of Information, he agreed to write a film script for David Selznick about England in wartime, material that first appeared as fiction in serial form in *Redbook* magazine in the winter of 1941–42 and then as a book in June 1942.

Maugham was not comfortable writing to order, and *The Hour Before the Dawn* required him to adopt stances he had always rejected in his writing: blind jingoism and belief in the value of the British upper class and imperialists. His mandate in the novel was to portray a typical British family's response to the war, but his household is typical only of that which appeared in his comedies of manners in the 1920s. The Hendersons live in a country house, complete with Italian statues, a tennis court, and a butler, on land that has been in the family for two hundred years. In the best tradition of the landed gentry, the family is prepared to sacrifice itself to hand down to its successors the land it holds in trust.

Maugham populates this family with what is meant to be a representation of various responses to the war. The patriarch, General Henderson, is too old for active service, but his son Roger works in counterespionage at the War Office and his son-in-law Ian is in the army. However, another son, Jim, has become a pacifist at Oxford, and his refusal to enlist distresses his family, though it respects his right as a Briton to do so. The youngest son,

Tommy, is still at school but eager to hear of the exploits of those in action. Mrs. Henderson is the long-suffering, generous-spirited British mother; Roger's wife, May, is unhappy in her marriage and in love with their friend Dick Murray; Ian's wife, Jane, is the plain-speaking comic member of the family; and Dora Friedberg is an Austrian whom Jim has secretly married.

The Hour Before the Dawn begins the day before war breaks out and covers such events as the sinking of the *Athenia*, the evacuation at Dunkirk, and the London Blitz. Ian is wounded in action and Roger, presumed dead, heroically escapes from France with the aid of a stereotypical little Cockney corporal, Knobby Clarke. The theme of the classes working together in the common cause is repeated later when Roger and Jane take refuge in a bomb shelter with Knobby and his wife and children. Moreover, Mrs. Henderson takes in thirty working-class children evacuated from London.

Many of the wartime sacrifices of the Henderson clan, however, involve their relationships. May decides to give up Dick because Roger is doing important war work and it would be selfish to pursue a divorce. Later, when Dick returns from action blinded, it is Roger's turn to be noble, and he tells May about her lover's wound so that she can care for him—even fidelity, it seems, can be part of the war effort. Jim, too, makes a sacrifice when he abandons his pacifism and murders Dora, who is discovered to be a German spy who has contributed to the death of Tommy in a bombing raid. Jim then spares everybody the humiliation of flight or a trial by taking his own life.

At the end of the novel, when the Henderson family has taken its blows, it is left to the general to offer a valedictory speech—undoubtedly directed toward American audiences—about the passing of his class and the coming classless society created by the war: "We haven't always been wise, we landowners, and I dare say we've been complacent and high-handed, but on the whole we've been decent and honest and haven't done badly by our country. Perhaps we've accepted the good things our happy lot provided us as though they were our due, but according to our lights we've tried, the best of us, I mean, and I think I may say the most of us, to do our duty. But . . . we've had a long innings. . . . The future belongs to the soldiers and sailors and workmen who will have won the war. Let's hope they'll make it a happier and better England for all the people who live in it."[24]

Maugham was paid $65,000 to write the screenplay, and he completed it in Hollywood in the summer of 1941, but certainly not to the satisfaction of Selznick's writing department. "I have read scripts and reviewed fiction since 1932 but never have I felt so speechless," reported one member. "It is impossible to credit Maugham with this formless, maundering, illiterate rubbish. It is so trite and dead; the characters are stock of the worst novelette type. I just do not know what to say or how to say it, except that for his own sake Mr. Maugham had better just tear this up and forget what must have been a bad dream." Selznick diplomatically relieved Maugham of his commission, a dismissal that the author greeted mostly with relief, though he confessed that he despised the film people and "I will never again have anything to do with pictures."[25] He did, however, film an introduction that the studio used at least in part in the final cut: a short scene in which he opens a leather binder with his famous Moorish symbol on it and puts his name to the screenplay. Privately, he showed his regard for Selznick by pointedly excluding him from a Hollywood party to which he invited the producer's wife.

Selznick, meanwhile, was left to find a suitable script, and in the delay, the progress of the war overtook the production of the film. It had been decided to focus on the character of Jim and his pacifism, a stance that would play well in isolationist America, but the attack on Pearl Harbor radically changed American attitudes to war, and the film was put on hold. By November 1942, the studio decided that public opinion had cooled to the point that a conscientious objector could be featured, particularly if by the film's end he joins the fight. The English author Richard Aldington was approached to adapt Maugham's novel, but eventually the task fell to Hollywood veteran screenwriters Lesser Samuels and Michael Hogan. The job was big enough that Samuels was credited for the adaptation and Hogan for the screenplay.

The scripting of the conscientious objector scene was a delicate matter because American Quakers were expecting the film to show the pacifist position in a positive light while most of the country was in a fighting mood. Samuels enlisted the English author Christopher Isherwood, who was thought to understand the conscientious objector mind, to write the tribunal scene, but in the end he learned that nothing remained of his script. "I saw the finished product," he said, "in the projection room at the studio, with a man who was Paramount's representative in England. It was ghastly. 'What'll they think of it, over there?' I asked him. 'Oh, they'll like it all right.' 'But how *can* they,' I protested, 'it isn't like England at all.'

'That doesn't matter,' he told me calmly, 'they never expect that. Not since Mrs. Miniver.'"[26]

Samuels and Hogan also made substantial changes to simplify Maugham's story, narrowing the focus to Jim, his anti-war position, and his discovery that Dora is a German agent. The characters of the matriarch of the family (here called Hetherton), Jim's brother Ian and his wife Jane, are completely eliminated, and Dick Murray is not present to test May's marriage to Roger. In the absence of Mrs. Hetherton, her lines calling for a respect for Jim's pacifism are given to General Hetherton, who in the novel is rigid and distraught about a son who won't join the battle. Tommy becomes May's and Roger's son, and he is not, as in the original, killed in a German bombing raid.

Selznick originally wanted Ray Milland to play Jim and Vera Zorina to portray Dora, and the dependable Herbert Marshall would be Jim's brother Roger. When they were unavailable, the studio assigned the roles to Franchot Tone, Veronica Lake, and John Sutton. With the casting of Tone, then thirty-eight, the character of Jim, a twenty-one-year-old university student in the novel, becomes nearly middle-aged. His pacifism, attributed on the page to his time at Oxford, a nod to the famous student debate there about war service in 1933, is simplified in the film by a scene in his boyhood where he accidentally shoots his dog. In all of this, Tone's performance is lifeless and unconvincing, and he does not persuade the viewer that he passionately loves Lake's Dora.

Lake was never a very skilled actress, and she was disastrous in *The Hour Before the Dawn*. She abandoned her famous peekaboo hairstyle—hair falling over one eye—for the upswept "victory roll" she had promoted at the request of the Office of War Information (to discourage women factory workers from risking entanglements with machinery). Seen from behind, as it was several times in the film, it formed a "V for Victory." For the part of a German secret agent and saboteur who infatuates a man, however, the alluring peekaboo style, suggesting hidden things, would have been more effective. Lake, moreover, is wooden, with only several expressions—boredom and contempt for the English she is duping—and her attempt at an Austrian accent is ludicrous.

Filming of *The Hour Before the Dawn* took place nearly two years after Maugham had completed his *Redbook* serialization and aborted screenplay, and the material needed to be brought up to date. The film followed the original in showing the Hethertons listening to the king's speech on the outbreak of war but added a parallel scene of the German agents listening to Hitler. And while deleting the general's paean of praise for the English upper class, it added a recording of one of Winston Churchill's rousing lion's roar radio broadcasts. And while Maugham's story recognized that Jim's strangling of Dora after she runs out of bullets would lead to criminal charges and public disgrace for the family, the film skates over such moral questions. Rather than taking his own life, Jim is next seen flying in a squadron with Roger, having not only abandoned his pacifism but completed what must be the fastest enlistment and training in Royal Air Force history.

Paramount's *The Hour Before the Dawn*, finally released in May 1944 was unsuccessful both with moviegoers and critics. The *New York Times* reviewer called it "superficial melodrama" with "dialogue and a basic plot situation which lack conviction,"[27] and he found Jim's sudden conversion from pacifism unbelievable. Edwin Schallert, in the *Los Angeles Times*, observed that the film lacked any truly interesting or riveting elements, and the source of its failure might be found in his comment that "its emphasis on the British note might almost lead one to believe it had been made abroad rather than here."[28] It had in fact been written as propaganda, meant originally to explain to Americans a country facing the fascist threat in Europe, but by the time that it was seen in theaters, the war had engulfed much of the world, and the British, even a caricatured version, were then not alone in the struggle.

The last line of Maugham's novel *Christmas Holiday*, published in February 1939, was intended to hit the reader like a hammer blow: "The bottom had fallen out of his world."[29] It was the perfect line for a year in which, for tens of millions of people in Europe—and ultimately millions of people elsewhere—the foundations of their world collapsed. In September, when the conflagration began, W. H. Auden looked back and famously called the period leading up to it "a low dishonest decade." Before that, *Christmas Holiday* provided a skillful depiction of the political forces, and the widespread complacency that allowed the worst of them to triumph, ending with a warning. Few readers, however, understood the message.

Christmas Holiday tells the story of a naive, inexperienced English youth, Charley Mason, who leaves the comforts of his upper-middle-class family home to spend Christmas in Paris. He intends to spend his days broadening his knowledge in the city's galleries and his nights gaining experience in the city's brothels, but he becomes immersed in a different and disturbing world. He meets a Russian émigré prostitute, Lydia, and through her hears the story of her father's death at the hands of the Bolsheviks as well as her marriage to Robert Berger and his arrest and conviction for the murder of a friend. Despite knowing her husband's guilt, she remains loyal to him and sends money to him in his prison in French Guiana. In Paris, too, Charley is reunited with a friend from his youth, Simon Fenimore, but is horrified to discover that he has become cynical and hard, full of hatred and contempt for people.

Maugham had wanted to write about murder and the psychology of a murderer ever since he attended the 1932 trial in Paris of Guy Davin, sentenced to life imprisonment for killing a friend. In 1936 he talked to Davin on a visit to the French penal colony of Saint-Laurent-de-Maroni, and a year later he spent a month in Paris gathering more information. The Davin story, which became Robert Berger's, would in itself have made an engrossing novella or possibly a novel, but by the time Maugham wrote it in 1938, the realities of a turbulent political decade found their way into his text. For much of his career he had avoided politics in his writing, but in the early 1930s he could see another war coming, and he wrote a very political play, *For Services Rendered*, to sound an alarm. *Christmas Holiday* became another warning, this one directed at those people who were complacently and comfortably oblivious to the realities of fascism and unrest. The Berger story remained the heart of the novel, but Maugham framed it with a tale of a young man meeting up with an old friend in Paris and then hearing an account of the homicide from the killer's wife. *Christmas Holiday*, in novelist Glenway Wescott's shrewd analysis, thus became very much more than merely a murder story:

> Maugham in this slight volume, less than a hundred thousand words long, with his air of having nothing on his mind except his eight characters—how they came together and what happened and what they said and how they felt—explains more of the human basis of nazism [*sic*] and communism than anyone else has done: the self-fascinated, intoxicated, insensible character of all that new leadership in Europe; the womanish passivity of the

unhappy masses dependent on it and devoted to it; the Anglo-Saxon bewilderment in the matter, which still generally prevails; and the seeds of historic evil yet to come, not at all extirpated in World War II but rather multiplied and flung with greater profusion in no less receptive soil farther afield, even beyond Europe. Europe the starting point, the womb and the cradle, as it has been for millenniums.[30]

In Wescott's analysis, *Christmas Holiday* is a political allegory with greater social significance than any other work of fiction in 1939. Charley Mason is a representative of the prosperous middle class, the predominant ruling caste in Europe between the wars. Robert Berger is a member of the new dictating class that grew out of the First World War, while his wife, the Russian émigré prostitute, Lydia, tortured by the need to expiate the sins of her husband, is a symbol of the mass of gullible common people. The most striking figure is Berger's intellectual apologist and propagandist, the embryonic revolutionary Simon. In this character, Maugham attempts to examine the early development of a dictator, and the relevance to the totalitarian regimes of the 1930s is obvious. Simon is an outsider driven by a force within him to achieve his ends, and thus, with an almost religious austerity, he purges himself of all human ties, to become completely detached from all basic human demands. Only when he is entirely free of emotion will he be capable of establishing a totalitarianism that will ignore decent human sympathies.

Unfortunately, most readers, including Graham Greene, who wrote his own fictional studies of politics, missed the political allegory in *Christmas Holiday*. Though much more topical than most of Maugham's work, its commentary on the ideological struggles in Europe is a subtext, an allegorical representation rather than a direct examination. Readers were thus much more interested in the characters: the strange psychological makeup of Berger, the frightening personality of Simon, the tormented psyche of Lydia, and the journey of discovery of Charley. The evocative Paris background against which their dramas were played also helped to create the impression that Maugham's focus was on people rather than ideas. It was only in the aftermath of the Second World War that the subtext of *Christmas Holiday* became generally recognized.

It is thus hardly surprising that, when Universal Pictures made a film version of the novel in 1943, there was not a trace of a political element in it. Focusing entirely on the Berger murder story, it created one of the earliest film noir pictures that developed and flourished in the 1940s. Walter Wanger had wanted to adapt *Christmas Holiday* in August 1939, but the Hays Office rejected it as "a story of gross sexual irregularities."[31] Universal's script, written by Herman Mankiewicz, was approved in October 1943 because Lydia's occupation was changed from prostitute to cabaret singer. For the most part, Mankiewicz's adaptation is unrecognizable to anyone familiar with the novel. The action takes place not in England and Paris but entirely in the United States, and Charley, here called "Charles," is a newly minted lieutenant in the American Army. The film begins with his receiving a Dear John letter from his girlfriend, and what he learns through his experience in the picture is that the bottom has not fallen out of his world, that he must accept this rejection and move on with his life. This lesson is gained not in the political meeting ground of Paris but in New Orleans, where he is grounded for several days by bad weather. He meets Simon Fenimore, who is not the ascetic and frightening revolutionary of the novel but simply a loud-talking American wise guy who takes an interest in him. Fenimore takes him to a dive, Maison Lafitte, where he meets a singer-hostess, Abigail Manette, a bland version of Lydia without any of the problems of an émigré with a tortured background of family troubles.

Through Abigail, Charles learns the story of her husband, Robert Manette, who is serving time in prison for the murder of a gambler. Robert is a scion of an old New Orleans family who, though suave and charming, is addicted to gambling, ruthless beneath the surface, and inordinately attached to his mother. When he is convicted of murder, his mother blames Abigail for failing to convert her son from his corrupt behavior, telling her that "you killed him" and slapping her face. Abigail already feels a vicarious guilt for Robert's crime and works in the cabaret as a form of atonement, a very mild form of self-punishment compared with Lydia's work as a prostitute.

The conclusion of *Christmas Holiday* bears no resemblance to Maugham's novel. Robert breaks out of prison and shows up at the nightclub, unshaven and tough-talking and completely different from the charming, polished man he was earlier. He confronts Abigail, resentful of her working at the club, where he thinks she might have also been a prostitute. He intends to kill her but is shot by the police, and once again looking and talking like the man she first fell in love with, he dies in Abigail's arms with the words,

"You can let go now, Abigail." Charles repeats the message, and the film ends with an absurdly soaring crescendo of music while she looks at the night sky as if she has seen a manifestation of the divine.

The casting of the lead characters in *Christmas Holiday* could hardly have been more unexpected. For Abigail, Universal turned to its singer-actress Deanna Durbin, who had become America's ideal teenage daughter—and thereby, it was said, saved the studio from bankruptcy—through thirteen light, musical films. At the age of twenty-two, she and producer Felix Jackson believed that she needed to move into adult roles, and so she took on the part of the troubled nightclub hostess. Maugham's much more complex Lydia would have been beyond Durbin and much better suited to more skillful actresses such as Bette Davis or Ida Lupino. Mankiewicz and the director, Robert Siodmak, seemed to have decided that, if their star could not handle Maugham, then Maugham's story would have to be adapted to fit her. Not surprisingly, this includes her singing two songs, "Spring Will Be a Little Late This Year," written for the film by Frank Loesser, and Irving Berlin's "Always."

When it comes to conveying depth of character, however, Durbin is ill-equipped both physically and emotionally. Film critic Arthur Pollock said that she has "a face as sophisticated as a honeydew melon" and "doesn't seem to suffer any more than Deanna Durbin reading a schoolbook."[32] In addition to this screen presence, according to Siodmak, she always wanted to look wholesome and untarnished regardless of the requirements of the role. This simplification of the character, among other things, makes ludicrous Charles's comment at the end that "I've learned a hundred years of life in the last twenty-four hours." With not much more experience of the realities of the world, this Abigail has little to teach him. Durbin always thought that the best performance of her career was in *Christmas Holiday*, but when the following four years failed to establish her as a mature actress, she retired.

The other unusual casting against type was that of Gene Kelly as Robert Manette. Having made his reputation as a song-and-dance performer on Broadway, he turned to film with MGM in 1941, and after several pictures he was cast as a Chinese character in *Dragon Seed*. When he proved entirely unconvincing as an Asian, he was loaned to Universal in exchange for Turhan Bey and was assigned to *Christmas Holiday*. He did not like the script but was bound by contract, and with Siodmak's ultimate approval, he played Robert with a touch of homosexuality. His handsome good looks, smooth charm, and simple likeability on screen made him perfect for the scenes in which Robert wins the heart of Abigail. The problem, however, is that Kelly fails to show that this persona is a facade, that there is a calculating, devious character beneath the surface, the one who gambles and murders and returns in the end to punish his supposedly unfaithful wife. The result is that the transformation to the tough-talking, vicious man seeking revenge at the end is too absolute and therefore unpersuasive.

The best performance in *Christmas Holiday* is that of Gale Sondergaard, who had played the biracial widow so effectively in *The Letter* four years earlier. Her portrayal of Robert's mother is controlled, subtle, and suggestive of much going on beneath the surface, stretching Maugham's idea of protective mother love to the edge of incest. The film benefited, too, from the Oscar-nominated music score of Hans J. Salter and from Siodmak's skillful direction: his use of light and shadow to create an atmosphere of menace and implicit threat. It was enough to make it a success at the American box offices, its two-million-dollar gross being better than anything Durbin's musicals had drawn. In the words of the *Brooklyn Daily Eagle* reviewer, however, "It makes a good enough movie but it would be a great deal better if more Maugham had been left in it."[33]

CHAPTER 8

The Greatest
Generation's Quest

The Razor's Edge

Published in April 1944, *The Razor's Edge* is the last important book of Maugham's long career, and though he was an author who carefully planned his writing, it seems to have forced itself on him. In his 1938 literary autobiography, *The Summing Up*, he announced that he had finished with fiction, but five years later, living in the United States in wartime and sick of doing propaganda work, he felt impelled to write a novel. When asked how long it took him to write it, he replied, "sixty years," suggesting that its concerns came deep from within and had developed over much of his life. Hearing him talk about it, Garson Kanin commented, "This work means a great deal to him, more than any of us suspected. He thinks of it as being, perhaps, his last major work. No matter what the critics or the public thought of its philosophical content, it is profound and meaningful to him."[1]

A clue to what impelled Maugham to write *The Razor's Edge* in 1942 can be found by examining "The Fall of Edward Barnard," his 1921 short story that provided the basic plot for the novel. There a young businessman from Chicago, a city characterized by Maugham as the bustling industrial and financial center of the United States, gives up a career of financial success, social status, and marriage to an attractive woman from an affluent family. He prefers the easy and leisurely life he has found in Tahiti, a milieu in which he believes he can find self-knowledge and self-expression. To the disappointment of his fiancée and the disbelief of his good friend, the story's narrator, he turns his back on the American Dream at a time when the United States is becoming the wealthiest, most powerful, and most influential country in the world.

The Razor's Edge also begins in Chicago in the 1920s, and it focuses on a young man, Larry Darrell, who is expected to marry the beautiful and wealthy Isabel Bradley and to go into business. To everyone's surprise, however, he decides to spend two years in Paris with the vaguely defined purpose of finding meaning and purpose in his life. This search stretches for years, which involves his working in a coal mine in the north of France, living in Germany and Spain, and then, most importantly, studying Vedanta in an ashram in India. Isabel, meanwhile, marries their mutual friend Gray Maturin, has children, and lives a life of wealth and privilege, but she still loves the elusive Larry. The novel ends with Larry, having found the peace and understanding of life he had pursued, returning to live in the United States, perhaps as he had suggested as a taxi driver or truck driver, but certainly inhabiting a different world from that of Isabel and Gray.

The plot, structure, and characterization of the protagonist are much more complex in *The Razor's Edge* than in "The Fall of Edward Barnard." Edward's decision to remain in Tahiti is the result of a relatively simple and understandable desire to opt out of the materialistic, commercial world of modern America—what a later generation called "the rat race." He talks briefly about finding meaning in life, but he is essentially escaping from what he sees as a form of enslavement rather than advancing toward some enlightened view of the world and himself. The catalyst for this change of life seems little more than the effect of two years of living in the idyllic, lotus-eating environment of Polynesia.

In 1921 Maugham understood that readers did not want to be reminded of the recent cataclysm of the First World War, and so there is no mention of it in "The Fall of Edward Barnard." Two decades later in *The Razor's Edge*, however, Maugham attributes Larry's restlessness with his life to his combat experience in that war. In particular, he is haunted by the death of a fellow pilot mortally wounded while saving him from being shot down, and this survivor syndrome causes him to seek meaning in his own spared life. In 1943 much of the world was caught up in the hostilities, either as combatants like Larry or as civilians inescapably affected by it. World War II, the second act of an immense tragedy, made casualties and battle fatigue relevant again, and readers could understand Larry's angst. Thus, as Alec Waugh pointed out, the actions of the central figures in each story are in keeping with the spirit of the times: "Whereas Edward Barnard made an escapist's choice, living on in Tahiti, idly, with a pretty Polynesian, the hero of *The Razor's Edge* refused the conventional pattern out of a discovery in himself of a sense of purpose, a working towards the life of a mystic and ascetic. It was a theme appropriate to the hour. Escapism is sympathetic to a decade of disenchanted lassitude, but it is not sympathetic to an hour of strain and action."[2]

The most significant difference between "The Fall of Edward Barnard" and *The Razor's Edge* is Larry's discovery of meaning and purpose in his life through Indian mysticism and Vedanta. Maugham had always been sensitive to changing ideas and beliefs, and he was familiar with the work of Gerald Heard, Aldous Huxley, and Christopher Isherwood in explaining Indian philosophy and yoga. He had, moreover, traveled extensively in India in 1938, making notes on the yogis he had met and the ashrams he had visited, material that became the basis of much of Larry's experience. Despite being nearly seventy years old, Maugham understood the appeal of Eastern mysticism, though it would be almost twenty years before a younger generation would make its own pilgrimages to the east and incorporate its art and culture into its music, writing, and lives.

Maugham complicates Larry's quest and enriches his novel with the addition of well-drawn characters. The most memorable is Elliott Templeton, a snob and a social climber in the mold of Ferdy Rabenstein in "The Alien Corn" and Thornton Clay in *Our Betters*. Like Larry, he has turned his back on the commercial enterprise and materialism of the New World, preferring to live in Paris and move in European social circles. In doing so, he has taken on a life equally opposed by Larry: the Old World of narrow conventions based on birthright, appearance, club membership, clothes, jewelry, and weekend house parties. Gray Maturin, a less important figure, has the easily recognized, more concrete goals of property, family, and wealth; and as such, he is the most suitable husband for the socially conscious, materialistic Isabel. Set against these figures are two women: Sophie Macdonald, a childhood friend of Isabel and Larry whose life falls apart when her husband and baby are killed; and Suzanne Rouvier, warm, generous, and maternal, with an amoral promiscuity.

Next to Larry, perhaps the most important figure in *The Razor's Edge* is a character called "Somerset Maugham." Maugham had first used the device of telling his story through a participant in *The Moon and Sixpence*, where an unnamed novelist with a personality and history very much like his own acts as an observer, chorus, and foil to the central figure. In *The Razor's Edge*, the narrator, who moves among the various characters and ties the story together, resembles the author even more and bears his name. He is not entirely autobiographical, that is, the man who moved in the real world, but, rather, Maugham as he would have liked to have been, and therefore the narrative voice is the most attractive of any of his works. Though there are qualities of caution, restraint, and guardedness, he is mellower and warmer and more playfully self-deprecating than in any other piece of writing. Detached in an avuncular way from the central conflicts of the story but sensitive to the difficulties of the characters, he is able to be compassionate and generous.

Such an intrusive narrator serves another very important purpose. *The Razor's Edge*, like *Of Human Bondage*, tells of a young man's journey to discover meaning in his life and a pattern for it. Maugham wrote the earlier novel when he was forty, however, and it was a fictional representation of someone he understood very well: the person he had become at that point. *The Razor's Edge* is another account of a youthful search for meaning and purpose, but the seventy-year-old Maugham, though he could show remarkable sensitivity and perception of the youths of a new era, was not one of them. As he confesses in the novel, "I am of the earth, earthy; I can only admire the radiance of such a rare creature, I cannot step into his shoes and enter into his inmost heart."[3] Inevitably, seeing Larry only through the eyes of the narrator and other characters instead of being given his inmost thoughts directly makes him somewhat elusive and mysterious. And this is one of the appeals of the novel: Larry's quest and the inner peace that he finds are vague enough that readers can formulate their own versions of self-discovery. This was not, however, a quality that translated easily to the movie screen.

When *The Razor's Edge* was published in 1944, it instantly became a best seller, acclaimed by reviewers and eagerly devoured by readers. Most film producers were leery of it, however, unsure of how to film Larry's spiritual and philosophical search and his interior life, but Darryl Zanuck, head of 20th Century Fox, thought that he could make a blockbuster movie of it. "There must be a reason," he said, "why the American public is reading this book more than it is reading any other book. Millions of people today are searching for contentment and peace in the same manner that Larry searches in the book."[4] He bought the rights for $250,000 and set the experienced screen writer Lamar Trotti to work on a script. And then the problems began.

Zanuck had told his production team that "as I see the basic story, it is an adventure picture, ... a melodramatic adventure, wherein a man searches the face of the earth for the hidden key to contentment."[5] Adventure seems to have been the key element, and as Trotti told his fellow writer Philip Dunne at the time, "Darryl can't bring himself to understand that his and Maugham's concepts of life are as far apart as the North and South poles."[6] Zanuck's views of the novel, it turned out, were far from those of other important players. Maugham's contract stipulated that the director should be someone respected in the film industry, and he suggested his good friend George Cukor, who had directed *Our Betters* and had recently done *Winged Victory* with Zanuck. Cukor, however, disliked Trotti's script, which, he said, "had what the studio called entertainment, which means dancing and country clubs and all that crap. Nothing to indicate you were supposed to sit down and listen to what was being said. Whatever important things this script retained were sandwiched between all sorts of nonsense."[7] Cukor told Zanuck that he would direct the film only if Maugham, who was also appalled by Trotti's adaptation, did the screenplay. Maugham surprised Zanuck by agreeing to write a script for nothing, seeing it as an opportunity, following the rebuff of his *The Hour Before the Dawn* screenplay, to conquer the cinema by devising a script that faithfully rendered a novel that he considered important.

Maugham moved to Hollywood in June 1945 and spent the summer living and working in Cukor's home. To ensure authenticity in the Paris scenes, he consulted his friend the French writer André David, and in Los Angeles he met with Swami Prabhavananda to learn precisely what instructions a holy man would give Larry. When he had agreed to work on the screenplay, he thought that he would be required only to offer some suggestions and make a few revisions, but when he learned that Zanuck wanted a whole new screenplay, he sat down and wrote one in longhand. Contrary to Hollywood folklore, Maugham's script was not intended to replace Trotti's but rather, as his introductory note to the manuscript now in the Berg Collection of the New York Public Library indicates, to amplify it:

"The following is not to be looked upon as a script and will be incomprehensible unless it is read in conjunction with Lamar Trotti's. It should be looked upon only as a story in dialogue. To save time I have left all descriptions of the various scenes and all indication of the feelings or expressions of the various characters. I know nothing about photographic effectiveness and so have left that to be dealt with by Lamar Trotti and George Cukor."[8] The result, said Cukor, was the kind of script that told the audience from the opening sequence that "'this is the kind of picture it's going to be, you'd better listen. You listen here!' A taxi drives up to a house, a man gets out, he goes inside and immediately starts a long conversation with someone in the house."[9]

This version of *The Razor's Edge*, however, did not seem to Zanuck to be an "adventure," and he found it too verbose and contemplative. It was a reaction, Cukor told Maugham, that was typical of the usual Hollywood attitude to filming books. "They are accustomed," he said, "to treating books and plays, etc., for pictures with either a matter-of-fact realism, sentimentality, or in a sanctimonious, Sunday-school way. They shy from any elevation of spirit. They are in strange territory with *The Razor's Edge*. Its approach is unfamiliar to them. That's what worries them."[10]

Zanuck rejected Maugham's adaptation and, though the author had demanded no payment, gave him $15,000, with which Maugham bought a painting by Matisse. Ironically, when the film was completed, Zanuck was so pleased that he asked Maugham to write a sequel that would describe Larry's life after his return to the United States. Not surprisingly, Maugham declined the invitation, telling the producer, "The only example in history of a sequel being as good as the original is 'Don Quixote.' So I'd be crazy to attempt it. I'd need a far greater knowledge of American life than I can possibly possess."[11]

In addition to the scrapping of Maugham's screenplay, Cukor was replaced by Edmund Goulding and, with some alterations, particularly to the dialogue, but without Swami Prabhavananda's advice, Trotti's original script was brought back. Zanuck had always seen Tyrone Power in the role of Larry, but since he had joined the Marine Corps in 1942 and was unavailable, he approached James Stewart. Fearing that the part was too saintly, Stewart declined, and so the studio delayed production until Power was discharged from active duty in January 1946. Power had been decorated for his considerable action in the South Pacific, and his war experience not only gave him a deeper understanding of Larry's character but he also recognized how he would strike a sympathetic nerve with millions of returned soldiers. In an article titled "This Is What I Believe," written for *Screenland* magazine in August 1946, he revealed why he was eminently suited to play Maugham's protagonist:

> The shooting war is over, but the war in men's hearts isn't. During my three years in the service, I discovered that many servicemen, given more time for introspection than they had ever had previously, were groping about for something in which they could believe. One reason I was anxious to make "The Razor's Edge" immediately upon my return from service was because it seems to me that in Larry Darrell, whose faith in his old way of life was shaken by the first World War, Somerset Maugham created a character similar in his reactions to hundreds of thousands of ex-servicemen today. They, too, are for the most part not content to go back to their old jobs in drug stores or banks or selling bonds. They are restless and confused. They don't know exactly what it is they are searching for.[12]

Power's understanding of his generation and its attraction to *The Razor's Edge* was sound, but he could not have anticipated that youthful restlessness and searching would stretch over the next two decades. Larry's rejection of the materialism of the American Dream, his pursuit of spiritual meaning, and his exploration of Eastern mysticism appealed as well to the Beat Generation. And in more general terms, his rebellion against conventional social expectations resonated with rebellious young people on both sides of the Atlantic.

Zanuck was determined to make *The Razor's Edge* a smash hit, and he surrounded Power with an impressive supporting cast. When Cukor was still involved, he made the case for Isabel to be played by Katharine Hepburn, who was said to be excited about the role, but she was committed to a long run in a Broadway play. Zanuck first wanted Olivia de Havilland and then Jennifer Jones, but the latter was under contract to David Selznick and turned down the part. Zanuck then considered borrowing Bette Davis from Warner Bros. because she was a major star and could play Isabel with some sizzle, but that idea fell through. At one point he told Maureen O'Hara that she had the part, but since he was mounting a huge publicity campaign, she was not to tell anyone. She could not, however, resist sharing the news with Linda Darnell, one of Zanuck's mistresses, and when he heard of O'Hara's indiscretion, he fired her.

In the end, Zanuck picked one of his studio's own stars, Gene Tierney, who had become well known for *Laura* in 1944 and received an Oscar nomination for *Leave Her to Heaven* in 1945. One of the most beautiful actresses in films, she was elegant, with high cheekbones, an appealing overbite (her contract prevented the studio requiring her to have her teeth fixed), and blue-green eyes. She was more attractive than Maugham's Isabel, but her patrician demeanor suited a pampered and privileged woman from the upper crust of Chicago society. Tierney played the part well, though her Isabel is haughtier and more consistently mean-spirited than the original.

The part of the free-spirited Suzanne Rouvier was dropped from the script but not before it was rejected by Constance Bennett and considered by Gloria Swanson. The richer part of the unfortunate Sophie first had Angela Lansbury's name attached to it, but before long Zanuck asked Louis B. Mayer for the loan of Judy Garland. When Garland's schedule was too full, he asked Betty Grable, who was wise enough to realize that she was wrong for the part, that moviegoers would expect her to rise from her suicide's deathbed singing and dancing as usual. Finally, Zanuck settled on Anne Baxter, whose more ordinary, girl-next-door looks made her a perfect foil to Tierney's Isabel. She was persuasive as the down-to-earth, insecure young woman whom tragedy turns into a drug-and-drink-addled woman of the streets. Baxter later said that the only really great film performance of her career was in the scene when she learns that her husband and child are dead. Most critics praised her work, and it garnered her an Oscar and a Golden Globe Award for Best Supporting Actress.

The best performance in *The Razor's Edge*, though it did not win an Oscar, was that of Clifton Webb as Elliott Templeton. Two months after the novel hit the bookstores, people were already telling Webb that he would be the perfect Templeton, and in November 1944, Hedda Hopper claimed that 20th Century Fox had bought the rights to the novel especially for him.[13] Webb had just received an Oscar nomination for playing the suave villain, Waldo Lydecker, in *Laura*, and minus the villainy, he was well-suited to play Maugham's condescending snob. Tall, slender, elegant, and articulate, he had appeared in Oscar Wilde and Noel Coward plays—as well as Cole Porter and George Gershwin musicals—on Broadway, and he delivered Maugham's lines not only with conviction but irony. He carried this supercilious but self-parodying persona into his next film, *Sitting Pretty*, and Bosley Crowther's description of his Lynn Belvedere could just as well be applied to his Elliott Templeton: "He does it with elegant detachment and a chilling coolness towards the common herd. Yet there slyly protrudes through his arrogance a flickering spoof of pomposity and a tentative benevolence toward humanity, of which he generously agrees to be one. A student of the fine shades of kidding will find a lot to admire in Mr. Webb."[14] If Baxter's hospital scene is heartrending, Webb makes Templeton's deathbed moments simultaneously comic, pathetic, and moving.

One of the critical decisions facing Trotti and Goulding in adapting *The Razor's Edge* was what to do with the novel's narrative voice, the character of "Somerset Maugham" within the story. They decided to retain the observer/narrator, and, for the fifth time, Herbert Marshall appeared in a Maugham film. Four years earlier, he had played a similar role—an unnamed observer and foil for the lead—in *The Moon and Sixpence*, and it was a natural progression for him to portray Maugham. Marshall knew Maugham, but not well, and so he wisely did not attempt to impersonate the real man. "I did not try to do a portrait of Maugham," he said, "I didn't try to be like him at all. What I did try to do was characterize his behavior as a character in his own book. That may be a fine point to some."[15] Fine point or not, it was an important distinction since the character is the author's view of himself, not as he was, but as he would have liked to have been.

The problem with the effectiveness of Baxter, Webb, Marshall, and to some degree Tierney is that their characters overshadow Larry. When he began *The Razor's Edge*, Zanuck said that the real challenge lay in dramatizing the central theme: Larry's search for meaning and spiritual contentment. Ultimately, though the film was popular with moviegoers, most critics concluded that it had not met Zanuck's challenge. Bosley Crowther's reaction was scathing but it reflected the response of many reviewers: "It is an overdressed, overtalked picture. . . . [The] spiritually troubled protagonist . . . is just a blankly superficial social misfit mooning about among his Elsa Maxwell friends. . . . And the return of this gent to the world of people reveals him more in the role of a pious and futile Mr. Fixit than that of a true evangelist."[16] Years later, film historian Roger Manvell referred to "the religious and moral hokum of such problem pictures as *The Razor's Edge*."[17]

It may be that the spiritual quest that Maugham suggested reasonably well on the printed page was not transferable to film, or at least not by Hollywood filmmakers in the 1940s. Even Crowther referred to the "basically illusory theme" of *The Razor's Edge*, and Philip K. Scheuer commented that "goodness is real; and when you find it, infinitely precious. Is it something that can be photographed or does it remain too abstract to be seen? . . . To achieve spirituality, it is not enough to talk about it, nor does an odor of sanctity necessarily exalt the soul."[18] What the film actually shows of Larry's quest and what he learned seems rather prosaic: he lives *la vie de bohéme* in Paris, works in a coal mine, stays in an ashram and consults a religious man in India, returns with a skill in curing headaches with a coin, and tries to save an old friend from self-destruction. What was given an aura of mysticism on the printed page does not stand up to the more direct eye of the camera.

Maugham had written of spiritual and philosophical quests before, and filmmakers had not found a way—or a desire—to represent his words in concrete images. The versions of *Of Human Bondage* completely avoided dealing with Philip Carey's search for meaning, and the film adaptations of *The Painted Veil* and *The Narrow Corner* paid scant attention to the Eastern religious beliefs that underpinned the novels. *The Razor's Edge*, however, could not be stripped of the spiritual elements and remain the story that had appealed to millions of readers. The attempt by 20th Century Fox to represent them led, perhaps inevitably, to the accusation of purveying "hokum," though it seems that one person's hokum is another's spiritual truth. Two weeks after the launch of *The Razor's Edge*, RKO released *It's a Wonderful Life*, in which an angel comes to earth to persuade an unhappy man that his life has been worthwhile and that he is important in the world. On the man's acceptance of this "truth," it is suddenly Christmas, and he is singing Christmas carols with his family and surrounded by friends and townspeople who have come bearing money. Watching this hokum has become an apparently spiritually enriching Christmas ritual for millions of people.

And sometimes hokum takes on cult status. Forty years after the publication of *The Razor's Edge*, the American comic actor Bill Murray played

Larry Darrell in a new film adaptation. Murray was not familiar with either the novel or the Power film, but when director and writer John Byrum gave him a copy of the book, his response was quick. "I knew right away that it was what I wanted to do. I knew what the guy was talking about. I wanted to make a dramatic film, and this is a story that works."[19] Murray's studio, Columbia Pictures, was understandably dubious about the project, but when the actor agreed to do the much more promising *Ghostbusters*, it gave lukewarm approval of his version of *The Razor's Edge*. Byrum and Murray wrote the script, and filming took place in England, France, and the mountainous Srinagar and Ladakh region of India.

It is not clear what Murray meant when he said that he knew what the "guy" (Larry or Maugham) was "talking about," and the film devotes little attention to the nature of Larry's beliefs. He is shown in an overly long war episode, where he is an ambulance driver on the edge of combat rather than a pilot in the midst of it, but little is made of this thereafter. As the film progresses, Larry seems to take his suggestion that he will "loaf" literally, and he is much more of a hippie dropout than a troubled combat veteran looking for inner peace.

Murray took on the role to prove to the studio and the public—and perhaps to himself—that he was more than a comic actor, that he could excel in a serious role. When the picture was complete, however, he explained that "I want people to laugh all the way. . . . We weren't trying to make a funny movie, but the intention was to show that this search doesn't mean you lose your sense of humor."[20] The problem is that Murray could not resist clowning in the manner for which he had become famous on *Saturday Night Live* and a number of feature films. When, for example, Larry is emerging from a swimming pool to have a serious conversation with Isabel about their relationship, Murray prefaces it with an imitation of a seal. In India, on his way to find spiritual understanding, he is chased through the village streets by a horde of children after giving a boy a rupee; and he clowns with village women selling vegetables in the Himalayas.

These moments, rather than showing that Larry has a sense of humor, simply detract from the seriousness that Murray claimed to have seen in Maugham's story. Most damaging, though, is the comic eulogy that Larry delivers on the death of a fellow ambulance driver, an ironic commentary that Murray's fans would recognize as a buried tribute to John Belushi, his good friend who died of a drug overdose two years earlier. "He was a slob," he intones. "Did you ever see him eat? Starving children could fill their bellies on the food that ended up on his beard and clothes. Dogs would gather to watch him eat. I never understood gluttony, but I hate it. I hated that about you. He enjoyed disgusting people, being disgusting, the thrill of offending people and making them uncomfortable. He was despicable. He will not be missed." It is the kind of ironic tribute that would have been fitting at Belushi's funeral, where everyone would recognize that the pain of loss was being blunted by comic reversal, that Belushi himself would have appreciated the joke, but it was entirely out of place when applied to the dead ambulance worker.

Two decades later, Murray showed that he could be a fine, subtle actor in *Lost in Translation*, but in *The Razor's Edge* he had not yet learned how to go beyond the persona of the hip ironist. His preeminent skill was in portraying insincerity and one of his greatest tools was the deadpan look. Larry's strongest trait is his genuine earnestness, however, and Murray is not convincing in the serious moments when he is supposed to be experiencing an epiphany or learning a fundamental truth. The deadpan is just dead; his face is blank and his eyes convey nothing. And by the end of the film, the search for enlightenment seems almost entirely forgotten as Murray's holy fool becomes much more fool than holy.

One of the fault lines in Murray's *The Razor's Edge* is the clash between his modern ironic performance and the film's setting: World War I and after. In 1946 the recent war had given relevance to Maugham's story of the earlier conflict, but by 1984 people were engaged in different struggles. Columbia had wanted a modern background, and Murray later came to realize that the appeal of Maugham's novel for him lay in what it had to say to people of his own era. "I saw people I knew in the book," he said, "people of my time and the Vietnam era, and that's one of the reasons it touched me."[21] The characters and milieus of the picture, however, were dated and irrelevant, especially when placed against Murray's modern persona. The supporting cast, while not as strong as in the earlier film, is capable. Catherine Hicks's Isabel lacks the beauty and spiteful presence of Tierney, James Keach does Gray Maturin as well as Payne, and Denholm Elliott's performance, fine as it is, still does not match Webb's. Perhaps wisely, Murray and Byrum eliminated the "Maugham" figure without any damage to the telling of the story.

Theresa Russell acquits herself well as Sophie, but in a larger and sexier role than that played by Baxter or envisaged by Maugham. The novel avoids any detailed description of what lies behind Larry's decision to marry Sophie except to attribute it to self-sacrifice to save her from dissolution and ruin. He seems to have little interest in sex, resisting Isabel's desperate attempt to seduce him in Paris, but the film shows the pair bedded down. Similarly, Murray pursues a joyful courtship of Sophie, and a strong emotional and physical attraction develops between the two. As in the original story, Isabel destroys Sophie through leaving her alone with the Polish liqueur, but the film then races to its conclusion by having her reject Larry the same evening and going on to have her throat cut by murderous thugs during the night. When he goes to confront Isabel, he discovers that Elliott is dying, and he pretends that he is bearing a party invitation from the old snob Princess Novemali, thus giving Elliott his triumphant death scene. The film ends with Larry bidding farewell to Isabel and Gray, and to their question about where he will go, he replies portentously, "America." In the novel it was a significant destination because, having secured inner peace through his spiritual search, he could thrive in the bustle and clamor of the United States. Here it seems simply a retreat from relationships with two women that have gone wrong.

The consensus of movie reviewers was that Murray's *The Razor's Edge* had missed the mark. Janet Maslin in the *New York Times* called it "slow, overlong and ridiculously overproduced,"[22] and for the *Baltimore Sun*'s Stephen Hunter it "is so banal and oafish, so mock profound and orotund, that it makes the minutes seem like hours and the hours . . . seem like geological epochs."[23] Some critics, however, seeing the picture as a Bill Murray platform rather than an adaptation of a Maugham story, praised it. Gene Siskel, for example, found it "a pleasant, thought-provoking surprise," a story in which Murray succeeds in disappearing into a character searching for meaning: "'The Razor's Edge' is Murray's movie, and the fact that he is now a complete movie star is really quite wonderful. . . . Murray simply walks through 'The Razor's Edge' and we follow."[24] For Murray's many fans, it is a path they happily continue to follow.

CHAPTER 9

Life in Short,
Sharp Strokes

The Omnibus Films

When television exploded as a popular medium of entertainment on both sides of the Atlantic in the 1950s, it was inevitable that it would exploit the work of Maugham. In the era before the development of serial dramas and sitcoms, television networks relied on anthology programs that offered a different play each week, many of them written by respected playwrights and performed live by well-known actors. These shows gave a cultural legitimacy to a medium trying to prove its artistic worth, and it led to the period being called "the Golden Age of Television."

Among Maugham's hundred or so short stories, there were many that were perfectly suited to the half-hour or full-hour format, and of course his name suggested sophistication. And so in the United States in 1950–51, CBS created "The Somerset Maugham TV Theatre," which, when taken over by NBC, presented forty of his tales, many of them directed by Martin Ritt and featuring such eminent actors as Lee J. Cobb, Grace Kelly, Anthony Quinn, and Jessica Tandy. The author's introductions were filmed at his villa at Cap Ferrat, and the stories were broadcast live from a New York studio. In 1960–62 the British Independent Television network presented thirty-eight stories in "The Somerset Maugham Hour," using many of the best British actors and directors. A decade later, in 1969–70, BBC TV offered more than twenty stories in a Maugham season, productions so well produced and acted that it won the Society of Film and Television Arts award for most outstanding drama series of 1969. Only Georges Simenon has had his works anthologized in so many television series.

While Maugham's short stories were ideally suited to a television format, most of them—with the exception of "Rain" and "The Letter"—had always been considered too slight to be expanded and made into feature films. In 1948, however, the head of Gainsborough Pictures, Sydney Box, anticipated the television success and decided to put five of the author's short stories in a single film. Groups of stories had occasionally been put on the screen before, but they were always linked by a common theme or device like a location or object. *If I Had a Million* (1932) comprised eight tales about what a gift of a million dollars would do for eight individuals, and *Tales of Manhattan* (1942) followed the experiences of a gentleman's dress coat as it was, in succession, owned by six men. These omnibus films were rare, though, leading Bosley Crowther to call for more in the *New York Times* in 1942.[1] Box's movie, to be called *Quintet*, would, however, comprise five entirely separate tales played by different casts and shaped by different directors. They would be held together by a common tone and attitude, that of Maugham himself, and thus the picture begins with the announcement that "the star of this film is not an actor or actress, but a writer."

To emphasize the importance of the author to the film's stories, Box became innovative, and Maugham was persuaded to provide an on-screen introduction to each episode. These were filmed in Pinewood Studio, in London, where the author's Cap Ferrat study was meticulously re-created, including a reproduction of his favorite armchair with its well-worn arms. Maugham spoke deliberately to avoid the stammer that had plagued him all his life, and he talked casually about his writing and his career. The famous Moorish symbol that had adorned all except his earliest books was featured in the opening credits, and each story was prefaced by a shot simulating his turning of the pages of a thick volume called "Quartet" (the film's eventual title). It was a faux book, with, in some cases, the opening lines on the page being the screenwriter, R. C. Sherriff's, modifications rather than Maugham's words.

It was a coup to enlist Maugham to appear in person, because at the age of seventy-four he had become a Grand Old Man of Letters, the second most respected author in the United States; and he had a distinguished presence. He had been represented on screen in some of his narrators, as in *The Moon and Sixpence* in 1942, and then as "Mr. Maugham" in *The Razor's*

Edge in 1946. It was a logical next step to put the man himself in front of the cameras, and it was so successful that CBS used the same device in 1950. A variation of it was also adopted in 1971 by PBS when it employed Alistair Cooke, an articulate and urbane Englishman, to introduce the stories of Masterpiece Theatre as if comfortably seated in his library.

Box was gambling on his audiences being entertained by these diverse, disconnected narratives, and he advertised the film as a moviegoer's bargain: "Four complete stories—each containing as much entertainment, as much drama, and as many stars as any one ordinary film!"[2] The danger, however, was that viewers would miss the sustained connection with the characters of the ordinary film. Film historian Raymond Durgnat, on the other hand, observed that the lack of a close identification with a few featured characters might make for a different and equally valuable movie experience. "One advantage of the formula," he said, "is that, since the audience get a varied bill of fare, identification need be less consistent. This might well facilitate characterizations and stories which are just a little odder, sadder, truer, and more, in a semi-Brechtian sense, alienating, yet recognizable, than the principal characters in a one-story feature."[3] Commenting on this idea in his excellent study *Omnibus Films: Theorizing Transauthorial Cinema*, David Scott Diffrient makes a sweeping claim that the Maugham films are "the oddest, saddest, truest, and most alienating yet recognizable . . . in terms of the quirkily drawn characters therein: disillusioned, needy, cautious, destructive, and self-loathing people whose 'muffled, seething, restrained, [and] polluting' spitefulness would not manifest so distinctly again until the 'angry young men' made their entrance a decade later."[4]

In casting the actors and actresses to play the often quirky, troubled, comic, and caricatured parts in the omnibus films, Gainsborough was able to draw on the rich theatrical life of London. The presence of so many playhouses in or near London ensured that there was a wealth of what, in North America, are called "character actors," essentially fine actors, often with unique screen presences, who usually played supporting roles. *Quartet* and its sequels, *Trio* and *Encore*, gave such actors as Nigel Patrick, Cecil Parker, James Hayter, Angela Baddeley, Nora Swinburne, John Laurie, Kay Walsh, George Cole, Françoise Rosay, and many others a chance to play leading roles, albeit in only a portion of a film. Occasionally the studio used a more prominent actor, such as Michael Rennie, or young performers such as Dirk Bogarde and Jean Simmons, who went on to film stardom.

The original list of short stories drawn up in 1947 to be considered for inclusion in the omnibus film comprised ten titles, and it is interesting to consider the ones not deemed suitable. "The Round Dozen," a tale of bigamy, was vetoed by the Hays Office, and "The Back of Beyond" (about sexual infidelity, and the need for the injured party to accept it) and "Footprints in the Jungle" (about adulterers and murderers who go unpunished) were not seen as acceptable replacements. There can be little doubt that "The Unconquered" (rape and child murder), "The Happy Couple" (unpunished murderers), "Force of Circumstance" (interracial sexual relationship), and "Red" (interracial sexual relationship) were dropped because of their subject matters.

Only four stories were ultimately chosen for what came to be retitled *Quartet*, and all were markedly changed to satisfy the censors or to appeal to popular tastes. Maugham explained later that "the necessary changes to satisfy government regulations of movie material were made by someone else,"[5] the other person being the veteran screenwriter Sherriff. Maugham agreed to the adaptations but did not like them, telling Garson Kanin that *Quartet* was "extremely good except for the fact that they had in each case absolutely removed the point of the story."[6] The most serious damage to his fiction was inflicted on "The Alien Corn," a perceptive and complex account of a Jewish family's attempt to become assimilated into the English upper middle class. In the original story, the parents change their name from "Bleiker" to "Bland" ("Miriam" becomes "Muriel"), and they aspire to a political career for their son George. As a foil to these pretensions, Maugham torments them with one of his most memorable creations: Ferdy Rabenstein, Lord Bland's brother and a man who retains and relishes his Jewish identity. In the middle of this tension is George, who the family hopes will assume his father's title and become a proper aristocratic English country gentleman.

These hopes are threatened when George announces that, rather than inheriting the title, he wishes to become a concert pianist. In desperation, his parents agree to an arrangement whereby he will study in Germany for two years and then play before an expert. If he then seems to have promise he will be free to pursue a career; if not, he will give up music and accept the pattern that the Blands have conceived for him. While in Germany he encounters the Jews of Frankfurt and Munich, who have maintained their culture, and he develops an urge to give up his family's English life and join these Jews in Germany. On his return, however, he performs for a famous pianist, is pronounced lacking in essential talent, and kills himself rather than return to the family fold.

"The Alien Corn" is a penetrating examination of Jewish assimilation in Britain (or anywhere else). Ludwig Lewisohn included it in his *Among the Nations: Three Tales and a Play about Jews* and wrote in the preface that "every other point and circumstances and turn of phrase in 'The Alien Corn' is of an unrivalled perspicacity and exactness. Yet Mr. Maugham, with an extraordinary humanity, never lets either the Rabensteins or the Blands become contemptible. He may himself be surprised to know how powerful to authentic Jews the moral of his story is, the moral, namely, that total assimilation is not only a shabby and degrading thing, but that it does not even work."[7]

Astonishing as it seems, Sherriff's screenplay for *Quartet* expunges all references to Jews and Jewishness. In place of the pseudo-county facade, the film offers a family of genuine English landed gentry. "Adolphus Bland" becomes "Sir Frederick Bland," "Ferdy Rabenstein" is replaced by "Uncle John," the Jewish *grande dame* Lady Bland is transformed into "Aunt Maud," and the narrator is replaced by "Paula," played by Honor Blackman, a young woman added to provide the conventional romantic interest. Instead of studying in Germany, George, portrayed very well by a young Dirk Bogarde, goes to Paris, and the conflict is now centered on the pretensions of conventional English society and the young man's overly ambitious desire to become a concert pianist. At the insistence of the Hays Office, his death is presented ambiguously, suggesting that it might have been an accident rather than a suicide.

In 1950 Maugham explained that "The Alien Corn" had eliminated any reference to Jews or Jewishness because the political and social climate of the time would not permit the filming of the story as he had written it in 1931. Lewisohn's *Among the Nations* had printed the story unchanged in 1948, the same year that *Quartet* was released, but readers were assumed to be more sophisticated than moviegoers. In the postwar years, with the revelation of Hitler's attitudes toward, and treatment of, the Jews, film-makers would not have been comfortable presenting Jews attempting to disguise their backgrounds by adopting the pretensions of a foreign culture. They could not have shown the protagonist going to Germany and succumbing to the culture of the Jewish ghettos in Frankfurt and Munich. By 1960, however, Britain's Independent Television felt free to offer a faithful depiction of Maugham's story, and its acute and shrewd observation of the Jewish Blands led the London *Times* reviewer rightly to see it as a sign of how much a popular medium like television had matured.[8]

None of the other stories in *Quartet* were as eviscerated as "The Alien Corn," but all were changed to meet the demands of the censor. In the original story of "The Facts of Life," a young Englishman, Nicky, goes to the Riviera and does three things that his straitlaced father warns him against: he gambles, lends money, and sleeps with a woman. To the chagrin of his moralistic father, he returns more experienced and richer, having won a substantial sum at the roulette table, loaned money to a coquette, and then, having bedded her, inadvertently taken some of her money while thwarting her attempt to steal his own. In the film adaptation, though, Nicky does not seek an affair, and he does not sleep with the woman, who is not presented as the "tart" or "coquette" of the story. She is a married woman whose husband is absent, and she invites him to her hotel room, a large suite, so that he can have a fine view of the city. The young man rather incredibly spends the night on a sofa in another room.

The makers of *Quartet* contrived to give happy endings to the other two stories by appending additional scenes, as if Maugham's last word was not the right one. "The Kite," called by Diffrient a "bizarre psychodrama of obsession, parental possessiveness, and the social pretensions of the lower middle class,"[9] is a tale of a young man, Herbert Sunbury, raised by an overprotective mother, who develops a monomania for kite flying. When his young wife, Betty, resents this pastime, he returns to the family home, thus driving her to retaliate by destroying his most prized kite. The story ends with Herbert stubbornly remaining in jail rather than paying his wife alimony. It was a conclusion apparently too acerbic for movie audiences, who expected estranged lovers always to be reconciled, and so a short scene was, almost apologetically, tacked on. The narrator says, "That's the story as Ned Preston told it to me, and I never knew what happened to Herbert and Betty; perhaps it was something like this." Herbert is then let out of prison, goes to the common where he discovers his wife herself flying a kite, and becomes reunited with her. Not only does this stretch dramatic plausibility, but if the Freudian overtones are as strongly present in the story as many critics claim, the additional scene destroys them or makes for a very bizarre psychological interpretation indeed.

In the screen adaptation of "The Colonel's Lady," equally serious damage is done to Maugham's story, dramatically and thematically. The original tale recounts how a middle-aged "Colonel Blimp," George Peregrine, discovers that his wife has written a book of poems describing a passionate affair she had several years earlier that ended in the death of her young lover. Peregrine is tormented by thoughts of her infidelity and, when he asks his lawyer what he should do, he is told: "Nothing." The affair was in the past, the young man is dead, and if Peregrine wants to keep his wife, he will forget the whole thing. Maugham's point, which is repeated in so much of his writing, is that infidelity, especially that committed in the distant past, should not be allowed to destroy a relationship that is otherwise satisfying and well-grounded. Peregrine accepts this position, but Maugham nonetheless ends his story with a twist: Peregrine tells his lawyer, "There's one thing I shall never understand till my dying day: What in the name of heaven did the fellow ever see in her?"[10]

Box decided that this conclusion was too cynical for the general cinema audiences and, with Maugham's agreement, wrote an additional scene in which Peregrine ignores his lawyer's advice and confronts his wife about the identity of her lover. He was, she replies, Peregrine himself! *He* was the passionate young man, one who had become dead to her over the years because she had not fully understood him. They are thus reconciled, and the audience, having been titillated throughout by the suggestion that an illicit affair has occurred, can leave the theater satisfied that there has been no impropriety. At the movies, it seems, one can indeed have one's affairs and moral smugness as well.

According to the director, Ken Annakin, the ending of "The Colonel's Lady" was not the only alteration made to Sherriff's script: he went back to Maugham's original dialogue because he found it more realistic than the screenwriter's version. Maugham was pleased to hear about this, pointing out that in real life people hesitate and repeat themselves, something not considered appropriate in fine writing. Aside from the modified ending, "The Colonel's Lady" is well done, with excellent performances by Cecil Parker (Peregrine) and Nora Swinburne (Evie). Annakin went on to a lengthy and distinguished directing career, but he looked back on the Maugham story as "one of the best pictures I ever made. . . . Of all my British films, I would like to be remembered for 'The Colonel's Lady.'"[11]

Thirty-six years after *Quartet*, in 1984, American producer/director Jon Bloom reworked Annakin's adaptation in a superb twenty-eight-minute film. With excellent performances by Robert Loggia as George Peregrine and Louise Fletcher as his wife, Evie, *Overnight Sensation* became an excellent example of how a creative work can be made new and relevant for a new generation. In this version the story is set not in England in the 1930s but in southern California in the 1980s, and George is not a colonel but a fashion photographer. After years of marriage, Evie has become almost an afterthought to him, a situation beautifully represented in the opening scene, when she is trying to type a story while cooking for him. When he blithely says that he won't be home for dinner, she sets the food preparation aside and returns to writing in greater earnest. Her first novel has been published, and she soon learns that the paperback rights have been bought for $85,000, both developments that George dismisses as a hobby.

As Evie attracts more and more acclaim, George's sizeable ego is dented, a development given more emphasis than in the original story. When he finally reads Evie's novel, he becomes enraged and demands to know the identity of the young man in the novel; and, as in Annakin's revised ending, she tells George that the hero was his younger self. Whereas Annakin offers the viewer a happy ending, one at odds with Maugham's story, Bloom's brilliant last shot is full of ambiguity. George pleads with Evie to keep their marriage intact, saying, "I can change; change is my middle name." He has used the "middle name" line several times before as part of his superficial patter, and it is a clear indication that he is not serious about changing. Evie knows this, and as she embraces him, the camera remains on her disbelieving face. It is the same expression that Katharine Ross has at the end of *The Graduate*, when Elaine begins to wonder what she has got herself in for by running off with Benjamin Braddock. The audience is thus given not the artificial happy ending of Annakin's dramatization but an ambiguous one that is so much more realistic and credible. So effective was

Overnight Sensation that it was nominated for an Oscar for Best Live Action Short Film.

In 1948 Box gambled with *Quartet*, but it paid off with great popular and critical success on both sides of the Atlantic. In the United States it enjoyed a large following in art house movie theaters such as New York's Sutton, where it sold out for eight months. Box worked quickly to re-create the winning formula by producing *Trio*, comprising two light comic stories, "The Verger" and "Mr. Know-All," and a much more serious tale, "Sanatorium."

"The Verger" is a wry little story of Albert Foreman, a man who is fired as a verger because he cannot read or write, though this deficiency does not hamper his work. Forced to find a living, he opens a tobacco shop, and when he does so well with it, he opens another and repeats this until he is the affluent owner of ten shops. When his bank manager learns that he is illiterate, he is stunned and asks him what he would be if he had learned to read and write. Albert's reply is the story's last line: "I'd be the verger of St. Peter's, Neville Square."[12]

The screenplay of "The Verger" was written by Maugham himself and is one of the very few of his attempts to write a script to be accepted by a film company. Not surprisingly, there are very few differences between the published story and the film version, the main one being that, while Albert is married in the former, the latter shows him proposing and marrying his landlady. In the main, Maugham's adaptation simply expands a brief tale, filling out the process by which Albert becomes a successful businessman.

"Mr. Know-All" is also a comic vignette, the story of Max Kelada, an obnoxious know-it-all who exasperates all his fellow passengers on a fourteen-day voyage from San Francisco to Yokohama. Among other things, he declares himself an expert on pearls, a talent put to the test when, in front of everyone he pronounces a woman's pearl necklace, which she has told her husband is composed of cheap imitations, genuine and worth a large sum of money. As he looks closer at them, he realizes that they are actually a gift from a lover and so, to maintain her secret, he says that he was mistaken: they are indeed imitation. The passengers enjoy Kelada's humiliation, but the narrator has a newfound respect and affection for him.

The screenplay, written by Sherriff, follows the original 1925 story closely except in one significant respect. Maugham's Kelada is not an Anglo-Saxon

Englishman but an outsider who is "dark skinned, with a fleshy, hooked nose and very large, lustrous and liquid eyes. His long black hair was sleek and curly. He spoke with a fluency in which there was nothing English and his gestures were exuberant. . . . Mr. Kelada was born under a bluer sky than is generally seen in England."[13] He is identified as a "Levantine," but Maugham's readers in 1925 would almost certainly have assumed that he was a Jew, and in any case a surprising figure to commit the gentlemanly act to save a woman's reputation. By 1950, however, public attitudes had changed. As in "The Alien Corn," the film eliminated any insinuation about Kelada's ethnic background, and the English actor Nigel Patrick plays him as simply a universal figure: the know-it-all loudmouth.

The third story of *Trio*, "Sanatorium," is the most serious, and it is substantial enough that it was once considered for a full-length feature film. It is based on Maugham's own experience as a tuberculosis patient in a sanatorium in Nordach-on-Dee, Scotland, in 1918. He discovered there that the shadow of death hanging over the sanatorium did not preclude the usual tragedies and comedies of human behavior. Even sexual misconduct crops up, and "Sanatorium" tells of a woman—"pretty hot stuff"—who, though married, is having an affair with another resident. To put an end to this improper behavior, the clinic administrator has the floor painted outside her room one night and the next day he expels the man with fresh paint on his slippers. As much as this comic scene lends itself to film, the subject matter was considered inappropriate, and it was excluded from the screenplay.

"Sanatorium" focuses on three relationships, and each is transferred with little change to the screen. One concerns two Scotsmen who have had an antagonistic relationship for seventeen years, Campbell envying McLeod's room and playing his violin to irritate him, and both fighting with each other over cards. When McLeod (Finlay Currie) suddenly dies of a heart attack, however, the other man (John Laurie) takes no pleasure in his new room nor in having no one to annoy with his music. Another pair are the Chesters, played by Raymond Huntley and Betty Ann Davies, who are coping with his deep bitterness over his illness, a resentment that turns into acceptance at the end.

The most moving relationship is that of a longtime patient, a pretty young woman named Evie Bishop, with Major Templeton, a rake with a disreputable past who has only a year or two to live. It does not take long for Templeton, the smooth and handsome Michael Rennie, to notice Evie, played beautifully and well by Jean Simmons, and tongues start wagging when their courtship begins. Evie, though, is not naive and knows her own mind, but she accepts Templeton's proposal even though both know that by leaving the sanatorium to pursue a normal marriage they are hastening their deaths.

Like *Quartet*, *Trio* was well received by both moviegoers and critics. Maugham traveled to New York in October 1950 to do extensive press, radio, and television interviews, and Paramount promoted the film heavily in the United States. By this time Two Cities Films, which had absorbed Gainsborough Studio under the J. Arthur Rank umbrella, was working on another Maugham omnibus film: *Encore*. It comprised three stories, each adapted and directed by different teams: "The Ant and the Grasshopper," written by T. E. B. Clarke and directed by Pat Jackson; "Winter Cruise," written by Arthur Macrae and directed by Anthony Pelissier; and "Gigolo and Gigolette," written by Eric Ambler and directed by Harold French. Each tale was revised to meet the demands of the censor and the perceived tastes of the moviegoing public.

"The Ant and the Grasshopper" is a droll story that gives an ironic twist to Aesop's fable of the hard-working ant carefully storing grain for the winter while the grasshopper spends the summer singing and then finds himself without food when winter comes. In Maugham's version, George Ramsay is a careful conservative lawyer with a feckless scapegrace brother, Tom, who has been sponging off him for years. Having saved his money carefully, George is convinced that he will have a comfortable retirement while Tom, who has not planned for the future, will be destitute. Then, however, Tom marries an aged woman who dies soon thereafter and bequeaths him a small fortune, leaving his brother distraught and feeling cheated by life.

With Nigel Patrick and Roland Culver playing Tom and George very capably, *Encore* provides a reasonably faithful adaptation of the story. Because the Hays code prohibited the depiction of characters benefiting from crimes, however, Tom's various extortion schemes had to be softened. Thus, a scene was added to show Tom repaying all his debts to George; though with almost a wink to the audience, the film ends with him trying to borrow another fiver. Moreover, his marriage to an older woman who dies was too cynical and harsh, so the film shows him opportunistically wooing and marrying a beautiful, rich young woman who remains very much alive. Thus Maugham's implication that pure luck saves the "grass-hopper" is changed to one where romantic attraction proves fortuitous. And in case the filmgoers might get the wrong idea, Maugham's introduction to the segment warns that Tom "is just the exception which proves the rule that, on the whole, honesty is the best policy and, in this hard world, if you want to eat you must work." Though he spoke the lines to satisfy the censors, Maugham, more than anybody, must have known that his story clearly shows the opposite.

"Winter Cruise" is more seriously altered to remove much of its point. Maugham's story tells of a middle-aged female passenger, Miss Reid, whose talkativeness drives the crew of a cargo ship nearly insane until they arrange for their young wireless operator to sleep with her.[14] The doctor's theory is that at her age all she needs is a lover. "That inordinate loquacity," he thinks, "that passion for information, the innumerable questions she asks, her prosiness, the way she goes on and on—it is all a sign of her clamour-ing virginity. A lover would bring her peace. Those jangled nerves of hers would relax. At least for an hour she would have lived. The deep satisfaction which her being demands would travel through those exacerbated centres of her speech, and we should have quiet."[15] In the film, however, the ship's company arranges to provide Miss Reid not sexual satisfaction but, rather, "romance." The film viewers are left with little doubt that not much has happened when she tells the captain: "I was highly amused. And, after all, who knows, your idea *might* have been a great success."

"Gigolo and Gigolette," first published in 1935, is a powerful indictment of the exploitation of people who prostitute themselves for the amusement of the idle, bored rich. It tells of a couple, Stella and Syd Cotman, who, after years of struggle as a gigolo and a paid dancer, are making decent money with a daring act performed in a luxury hotel along the French Riviera. The performance consists of Stella diving from a height of sixty feet into a five-foot-deep pool covered in flames, and it draws crowds of affluent customers wanting to be present the evening when she kills herself. Stella eventually loses her nerve, but Syd, who is her manager as well as husband, insists that she continue, and she agrees to do so "every night till I kill myself. . . . I mustn't disappoint my public."[16]

The story was adapted for the screen by the experienced and capable Eric Ambler—he'd received an Oscar nomination for his script of *The Cruel Sea*—whom Maugham called "my favorite screenplay writer."[17] For his part, Ambler, who admired the author a great deal, was apprehensive because the studio required several modifications of the story and the insertion of entirely new material and scenes. Had he known him better, he would have realized that Maugham understood that the right to make changes to his work was inherent in his contract with the studio.

Ambler's revisions were extensive and, unfortunately, weakened the effect of "Gigolo and Gigolette." In Maugham's version Stella suddenly suffers an attack of nerves, like an actor attacked by stage fright or an author suffering writer's block, and she is terrified of going on. The film, however, expands the role of Flora Panezzi, a retired performer who was once "The Human Cannonball," and has her frighten Stella with the tale of a trapeze artist who lost her nerve and fell to her death. Another added scene shows a desperate Stella gambling Syd's and her savings at the roulette table and losing everything. Thus, rather than going ahead with her evening dive because she is urged on by her avaricious husband, she does so as an act of atonement for having lost the money. Furthermore, Syd rushes to try to prevent her dive, climbing up to the platform to exhort her to stop; but she says, "I'm all right now," and plunges into the tank. When she safely surfaces, she is beaming at Syd, suggesting that all is well with them and that she is no longer in danger. As the screenplay direction says, "We know Stella is safe."[18] A lot safer, one might say, than Maugham's script was in Ambler's hands.

On the whole, and apart from the euphemizing of Maugham's stories required by censorship and public taste, *Encore* was well done and well received. It was, though, the last of the Maugham omnibus films, as CBS's "The Somerset Maugham TV Theatre" proved to be a better venue for short story dramatization than the feature film. One more Maugham short story ended up in an omnibus film, *Three Cases of Murder*, produced by Wessex Film Productions in 1955. Four years earlier, Fidelity Pictures had announced that it would film three stories: Balzac's "The Mysterious Mansion," Faulkner's "A Rose for Emily" (with Joan Crawford), and Maugham's "Lord Mountdrago" (with Ralph Richardson). This project fell apart, however, and Wessex was able to put together a film that included only "Lord

Mountdrago" and two stories by the much lesser-known Brett Halliday and Roderick Wilson. Richardson was replaced by Orson Welles, who, though the boy genius gloss had long worn off, was still someone who could carry a film—or in this case, part of one. George More O'Ferrall was credited with the direction of "Lord Mountdrago," but Wells soon complained about the slow pace of the filming, pointing out that it was taking almost twenty times as long as it had taken Maugham to write the story.[19] Within a few days he was running the lighting and within a week he was in control of the whole production, having ordered O'Ferrall into a corner.

"Lord Mountdrago," pretty much the only supernatural story Maugham ever wrote, tells of a prominent English cabinet minister who, after humiliating a Welsh working-class opposition member, Owen, in the Commons, begins to have nightmares about him. Mountdrago dreams that he is caught at a prominent social gathering without any trousers, that he breaks off a speech in the Commons to sing some verses of "A Bicycle Built for Two," and that he behaves bawdily in a seedy nightclub. He is appalled to discover that, on the day following each nightmare, Owen seems to know their contents, as if he shares the same dream, and laughs at him. Consulting an analyst, he is told that the dreams are a working out of unresolved guilt and that he should settle things with the Welshman, but he threatens instead to kill him in his dream. The next day Owen dies from a mysterious illness, and Mountdrago throws himself in front of a tube train.

Though it is the best of the tales in *Three Cases of Murder*, the "Lord Mountdrago" segment is not memorable. Alan Badel and André Morell were both excellent as Owen and as the analyst, Dr. Audlin, but Mountdrago is the center of the picture and Welles chews up the scenery. Feeling that his own modestly formed nose was insufficient for his character to look down on others with, he donned a more substantial fake one. His performance, though capable, was no more persuasive, and the film was so poor that J. Arthur Rank, concluding that Welles was no longer enough of a box office draw to make up for a weak production, announced that "we are refusing to handle *Three Cases of Murder* because it's a mediocre film."[20]

The Welles "Lord Mountdrago" became a coda to the Maugham omnibus films. Since then there have been only the occasional attempt to present a group of stories in a feature film, notably *Paris, je t'aime* in 2006 and *The Ballad of Buster Scruggs* in 2018. Though there were dozens of other

Maugham short stories suitable for filming, Gainsborough Pictures had discovered the successful formula a bit too late to avoid being preempted by television. But *Quartet, Trio,* and *Encore* remain watchable today, and as David Diffrient points out, they are among the most important examples of episodic cinema in history: "As historical touchstones . . . they were so unlike anything that had come before and so popular with mainstream audiences and critics alike at the time of their theatrical runs that, for years afterwards, they would serve as a kind of template for adducing the relative failure or success of subsequent multi-story omnibus productions. Indeed, in the annals of episodic cinema, few films have been so frequently referenced by critics in English-language reviews as *Quartet* and its two sequels, *Trio* and *Encore*."[21]

CHAPTER 10

Twenty-First-Century
Perspectives

Up at the Villa and Being Julia

Next to *The Hour Before the Dawn*, published in 1942, *Up at the Villa* is one of Maugham's least impressive works. He hated writing fiction to order, and both were commissioned pieces, the former being a propaganda novel written at the request of the British government and the latter a novella published serially in early 1941 by the American magazine *Redbook*. He had agreed to *Redbook*'s request in early 1939, but, exhausted after a lengthy trip across the United States and a month's stay in London in early summer, Maugham hated the task. Moreover, by late July the threat of war in Europe had become very real and he knew that he would soon be embroiled in intelligence work in France for the British government. Thus he found it expedient to rework and expand a short story called "A Night in June," which he had finished many years earlier but had lain in his files unpublished. With his heart not really in his task, he produced a book that was, in Morton Dauwen Zabel's words, "as unmitigated a specimen of fictional drivel as has appeared under respectable authorship within living memory."[1]

The incident at the heart of *Up at the Villa* could have made an excellent short story along the lines of "The Letter," or "Rain": like them, it tells of a sexual encounter that leads to the death of the man involved and peril for the woman. But in addition to their dramatic centers, "The Letter" offers a perspective on British colonialism and racism and "Rain" reveals the hypocrisy of rigid, prudish religious practices. *Up at the Villa*, however, is set in Florence among the decadent set of British and Americans enjoying their privileged lives among the art galleries, in the luxurious restaurants, and in the endlessly sunny, gossip-filled gardens. It is a world already familiar to readers of Henry James, E. M. Forster, Edith Wharton, and others, and Maugham adds nothing original to it. Even the political upheaval and threat of war gripping the world during its writing appears in *Up at the Villa* only in one brief allusion to the Anschluss. *Christmas Holiday*, published a few months earlier in *Redbook*, can be read as an allegory of the various political forces at work in Europe, but it is hard to see any such broader implications in the novella. Instead, Maugham simply pads his short story with dialogue and characters of the sort that used to populate his plays and that he could create almost in his sleep.

The protagonist of *Up at the Villa* is Mary Panton, recently widowed after an unhappy marriage and living in a borrowed house in Florence. She is being courted by Sir Edgar Swift, a rising star in the Indian Civil Service who is in line to become the governor of Bengal and perhaps eventually the viceroy. Though he is a good many years older than her, she is encouraged to accept his proposal by the Princess San Ferdinando, a character out of *Our Betters*: that is, an American who married a Roman prince and is now a gossipy grande dame in Florence. At one of the princess's parties, Mary meets Rowley Flint, a rogue (said to be based on Maugham's lover Gerald Haxton) and a womanizer. She resists his advances but later needs his help when, after she has impetuously gone to bed with a young Austrian refugee, thinking that she was giving him one night of beauty and happiness, the youth has killed himself. Flint and Mary surreptitiously move the body from her bedroom to the countryside, and since there is nothing to implicate her in the death, life goes on as usual in Florence's foreign enclave. When she next sees Sir Edgar, however, she feels impelled to tell him the unhappy story, and even though he nobly agrees to marry her anyway, she recognizes his barely hidden reluctance and releases him from his proposal. All is not lost, however, because Flint, who it seems has an estate in Kenya, invites her to join him there.

Up at the Villa is not as bad as Zabel's scathing comment would suggest, but it is essentially a hollow story told blandly and tritely. Mary is a superficial young woman who gets off scot-free and learns very little from the experience. The other characters—the princess, Edgar, and Rowley—make their moves as predictably as pieces on a chess board, and the young Austrian is treated as no more than a pawn. Some reviewers found melodramatic interest in the suicide and coverup, but most considered *Up at the Villa* to be shabby work. Maugham himself came to regret having written it, telling his friend Glenway Wescott, "It's the only thing I've ever done for money, and you pretend to be such an appreciator of my work, and you praise that story, you don't know hack-work when you see it. I'm ashamed ever to have done it."[2]

Despite its weaknesses as a work of literature, Warner Bros. saw promise in *Up at the Villa*, and they optioned it for $30,000 in the summer of 1939 with the idea of Anatole Litvak directing Bette Davis in the lead. As much as she liked Maugham's female protagonists, however, Davis turned down the part and the studio gave it to Merle Oberon. Filming of what was now called *The House on the Hill* was scheduled to begin on April 1, 1940, but when severe side effects from a sulfa drug disfigured Oberon's face, production was canceled and the project abandoned. By 1945 the rights had been bought by MGM, whose screenwriter, Christopher Isherwood, soon complained to a friend that he was working on "a bad script of a bad story."[3] This endeavor died as well, not because the story was bad but because the Hays Office was never going to approve a film about a woman who casually has sex with a man who responds by killing himself and, then, rather than being punished, runs off with a rogue. In 1951 Maugham himself concluded that, to satisfy the censors, the story would have to be entirely rewritten and it would become implausible. Joan Fontaine was nonetheless asked to star in an adaptation to be filmed in Italy in May 1955, but this project never got beyond the planning stage.

In December 1968, BBC-1 broadcast a fifty-minute adaptation of *Up at the Villa*, with a screenplay by Stanley Miller and the lead played by Claire Nielsen. It was a strange choice for inclusion in a series of love stories called *Boy Meets Girl* that ran on British television from 1967 to 1969; and since no recording of the production exists, we cannot know whether the "boy" of the story is Sir Edgar, Rowley Flint, or the young Austrian who kills himself. Mary Panton, though, is surely, though implausibly, the "girl."

Thirty-two years went by before, in 2000, director Philip Haas and his wife, the screenwriter Belinda Haas, put a version of *Up at the Villa* on the screen. The cast could hardly have been more distinguished: Mary was played by Kristin Scott Thomas, Rowley by Sean Penn, Princess San Ferdinando by Anne Bancroft, Sir Edgar by James Fox, and a newly created character, Lucky Leadbetter, by Derek Jacobi. It was stunningly filmed in luxurious interiors, among the famous streets and architecture of Florence and Siena, and in the beautiful Tuscan countryside. Unfortunately, nothing else in the film matches the cinematography.

Maugham's novella was almost sixty years old when the Haas team tackled it, and rather than recontextualize it for a new age, they decided to keep the setting in the late 1930s. Where Maugham had only briefly alluded to the German occupation of Austria, however, Belinda Haas's script added substantial references and scenes showing Fascism beginning to grip Italy. Philip Haas explained the intent: "A woman gets entangled with several men. Yet the action is reflected by what's going on in history. The personal and historical dilemmas reverberate."[4] This could have been an admirable and ambitious amplification of the original story, but the film simply does not provide any plausible parallel between Mary's relationships with the men and the political turbulence in Italy and beyond. The representative of the Fascist regime in Italy is an invented character, Beppino Leopardi, but he is no more than the traditional corrupt police officer of a thousand melodramas. He knows that Mary and Rowley have been involved in the young Austrian's death and the disposal of his body, and he knows that the ensuing scandal would destroy Sir Edgar's career. He arrests Rowley for illegal possession of a pistol, and he insinuates that Mary should give herself to him sexually. In a reversal of *The Letter*, however, she produces correspondence that reveals Leopardi's corrupt past and thus blackmails him into taking no action against them. If only it had been that easy to get rid of Mussolini.

Belinda Haas said that "the key for us was the context. Taking the main event and filling around it."[5] The problem, however, is that she was working with a story that had already been puffed up when its author turned his short story into a novella. Some of her further "filling" involves the Leopardi threat and Mary's efforts to pump the princess for information about his illicit past and her theft of incriminating letters from the princess's house. It also appears in the expansion of the latter's role as a scandal-loving, acerbic-tongued social matriarch of the expatriates of Florence. The film even attributes the story's crisis to her when she tells Mary that she once gave herself to a man out of generous pity. After Mary has emulated the action to calamitous effect, the princess flippantly says that she made up the story.

The unnecessary amplification is there, too, in the fey, homosexual Lucky Leadbetter, a meaningless part played well by Jacobi, but one with no integral connection to the central story. The result of these embellishments is not to add muscle to the story but to weigh it down with flab and make a poor Maugham tale even worse. The Haases, wrote A. O. Scott, "turn Maugham—an efficient, unfussy storyteller, whose fiction has, over the years, proved perfectly congenial to filmmakers—into a third-rate Henry James, a doddering, half-awake observer of the bottled-up passions of twittering Anglophones in a foreign clime."[6]

Scott Thomas, as she always does, plays Mary superbly as a beautiful and intelligent woman who makes a tragic error from a generous impulse and then, panic stricken, has to extricate herself not only from the reach of the law but also from her expected marriage to Sir Edgar. Of her work with Penn, Belinda Haas said, "They're a fantastic pairing. She with her English reserve and spikiness, he with his American intensity."[7] Despite this claim, however, one of the major problems with the film is a lack of intensity in Penn's performance, a sense that he is merely walking through the role and, as he admitted later, that he had a lack of commitment to it: "I wanted to approach it in a different way, actually. But when you're working with people you like and have respect for as I was—and it paid quite well, and I wasn't the whole movie—I didn't want to be disruptive. See, another part of it was that I was preparing another movie [*Sweet and Lowdown*] at the time, and there's an infidelity in that which I think takes you off your game. I maybe wasn't giving the commitment that I otherwise would have liked to."[8]

Rather than inhabiting Rowley, Penn seems to be at one remove from the character, playing an actor from the 1940s, Bogart perhaps, playing Rowley. One reviewer called him a poor man's Cary Grant, but the more apt comparison is with Robert Mitchum, who, like Penn in *Up at the Villa*, would cast an eye over a scene and the other characters with a skeptical raised eyebrow. But Mitchum, like Bogart and John Garfield, conveyed an intensity, the sense of a tightly wound coil that might spring at any moment. Penn simply suggests boredom, and part of the problem is that, though Maugham's Rowley is a bad hat, a notorious rogue, the film never shows him misbehaving.

Nearing the end of her film career and seemingly coasting through roles, Bancroft plays Princess San Ferdinando as a caricature, "coming on like a drag queen,"[9] in the words of Joe Baltake. Fox is excellent as Sir Edgar, the perfect embodiment of the English stiff upper lip in the face of unsettling or disappointing news. Mary, like the film's audience, can see his registering of her news about the young man's death and its implications for their marriage, but his good breeding prevents him from saying what he really thinks. The young Austrian, though not on the screen for long, is played persuasively by Jeremy Davies, and the experienced Jacobi, though given little to do but be one of the colorful outcasts adding to the intrigue of Florence, leaves the viewer wanting to see more of him in a more meaningful role.

The reviews of *Up at the Villa* were generally lukewarm, and some were strongly negative. The cinematography was rightly praised, as were the performances of most of the excellent cast, though the combination added up to a poor imitation of Merchant Ivory gentility for some reviewers. The most common criticism focused on the plot, which many commentators found inflated, meandering, or slowly paced. The result, they said, is a film that lacks the emotional intensity to draw the viewer into its world. It has, said Baltake, "attractive, sometimes even colorful characters who speak eloquently and articulately, often about passion, and yet it leaves you cold."[10] "The film is fine," observed Ann Hornaday, "for filmgoers satisfied with splendid scenery and a mildly diverting tale, but for real heat, Maugham still knows best."[11]

The last of Maugham's thirty-two plays, *Sheppey*, was mounted in London in 1933, after which he devoted his remaining years to fiction and autobiographical works, two genres that gave him much more creative freedom than writing for the stage. The theater had occupied much of his interest for thirty years, and he had seen all the great actors of his time, many of them in his own plays, in rehearsals, and in their social lives. It was the acclaimed actresses, though, for whom he created so many excellent roles—Marie Tempest, Irene Vanbrugh, Ethel Barrymore, Gladys Cooper, and others— who were the most memorable.

This was the era in which actresses were very conscious of their image on and off stage, when they declined roles that portrayed them as common or unattractive, and when they would not dream of being seen in the street without being well-dressed and elegant. It was a period when a celebrated actress would be applauded on her first entrance to a play, applauded even while making her way to a seat in the audience for someone else's production, and more quietly acknowledged as she made her way to a choice seat in a posh restaurant. Maugham had seen it all, and in 1937 he turned from writing *for* the great ladies of the stage to writing *about* them. His novel *Theatre* became his valedictory tribute both to the actresses who had shone in his plays and to the London theatrical world that had made him acclaimed and wealthy.

The central figure in *Theatre* is Julia Lambert, a middle-aged actress at the peak of her fame on the London stage. Her husband, Michael Gosselyn, is a much less talented actor, best known for his slim good looks, and he spends most of his time as their company's theater manager, seemingly more interested in account books than in sex with his wife. Their business partner, a stout widow of sixty named Dolly de Vries, has an amateur's love of the theater and a lesbian's attraction to Julia. Another of Julia's admirers is Lord Charles Tamerley, an erudite lover of the arts who for twenty years has had to settle for a platonic relationship with her. Michael and Julia have a seventeen-year-old son, Roger, who is fresh out of Eton and headed for Cambridge.

Joining this group is Tom Fennell, a young accountant brought in to examine the theater company's books and with whom Julia falls deeply in love. He is in awe of her as their affair begins, but soon it is Julia who is so besotted with him that she is jealous even of the time he spends with Roger. Having gained the upper hand emotionally, Tom uses her to advance his career and that of his actress girlfriend, Avice Crichton, humiliating Julia in the process. Adding to her mortification, when she finally offers her body to Lord Charles, he shows no interest and she realizes that he has never been interested in a sexual affair. The novel ends when, after she has allowed her emotional life to damage her ability to act, she regains control and completely humiliates Avice on stage. She avoids the opening night party, preferring to dine by herself in a restaurant and exult in her emotional and artistic freedom.

At the heart of *Theatre* is Maugham's lifelong concern with intellectual, emotional, and physical freedom, and here, as in *The Moon and Sixpence*, the protagonist's liberation is found in art. But where Charles Strickland's creativity is an almost autonomous force that erupts from within, takes possession, and demands expression if the artist is to feel free, Julia's is an innate natural talent that has been trained and refined for the theater. Her mentor, the company manager who first recognized her talent, Jimmie Langton, told her "Don't *be* natural. The stage isn't the place for that. The stage is make-believe. But *seem* natural."[12] She has become so skilled at seeming on the stage that it has become the one area of her life in which she is in absolute control: "There, in her dressing-room, she regained possession of herself and the affairs of the common round of daily life faded to insignificance. Nothing really mattered when she had within her grasp this possibility of freedom."[13]

With repeated success and acclaim in the theater, Julia has come to see herself as two people: "the actress, the popular favourite, the best-dressed woman in London, and that was the shadow; and the woman she was playing at night, and that was the substance."[14] Offstage, she is surrounded by people, but all of them are no more than a supporting cast in her life: a husband/manager with whom she has a platonic relationship, an infatuated lesbian business partner, a devoted aristocrat with whom she's never consummated their friendship, and a son with whom she has never been close. And it is Roger who, as he approaches manhood, objects to being treated as a juvenile player to her role as loving parent. "To me you act the part of the fond, indulgent, celebrated mother," he complains. "You don't exist, you're only the innumerable parts you've played. I've often wondered if there was ever a you or if you were never anything more than a vehicle for all those other people you pretend to be. When I've seen you go into an empty room I've sometimes wanted to open the door suddenly, but I've been afraid to in case I found nobody there."[15] Though disconcerted by this suggestion, when she has celebrated another triumph in the theater, Julia rejects his claim: "Roger says we don't exist. Why, it's only we who do exist. They are the shadows and we give them substance. We are the symbols of all this confused, aimless struggling that they call life, and it's only the symbol which is real. They say acting is only make-believe. That make-believe is the only reality."[16]

As she sits in the restaurant, Julia feels as if she is on a mountaintop, free from all earthly ties, like some ethereal spirit in heaven. This sense of freedom has come, however, after a near-disastrous encounter with the real world, her affair with Tom, which is the crisis of the novel. She had let her guard down, becoming a prisoner of an infatuation and subsequently losing control of her life and experiencing the real pain of unrequited love. It is a situation that lets Maugham make an interesting commentary on acting and how a performer's real-life experiences might enrich or damage her professional work. When Julia next goes onstage and plays a key scene of lovers parting, she pours all her own agony over Tom into her acting, convinced that its reality makes her performance greater than ever. Being a shrewd judge of acting, however, Michael tells her that she has been over-acting and, lacking conviction, the portrayal rang false. She has forgotten Jimmie's exhortation not to *be* natural on stage but to *seem* natural; she has been feeling, not acting.

On the surface, this part of *Theatre* would seem to be a criticism of Method acting started by Konstantin Stanislavski and developed in the United States by Lee Strasberg, Stella Adler, and others in the 1930s. In particular, it seems to point to the dangers of following Strasberg's in-junction to actors to search their memories for emotions—pain, joy, anger, disappointment—and use them onstage or on the screen. What Maugham seems to be pointing out, however, is that Julia takes her pain directly into the theater, where her raw emotion overwhelms her acting skills, the lan-guage of the stage. When her distress over Tom's betrayal has receded and become "emotion recollected in tranquility," the famous Wordsworth defi-nition of poetry quoted to her by Charles, she regains control of her art, and her acting again becomes an expression of her creative instincts. Hence her feeling of triumph as she sits alone in the restaurant.

Within months of the publication of *Theatre*, playwright Guy Bolton persuaded Maugham that his novel would make an excellent play, and Bolton produced a script that followed the story with one significant alter-ation. As the play begins, it is revealed that Julia and Michael have been secretly divorced for two years, a change presumably to account for the absence of sex in their relationship. This modification removes the adul-tery from Julia's affair with Tom and allows for a happy ending when Michael proposes to her again and they leave for dinner together. This version was mounted in the United States in 1941 with Cornelia Otis Skin-ner playing the lead and then, in 1950, as *Larger Than Life* in London with Jessie Royce Landis.

Bolton's play was the basis of the first film version of *Theatre*, an Austrian-French, German-language production made in London called *Adorable*

Julia. The cast was almost entirely French and German, with Lilli Palmer as Julia, Charles Boyer as Michael, and Jean Sorel as Tom. Palmer, then in her late forties but still glamorous, looks the part of Julia, and she convincingly portrays a diva always aware of her star power. Boyer is given little to do but look managerial and let Palmer dominate the scenes, and the handsome young Sorel is very much the social-climbing young lover.

Adorable Julia follows Maugham's novel fairly closely, with only a few significant differences. Julia's attempted seduction of Charles and her embarrassed retreat from it, is well done, but their relationship is not fully enough delineated to give the scene the force it should have. On the other hand, Julia's onstage humiliation of Avice is not shown at all, reduced merely to an allusion after the performance. Tom, though, is shown wanting to resume his affair with Julia but having her dressing room door closed in his face; and at the end she does not enjoy her celebratory dinner alone but in the company of Michael, suggesting that their marriage has been reinvigorated.

Adorable Julia contains little of the novel's examination of the art of acting, restricting itself almost entirely to its public and professional side. Julia's thoughts are frequently conveyed not through movement or gesture but through voice-over, which some critics found tedious. The device is awkwardly employed when Julia tells the movie's audience that she is acting a part in her exchanges with Tom, Charles, and Dolly. The challenge for an actress here is subtly conveying to the film viewer that she is performing, while never letting the other characters know that, and the voice-over is a poor substitute. It was a challenge superbly met forty years later by Annette Bening.

In 2004 the Hungarian Canadian producer Robert Lantos put together a film with a mainly English and Canadian cast and directed by the Hungarian István Szabó. It was shot in Budapest, with the exterior scenes filmed in London. Szabó had experience in making movies about actors, having won an Oscar for Best Foreign Film for *Mephisto* (1981), and *Being Julia*'s screenwriter, Ronald Harwood, had written *The Dresser*, a play and then a film about an imperious actor-manager. Together, they opted for setting the action in 1938, the year after the publication of *Theatre* rather than updating it for contemporary audiences. The theatrical life celebrated in the novel was already beginning to vanish when the book was published, and it would not have been possible to recontextualize it without making the story unrecognizable. The interior scenes were shot in buildings designed in the early twentieth century, and the period feeling was enhanced both by the soft, warm lighting of Lajos Koltai's cinematography and by the music: songs like "Mad About the Boy" and "Smoke Gets in Your Eyes."

Harwood essentially follows the plot of the novel but there are some significant changes. Where Maugham shows Michael casting Avice in the next play because he thinks that she is genuinely talented, the film attributes his decision to their having an affair. This makes Julia doubly resentful of her and allows Harwood to make her revenge on the young actress much more complex. Another alteration, however, robs the film of one of Julia's most skillful performances in one of the novel's most clever scenes: when, having finally offered herself to Lord Charles, she discovers that, after all the years, he really is not interested in bedding her, and she must extricate herself tactfully. Harwood preferred to credit Charles's reluctance to homosexuality rather than asexuality, and his revelation of this to Julia takes place in a rather flat scene at the seaside. Their relationship remains ideal for her, however, because he offers encouragement, companionship, and artistic taste without sexual demands or conflicts. In this Charles is much like Maugham himself, who had many women friends—the actress Ruth Gordon, for example—because they were comfortable with him.

The most clever and useful modification of Maugham's story is the presence of Jimmie Langton, Julia's mentor who has been dead for fifteen years, as a spirit/conscience/chorus. Well played by Michael Gambon, he reminds her of the acting principles he laid down for her, but he also advises her how to perform in her real-life conflicts and dramas. In this way, he is sometimes speaking for the narrative voice in the novel and sometimes representing Julia's own memories or thoughts. His applause when she has seen someone off with some calculated histrionics is really her own self-satisfaction at her off-stage performance. Whatever he represents, Jimmie is one of only two people—Roger being the other—with whom Julia has an honest conversation.

With one exception, the cast of *Being Julia* is strong and admirably brings Maugham's characters to life. Jeremy Irons, dapper in his well-cut suits and smoothly ironic in the delivery of his lines, perfectly conveys Michael's concern for Julia's performances as they affect the company's account books and his nonchalance about her role as his wife. Miriam Margolyes is the embodiment of Dolly de Vries, both comically absurd and movingly pathetic in her adoration of Julia; and Juliet Stevenson turns the supporting part of Evie into a wry and knowing, yet affectionate commentary on the diva she serves. Bruce Greenwood is well suited as the discreetly gay, loyal Lord Charles, and Tom Sturridge is excellent as Roger, absolutely persuasive as a young man coming to maturity and willing to confront his mother about the shallowness of their relationship.

The glaring weakness of the cast is Shaun Evans's portrayal of Tom. For reasons hard to discern, his character is changed from a young English accountant brought in to work on the theater's books to an earnest young stage-struck American. The problem is that, as A. O. Scott wrote in the *New York Times*, this earnestness is not enough to persuade audiences that he could turn Julia's world upside down: "Apart from his collegiate good looks, Mr. Evans brings nothing to the part to convince you that this boy could win Julia's heart, much less break it. He has all the sexual magnetism of a boiled potato, and it is hard to believe that such a bland fellow could throw the likes of her into such a swivet."[17] Indeed, when Tom suddenly kisses Julia in his room, she is more surprised than aroused, and she flees with a disconcerted haste not believable in a beautiful actress who has always had a host of admirers and would-be suitors.

The success of any film adaptation of *Theatre* will always rest on the actress who plays Julia, and *Being Julia* is Bening's triumph. The English Miranda Richardson seemed more suited to the role, but when illness prevented this, the American Bening took over and played the part to widespread acclaim. In doing so, she avoided several potential disasters: unlike Kim Novak, she did not attempt an English accent, adopting a safer, more relaxed mid-Atlantic one; and she did not, as many actresses would have, play Julia as simply an overacting diva. "It's such an actressy part," said Bening, "and just begs for that kind of thing. And I knew that if it was phony, that would be a disaster. Also, how do you do a performance for camera that's supposed to be for theater? Finding that balance, in terms of making it plausible, took a lot of time."

Bening referred to the role as "a feast . . . that I'd just been asked to dive into,"[18] but it is in fact one of the trickiest parts in any of Maugham's film adaptations. Bening had to navigate being an actress playing an actress who performs on stage as well as in most of her life offstage. Moreover, she had to portray Julia first acting well in her play and later overacting the same scene in her distress over Tom; the difference has to be apparent to the film's audience and to Michael, but not the fictional audience at the play. Similarly, Bening had to show Julia acting in her exchanges with those in her real life but subtly enough that the other characters do not recognize the performance. This is especially well done when she tries to persuade Tom not to leave her. "You're everything in the world to me," she tells him. "You know that. I love being with you. I don't want to lose you. . . . You're the only person in my life with whom I can be entirely myself." Bening delivers these lines with enough of a glint in her eyes to suggest that they might just have come from some romantic play in her past. When Tom later ends their relationship, she matches his irritating nonchalance with perfectly feigned indifference masking the pain that we can see in her. On a few other occasions, however, she has to let the mask fall and express real, honest emotion. Szabó rightly described it as a multilayered performance— "the real face, the mask to please the society around her, and the great actress onstage; three different challenges"[19]—one that Bening manages with subtlety and nuance.

Bening manages another juggling act: playing a self-centered, manipulative diva while at the same time displaying fragility and the vulnerability to wounds. Her faults are numerous and obvious, but the film viewer cannot help but be won over by her energy and joy in both her circle of friends— including an affectionate relationship with Evie—and her life on the stage. All of this comes together in the film's climactic episode when Julia gains her revenge on Avice onstage, a scene considerably expanded and broadened over Maugham's original. There Julia upstages her young partner by drawing the audience's attention with a large scarlet handkerchief, forcing Avice to reveal an unflattering profile, and prematurely cutting in with her replies to destroy the humor in Avice's speech. In the film Julia essentially rechoreographs the whole scene, taking the swing intended for Avice, sneezing outrageously to undercut the comic effect of Avice's own subsequent sneeze, and substantially changing the dialogue. Julia's new version of the script refers to Avice's character as having affairs with both an older man and with a young lover, unmistakable allusions to the young actress's affairs with Michael and Tom, both of whom are in the theater. The audience loves the revised script, and everyone in Julia's life—Roger, Charles, Jimmie, Dolly, and Evie—rise to their feet to celebrate her. The film's viewers cannot help but relish her triumph as well.

Being Julia was generally well received by audiences and critics, though some reviewers were disappointed that it was a historical piece rather than a more contemporary examination of the acting life and profession. The overwhelming consensus was that the film was distinguished by Bening's performance, for which she received a Best Actress Oscar nomination and was awarded a Golden Globe for Best Actress Comedy or Musical.

Conclusion

Looking Back and Looking Forward

If Gore Vidal was right that there was an era when Maugham dominated the movies, when a generation was in thrall to his sensuous, unusual stories, it was the period from 1920 to 1960. Those four decades saw the making of thirty-nine feature films from his material, a remarkable twelve being produced in the 1930s. Coincidentally, the period of Maugham's ubiquity has come to be called the Golden Age of Hollywood Cinema or, by critics focusing on its narrative and visual styles, Classic Hollywood. Maugham's works gave Hollywood subject matter—criminals, artists, spiritual seekers, and tortured souls—and a narrative style that translated relatively easily to the movie screen. And of course, it found in him an author whose widespread popularity was guaranteed to fill movie houses across America and beyond.

By 1960, however, the film industry had lost interest in Maugham as a source of material, and in the past sixty-three years there have been only seven feature film adaptations of his works. This decline can, in part, be attributed to the lack of any new plays from his pen after 1933 and no new fiction after 1948, when he published *Catalina*, an undistinguished novel that excited little interest from filmmakers. His last substantial piece of fiction was *The Razor's Edge* (1944), and though his penultimate novel, *Then and Now* (1946), was optioned for film treatment, it was abandoned because of censorship demands. Maugham quietly closed out his writing career with a volume of entries from his writer's notebook and several collections of essays, and there were no new Maugham novels to capture a large reading public and bring the viewers into the movie theaters.

Coinciding with the disappearance of Maugham's name from theater marquees and from new fiction bookshelves was his diminished presence

in the world's media. For much of the century he had been, like Bernard
Shaw and H. G. Wells, a public figure sought out by journalists, not just
for his views of drama, fiction, and art but also for his opinions on politics
and social issues. Serving as a spokesman for the British cause in the United
States during the Second World War, he appeared at countless university
campuses, women's book groups, service club luncheons, and war bond
rallies, and he was frequently heard on American radio broadcasts. At the
war's end he returned to his home in the south of France, and as he moved
into his eighth decade, his travels outside of western Europe became fewer.
Finally, as dementia set in during the last decade of his life, the public
heard less and less from him until in his last five years the only communi-
cations coming from the Villa Mauresque were the brief, tactful messages
written by his lover, Alan Searle.

The seemingly endless stream of film versions of Shakespeare, Jane
Austen, and others, however, shows that an author need not be alive and
producing new fiction to interest Hollywood. As film critic James M. Welsh
points out, "The whole process of [film] adaptation is like a round or a
circular dance. The best stories and legends, the most popular histories and
mysteries, will constantly be told and retold, setting all the Draculas to dancing in the dark as their ghastly stories are spun."[1] Indeed, the hundreds,
perhaps thousands, of cinematic Draculas, Frankensteins, and Sherlock
Holmeses exist because they became timeless archetypes, their authors having unwittingly created characters and stories that touched some primal
fear, anxiety, or desire in people.

Maugham might have created an archetype in Sadie Thompson, but the
prostitute, even one assaulted by a man of the cloth, was hardly an original
figure in literature or film. He came closer with the creation of a nearly
unique world often called "Maughamesque": Kipling's colonial empire
turned upside down by depictions of louche, adulterous, corrupt British
administrators. Few authors wrote so frequently about the imperialism conducted by the European rulers and, to a lesser degree, experienced by their
indigenous subjects. It was a world, however, that, for Great Britain at
least, began to vanish in the postcolonialism that emerged in the last half
of the twentieth century. The pukka sahibs retreated to English towns and
villages, where they could wax sentimental about their days in the sun in
Malaya, Burma, India, and elsewhere. Filmmakers came to see them almost

as comic museum pieces, and films about that colonial world were likely to look like exercises in nostalgia.

Imperialism and colonialism, however, has hardly disappeared in the twenty-first century; it has simply changed its shapes and its strategies. Physical occupation backed by military force still exists, but more often indigenous populations are controlled and manipulated by new, more sophisticated forms of propaganda and by economic infiltration. With creative adaptation, it may be that some of Maugham's colonial stories could become commentaries on the contemporary world. *Caesar's Wife*, in which a young woman abandons a passionate affair so as not to imperil the colonial mission of her husband, could be reworked to fit the modern world of diplomacy. The depiction of a corrupt judicial system in "The Letter," in which evidence can be suppressed and justice subverted, might be refashioned in terms of newer forms of foreign occupation in countries like Iraq and Afghanistan.

At the same time as the European colonial empires were dissolving, developments in critical theory, feminism, and race relations were revising attitudes to colonialism and to the art that represented it. Philip Holden's 1996 groundbreaking *Orienting Masculinity, Orienting Nation* examined Maugham's South Seas and Asian fiction in light of postcolonial, gender, and cultural theory, in particular exposing the homoeroticism within the presentation of colonial masculinity.[2] Among other things, Holden's careful reading of *The Narrow Corner* is a reminder that Maugham's novel could provide the basis for an excellent cinematic exploration of male homosexuality. In the 1960s Robin Maugham and Christopher Isherwood both wanted to create a film version that would reveal the novel's homosexual elements, and surely, post–*Brokeback Mountain* and other movies, the time is right for such a venture.

In the same year as Holden's study, Douglas Heil published a careful dissection of racial attitudes in the 1940 film of *The Letter* in "The Construction of Racism through Narrative and Cinematography in 'The Letter'" in *Literature/Film Quarterly*. Maugham, he said, had realistically portrayed racist attitudes in his English characters and had treated the Asian ones objectively: "Without exception . . . both the Asian and Caucasian characters are invested with dimensional ambiguity in 'The Letter': with Maugham, any human being is a complex phenomenon."[3]

The screenwriter, however, had abandoned the realism and structured his script along the Classic Hollywood narrative model and, in doing so, "without exception, Koch turns each Asian character into a Hollywood stereotype."[4] The plantation workers are portrayed as inferior to the white community, the excessively obsequious and smiling On Chi Seng is made as repellent as possible, and the biracial Mrs. Hammond is described by Leslie as having eyes like a cobra. The result, says Heil, is that, though *The Letter* is a superior melodrama, "it is also irresponsible, content to entertain, and indifferent to its status as a means of communication. What it does communicate is a notion that Asians may be indolent, over-excited, insidious, or menacing; none of them, however, are wholly human. In addition, it communicates that a lying, racist, adulterous white murderer is ultimately more deserving of empathy than anyone who is not white."[5]

Heil's criticism of the 1940 film version of *The Letter* could well be extended to many of the cinematic adaptations of Maugham's other works. Asian characters were often portrayed as caricatures by actors of white European descent: the Swedish American Warner Oland, famous for playing Dr. Fu Manchu and Charley Chan, was Osman Pasha in *Infatuation* and General Yu in Garbo's *The Painted Veil*; *East of Suez* saw Pola Negri playing the Asian Daisy; *Rain* had Mary Shaw as the Indigenous Ameera. In the 1942 version of *The Moon and Sixpence*, the Polynesian woman Tiara Johnson was played by Florence Bates, while Elena Verdugo was her daughter Ata. Even in the 1959 television production of *The Moon and Sixpence*, Tiara was portrayed by Judith Anderson, while the young English actress Jean Marsh was Ata.

These distorted performances are disconcerting to the twenty-first-century viewer, but they can be seen in thousands of films from the Classic Hollywood era. Thankfully, contemporary moviemakers have abandoned the practice, and so in the 2006 *The Painted Veil* all the Asian characters are rendered by Asian actors. And I would suggest that such portrayals more closely represent what Maugham, who had a fascination and respect for Southeast Asia and its culture, put on the page. As Heil pointed out, Maugham's depiction of the Asians in "The Letter" is more objective than the treatment of them in the 1940 production, and it can be argued that this objectivity runs through all his fiction, that his criticism is in fact directed at the abusive and exploitative British colonists.

Another important contemporary perspective by which the cinematic adaptations of Maugham should be judged is that of feminist film criticism. Beginning in the 1970s, feminist critics started to recover women's film history and to examine the stereotypes of women prominently featured in the movies of Classic Hollywood. They began to identify the sexist images and gendered value systems that had dominated the movie industry for decades and that were becoming increasingly dissonant with the increasing awareness of the place of women in society as a whole. In particular, they argued against the passive roles of female characters in countless films, referring to "to-be-looked-at-ness," the "final girl," and most often "the male gaze." "The gaze," as it is often called, describes the presentation of the male actor as the active figure and the female as a sexual object to be observed, fought over, and taken, even benignly in romantic comedies, as a prize.

For the most part, feminist critics have ignored the Maugham films, perhaps finding more important, provocative targets in movies such as *Gone with the Wind*, *Mildred Pierce*, *Last Tango in Paris*, and the personae of Mae West and Marlene Dietrich. In 1973, though, Marjorie Rosen fired a salvo at the 1934 *Of Human Bondage* in her influential book *Popcorn Venus*:

> Not unlike [Josef] von Sternberg, Maugham bases his treatment of women on his fear of their sexuality and its crushing, binding tentacles. But rather than deal with the complexities of female nature and sociosexual jockeying for power or freedom, he simplifies his women, dismissing them as emotional and moral Frankensteins (e.g., *Rain*, adapted for the screen in 1928, 1932, and 1956 as *Miss Sadie Thompson*; *The Letter*, adapted in 1929 and 1940). Bette Davis's *Bondage* impersonation firmly recalls the base of power wielded by the Mysterious Woman, but she flails her sexuality with a psychotic irrationality, laying bare (without motivation) every possible human flaw, which is then passed off as a female shortcoming.[6]

Even assuming that by "Maugham" Rosen is meaning his narratives as presented in the film adaptations rather than his original stories or, indeed, the man himself, her assessment is harsh. One can argue that Mildred and Leslie Crosbie are formidable, if destructive, and that Sadie is the survivor in *Rain* while the man proves weak and self-destructs. In any case, Maugham's plays and fiction certainly provide a great many strong, complex women who, in the hands of sensitive and perceptive filmmakers, could be—or could have been—the basis of meaningful films. The Maugham scholar Anthony Curtis makes a convincing argument that Maugham had a "most remarkable empathy" with women:

> Maugham understood women much better than any playwright of [his] period whether it was women of the political and social aristocracy, the wives of the professional middle class or the common prostitute. . . . It was Maugham who dramatized the actual reality of their situation at the time when they achieved their political and social independence. Maugham captured in all its most elusive forms that frightening new species—twentieth-century woman. He peopled his stage with dissatisfied women, heartless women, self-sacrificing women, Anglo-American women and one mercy-killing maternal woman. He agreed that the only profession open to most women was that of marriage, and he examined the nature of marriage from a point of view foreign to that of Pinero and Henry Arthur Jones, that of women.

Etching his female characters with a sharper and subtler needle than his predecessors, said Curtis, he was "indeed God's gift to the great actresses of his day."[7] Actresses fought, some desperately, to play these women on stage and in the films.

It may be that many of Maugham's works featuring women are now too dated to interest twenty-first-century viewers, but the 2004 adaptation of his novel *Theatre, Being Julia*, is anything but a musty museum piece. The novel's theater world and its conventions were already outdated when the book appeared more than eight decades ago, but its central story of a woman fighting to regain her emotional independence and preserve her creative freedom was made fresh in the film by some judicious adaptation. Contemporary viewers can celebrate the film's restoration of Maugham's ending: Julia, the actress, sitting alone in a restaurant relishing her triumph as a professional and her independence from lover and husband.

Similarly, the 2006 version of *The Painted Veil*, though set in the remote past of British-occupied China, focuses on the heart of Maugham's story: an English woman's emergence from her shallow, upper-class background to become strong-willed and independent of any man. Where the

1934 version twisted Maugham's narrative to make the woman discover her love for her cold and distant husband, giving Garbo the chance to portray glowing saintliness as the film ends, the remake remains faithful to Maugham's depiction of an irrevocably broken marriage. Its final scene, however, while showing the heroine's independence from her passion for her former lover, does little to show the spiritual growth and intellectual maturity that Maugham gave her. For all its virtues, the new version could have gone much further in this regard.

The 1984 remake of "The Colonel's Lady," a story in which a man's complacent married life is shattered by his wife's creativity, showed how Maugham's stories could be effectively reimagined in a modern setting. A similar approach could bear fruit with other of the author's works, notably *The Constant Wife* in which a woman demands equality in her marriage. Ibsen's *A Doll's House*, written nearly 150 years ago, continues to be tackled by filmmakers because its portrayal of a stifling marriage of inequality is still relevant; and Maugham's play could be reconfigured for the same reason. So too could *The Circle*, in which a young couple's defiance of social expectations is carried out against the cautionary yet encouraging example of an older pair whose romance has long since dissipated. And in an age when assisted suicide is becoming more common and problematic, *The Sacred Flame*'s story of a mother's dilemma could, like Clint Eastwood's *Million Dollar Baby*, provide a useful perspective.

For contemporary filmmakers wishing to tackle a significant Maugham work that has never been made into a feature film, there is *Cakes and Ale*. The title, of course, refers to a subplot of Shakespeare's play *Twelfth Night* in which the prudish Malvolio attempts to stifle the drinking and carousing of several characters. One of them, aptly named Sir Toby Belch, challenges him by saying, "Dost thou think, because thou are virtuous, there shall be no more cakes and ale?"[8] Ironically, Maugham's novel, which celebrated the life force as exhibited in drinking, carousing, and uninhibited sexual conduct, proved impossible to film during the years of the Hays Office censorship of the movie industry. With the Hays restrictions being long gone, *Cakes and Ale* could now be put on the movie screen, though the sexual openness of its central female character, Rosie, would not be as provocative as it would have been in the twentieth century. Her sense of freedom, her unwillingness to be captive to any man, her warmth, generosity of spirit, and beauty make her a role that the right kind of actress, for example Margot Robbie or Scarlett Johansson, could make memorable.

Finally, the development of the format of the limited series on regular television channels like PBS and especially on cable networks and streaming services has opened the door to presenting film versions of fiction more comprehensively than the conventional theater release movie can do. Within the two or two-and-a-half-hour theater format, a novel of even modest length must necessarily lose a good deal of its substance, and it is impossible to render long nineteenth-century novels fully. In recent years, there have been excellent six-, eight-, and ten-part serial versions of Dickens novels, *Les Miserables*, *Howards End*, *Jane Eyre*, and others.

It seems to me inevitable that television producers will turn to *Of Human Bondage*, an eight-hundred-page novel that could not be faithfully rendered in any of its three film versions. The protagonist Philip's early life as an orphan in his uncle's house in Whitstable, his miserable days at an English boarding school, his intellectual awakening in Heidelberg, his life among the artists in Paris, his training in medicine in London, and his arrival at a philosophy that gives him a foundation for a satisfying life; all these experiences, which were largely ignored in the film versions, provide rich episodic material. His tortured relationship with Mildred would still be an important, even central, part of the series but placed in the proper context of his development from early youth to independent adulthood. It is a treatment, moreover, that might profitably be applied to other Maugham novels such as *The Razor's Edge*, *The Moon and Sixpence*, *The Narrow Corner*, and others.

Though Maugham's reputation and readership inevitably declined following his death, readers in the twenty-first century are still discovering his fiction. It is not unreasonable to think that contemporary filmmakers can find ways to recontextualize and adapt his best work for a new generation of moviegoers.

Appendix

Film Productions of Maugham Works

The Explorer (Paramount Pictures) (lost film)

DIRECTOR: George Melford
SCREENPLAY: William C. DeMille
CAST: Lou Tellegen
    Tom Foreman
    Dorothy Davenport
    James Neill
    Horace B. Carpenter
    Alec McKenzie
    George Allerton
    Lucy Allerton
    Dr. Adamson
    McInnery
RELEASE DATE: September 27, 1915

The Land of Promise (Famous Players-Lasky) (lost film)

DIRECTOR: Joseph Kaufman
SCREENPLAY: Charles Whittaker
CAST: Billie Burke
    Thomas Meighan
    Helen Tracy
    Jack W. Johnston
    Mary Alden
    Margaret Seddon
    Walter McEwen
    Grace Studdiford
    John Raymond
    Nora Marsh
    Frank Taylor
    Miss Eunice Wickam
    Edward Marsh
    Gertie Marsh
    Miss Pringle
    James Wickham
    Mrs. Wickham
    Reginald Hornby
RELEASE DATE: December 9, 1917

Smith (London Film Company) (lost film)

DIRECTOR: Maurice Elvey

CAST: Elisabeth Risdon — Smith
Fred Groves — Tom Freeman
Manora Thew — Rose Baker
Guy Newall — Algy Peppercorn
Douglas Munro — Otto Rosenburg
Lydia Bilbrook — Mrs. Rosenburg

RELEASE DATE: 1917

The Divorcee (Metro Pictures) (lost film)

DIRECTOR: Herbert Blaché

SCREENPLAY: June Mathis

CAST: Ethel Barrymore — Lady Frederick Berolles
E. J. Ratcliffe — Lord Frederick Berolles
H. E. Herbert — Sir Paradine Fuldes
Naomi Childers — Kitty Beresford
John Goldsworthy — Horace Beresford
Joseph Kilgour — Robert Montgomery
Maude Turner Gordon — Lady Mereston
Harold Entwistle — Lord Mereston
Eugene Strong — Young Lord Mereston
Ricca Allen — Madame Claude

RELEASE DATE: January 20, 1919

Jack Straw (Famous Players-Lasky) (lost film)

DIRECTOR: William C. DeMille

SCREENPLAY: Olga Printzlau
Elmer Harris

CAST: Robert Warwick — Jack Straw
Carroll McComas — Ethel Parker Jennings
Charles Ogle — Mr. Parker Jennings
Irene Sullivan — Mrs. Wanley
Monte du Mont — Ambrose Holland
Frances Parks — Rose

Lucien Littlefield	Sherlo
Robert Brower	Count of Pomerania
Sybil Ashton	Mrs. Parker Jennings

RELEASE DATE: March 14, 1920

The Ordeal (Famous Players-Lasky) (lost film)

DIRECTOR: Paul Powell
SCREENPLAY: Beulah Marie Dix

CAST: Agnes Ayres	Sybil Bruce
Clarence Burton	George Bruce
Conrad Nagel	Dr. Robert Acton
Edna Murphy	Helen Brayshaw
Anne Schaeffer	Minnie
Gino Corrado	Gene
Adele Farrington	Madame St. Levis
Edward Martindel	Sir Francis Maynard
Shannon Day	Kitty
Claire du Brey	Elise
Edward Sutherland	Victim

RELEASE DATE: May 21, 1922

East of Suez (Famous Players-Lasky) (lost film)

DIRECTOR: Raoul Walsh
SCREENPLAY: Sada Cowen

CAST: Pola Negri	Daisy Forbes
Edmund Lowe	George Tevis
Rockcliffe Fellowes	Harry Anderson
Noah Beery	British Consul
Sojin Kamiyama	Lee Tai
Mrs. Wong Wing	Amah
Florence Regnart	Sylvia Knox
Charles Requa	Harold Knox
E. H. Calvert	Sidney Forbes

RELEASE DATE: January 12, 1925

The Circle (Metro-Goldwyn-Mayer)

DIRECTOR: Frank Borzage
SCREENPLAY: Kenneth B. Clarke
CAST: Eleanor Boardman — Elizabeth Cheney
Malcolm McGregor — Edward "Teddy" Luton
Alec B. Francis — Lord Clive Cheney
Eugenie Besserer — Lady Catherine "Kitty" Cheney
George Fawcett — Lord Hugh "Hughie" Porteous
Creighton Hale — Arnold Cheney
Otto Hoffman — Dorker
Eulalie Jensen — Mrs. Alice Shenstone
Buddy Smith — Young Arnold
Joan Crawford — Young Lady Catherine
Frank Braidwood — Young Porteous
Derek Glynne — Young Cheney
RELEASE DATE: September 22, 1925

Infatuation (First National Pictures) (lost film)

DIRECTOR: Irving Cummings
SCREENPLAY: W. Somerset Maugham
CAST: Corinne Griffiths — Violet Bancroft
Percy Marmont — Sir Arthur Little
Malcolm McGregor — Ronald Perry
Warner Oland — Osman Pasha
Clarissa Selwynne — Lady Etheridge
Leota Lorraine — Ronny's Sister
Claire du Brey — Pasha's Wife
Howard Davies — Khedive
RELEASE DATE: December 27, 1925

The Magician (Metro-Goldwyn)

DIRECTOR: Rex Ingram
SCREENPLAY: Rex Ingram
CAST: Alice Terry — Margaret Dauncey
Paul Wegener — Oliver Haddo

Firmin Gémier	Doctor Porhoet
Ivan Petrovich	Arthur Burdon
Gladys Hamer	Susie Boyd
Henry Wilson	Haddo's Assistant
Hubert Stowitts	Dancing Faun

RELEASE DATE: October 24, 1926

The Canadian (Paramount Pictures)

DIRECTOR: William Beaudine
SCREENPLAY: Arthur Stringer

CAST: Thomas Meighan	Frank Taylor
Mona Palma	Nora
Wyndham Standing	Ed Marsh
Dale Fuller	Gertie
Charles Winninger	Pop Tyson
Billy Butts	Buck Golder

RELEASE DATE: November 27, 1926

Sadie Thompson (Gloria Swanson Productions)

DIRECTOR: Raoul Walsh
SCREENPLAY: Gloria Swanson
    Raoul Walsh

CAST: Gloria Swanson	Sadie Thompson
Lionel Barrymore	Alfred Davidson
Blanche Friderici	Mrs. Davidson
Charles Willis Lane	Dr. Angus McPhail
Florence Midgeley	Mrs. McPhail
James A. Marcus	Joe Horn
Sophia Artega	Ameena
Will Stanton	Quartermaster Bates
Raoul Walsh	Sergeant Timothy O'Hara

RELEASE DATE: January 7, 1928

The Letter (Paramount Pictures)

DIRECTOR: Jean de Limur
SCREENPLAY: Garrett Fort
CAST: Jeanne Eagels — Leslie Crosbie
Reginald Owen — Robert Crosbie
Herbert Marshall — Geoffrey Hammond
Irene Browne — Mrs. Joyce
O. P. Heggie — Mr. Joyce
Lady Tsen Mei — Li-Ti
Tamaki Yoshiwara — Ong Chi Seng
RELEASE DATE: April 13, 1929

Charming Sinners (Paramount)

DIRECTOR: Robert Milton
Dorothy Arzner
SCREENPLAY: Doris Anderson
MUSIC: Karl Hajos
W. Franke Harling
CAST: Ruth Chatterton — Kathryn Miles
Clive Brook — Robert Miles
Mary Nolan — Anne-Marie Whitley
William Powell — Karl Kraley
Laura Hope Crews — Mrs. Carr
Florence Eldridge — Helen Carr
Montagu Love — George Whitley
Juliette Crosby — Margaret
Lorraine MacLean — Alice
Claud Allister — Gregson
RELEASE DATE: August 17, 1929

The Sacred Flame (Warner Bros.) (lost film)

DIRECTOR: Archie Mayo
SCREENPLAY: Harvey F. Thew
CAST: Pauline Frederick — Mrs. Taylor
Conrad Nagel — Colonel Maurice Taylor

Lila Lee	Stella Taylor
William Courtenay	Major Laconda
Walter Byron	Colin Taylor
Dale Fuller	Nurse Wayland
Alec B. Francis	Doctor Harvester

RELEASE DATE: November 24, 1929

Strictly Unconventional (Metro-Goldwyn-Mayer)

DIRECTOR: David Burton
SCREENPLAY: Sylvia Thalberg
   Frank Butler

CAST: Lewis Stone	Clive Champion-Cheney
Catherine Dale Owen	Elizabeth
Paul Cavanagh	Ted
Ernest Torrence	Lord Porteous
Tyrell Davis	Arnold Champion-Cheney
Alison Skipworth	Lady Catherine Champion-Cheney
Mary Forbes	Mrs. Anna Shenstone
Wilfred Noye	Butler
William H. O'Brien	Footman

RELEASE DATE: May 3, 1930

Rain (United Artists)

DIRECTOR: Lewis Milestone
SCREENPLAY: Maxwell Anderson
MUSIC: Alfred Newman

CAST: Joan Crawford	Sadie Thompson
Fred Howard	Hodgson
Ben Hendricks Jr.	Griggs
William Gargan	Sergeant Tim O'Hara
Mary Shaw	Ameena
Guy Kibbee	Joe Horn
Kendall Lee	Mrs. Robert McPhail
Beulah Bondi	Mrs. Alfred Davidson
Matt Moore	Dr. Robert McPhail

Walter Huston   Alfred Davidson
Walter Catlett   Quartermaster Bates
RELEASE DATE: October 12, 1932

Our Betters (RKO)

DIRECTOR: George Cukor
SCREENPLAY: Jane Murfin
   Henry Wagstaff Gribble
MUSIC: Bernhard Kaun
   Roy Webb

CAST:	
Constance Bennett	Pearl, Lady Grayston
Anita Louise	Bessie Saunders
Gilbert Roland	Pepi D'Costa
Violet Kemble-Cooper	Duchess Minnie
Charles Starrett	Fleming Harvey
Grant Mitchell	Thornton Clay
Minor Watson	Arthur Fenwick
Hugh Sinclair	Lord Harry Bleane
Alan Mowbray	Lord George Grayston
Tyrell Davis	Ernest
Finis Barton	Diana
May Beatty	Duchess of Hightower

RELEASE DATE: February 23, 1933

The Narrow Corner (Warner Bros.)

DIRECTOR: Alfred E. Green
SCREENPLAY: Robert Presnell
MUSIC: Bernhard Kaun

CAST:	
Douglas Fairbanks Jr.	Fred Blake
Patricia Ellis	Louise Frith
Ralph Bellamy	Eric Whittenson
Dudley Digges	Doctor Saunders
Arthur Hohl	Captain Nichols
Reginald Owen	Mr. Frith
Henry Kolker	Mr. Blake
William V. Mong	Jack Swan

Willie Fung   Ah Kay
Sidney Toler   Ryan
RELEASE DATE: July 8, 1933

Of Human Bondage (RKO Pictures)

DIRECTOR: John Cromwell
SCREENPLAY: Lester Cohen
MUSIC: Max Steiner
CAST: Leslie Howard   Philip Carey
    Bette Davis   Mildred Rogers
    Frances Dee   Sally Athelny
    Kay Johnson   Norah
    Reginald Denny   Harry Griffiths
    Alan Hale   Emil Miller
    Reginald Sheffield   Cyril Dunsford
    Reginald Owen   Thorpe Athelny
    Tempe Pigott   Agnes Hollet
    Desmond Roberts   Dr. Jacobs
RELEASE DATE: June 28, 1934

The Painted Veil (Metro-Goldwyn-Mayer)

DIRECTOR: Richard Boleslawski
SCREENPLAY: John Meehan
   Salka Viertel
   Edith Fitzgerald
CAST: Greta Garbo   Katrin Koerber Fane
    Herbert Marshall   Dr. Walter Fane
    George Brent   Jack Townsend
    Warner Oland   General Yu
    Jean Hersholt   Herr Koerber
    Bodil Rosing   Frau Koerber
    Katherine Alexander   Mrs. Townsend
    Cecilia Parker   Olga Koerber
    Soo Yong   Amah
    Forrester Harvey   Tim Waddington
RELEASE DATE: November 23, 1934

The Right to Live (Warner Bros.)

DIRECTOR: William Keighley
SCREENPLAY: Ralph Block
MUSIC: Bernhard Kaun
CAST: Josephine Hutchinson — Stella Trent
    George Brent — Colin Trent
    Colin Clive — Maurice
    Peggy Wood — Nurse Wayland
    Henrietta Crossman — Mrs. Trent
    Aubrey Smith — Major Liconda
    Leo G. Carroll — Dr. Harvester
    Phyllis Coghlan — Alice
    Claude King — Mr. Pride
    Nella Walker — Mrs. Pride
    Halliwell Hobbes — Sir Stephen Barr
    J. Gunnis Davis — Harvey
RELEASE DATE: January 26, 1935

Secret Agent (British International Pictures)

DIRECTOR: Alfred Hitchcock
SCREENPLAY: Charles Bennett
  Alma Reville
  Ian Hay
  Jesse Lasky Jr.
MUSIC: John Greenwood
CAST: John Gielgud — Edgar Brodie/Richard Ashenden
    Peter Lorre — Hairless Mexican
    Madeleine Carroll — Elsa Carrington
    Robert Young — Robert Marvin
    Percy Marmont — Caypor
    Florence Kahn — Mrs. Caypor
    Charles Carson — "R"
    Lilli Palmer — Lilli
RELEASE DATE: June 15, 1936

The Tenth Man (British International Pictures)

DIRECTOR: Brian Desmond Hurst

SCREENPLAY: Dudley Lesley
   Marjorie Deans
   Jack Davies
   Geoffrey Kerr

MUSIC: Harry Acres

CAST:	
John Lodge	George Winter
Antoinette Cellier	Catherine Winter
Athole Stewart	Lord Etchingham
Clifford Evans	Ford
Iris Hoey	Lady Etchingham
Aileen Marson	Anne Etchingham
Frank Cochrane	Bennett
George Graves	Colonel Trent
Bruce Lester	Edward O'Donnell
Barry Sinclair	Robert Colby
Antony Holles	Swalescliffe
Aubrey Mallalieu	Bank Manager

RELEASE DATE: August 12, 1936

Isle of Fury (Warner Bros.)

DIRECTOR: Frank McDonald

SCREENPLAY: Robert Hardy Andrews
   William Jacobs

MUSIC: Howard Jackson

CAST:	
Humphrey Bogart	Val Stevens
Margaret Lindsay	Lucille Gordon
Donald Woods	Eric Blake
E. E. Clive	Dr. Hardy
Paul Graetz	Captain Deever
Gordan Hart	Chris Anderson
George Regas	Otar
Sidney Bracey	Sam
Tetsu Komai	Kim Lee
Miki Morita	Ah Kay

Houseley Stevenson	Rector
Frank Lackteen	Old Native Lanar

RELEASE DATE: October 10, 1936

Another Dawn (Warner Bros.)

DIRECTOR: William Dieterle
SCREENPLAY: Laird Doyle
MUSIC: Erich Wolfgang Korngold

CAST: Kay Francis	Julia Ashton Wister
Errol Flynn	Captain Danny Roark
Ian Hunter	Colonel John Wister
Frieda Inescort	Grace Roark
Herbert Mundin	Wilkins
G. P. Huntley	Lord Alden
Billy Bevan	Private Hawkins
Clyde Cook	Sergeant Murphy
Richard Powell	Private Henderson
Kenneth Hunter	Sir Charles Benton
Mary Forbes	Lady Lynda Benton
Eily Malyon	Mrs. Farnold

RELEASE DATE: June 18, 1937

Vessel of Wrath (*The Beachcomber* in the United States)
(Mayflower Productions)

DIRECTOR: Eric Pommer
SCREENPLAY: Bartlett Cormack
MUSIC: Richard Addinsell

CAST: Charles Laughton	Ginger Ted
Elsa Lanchester	Martha Jones
Robert Newton	The Controleur (Gruyter)
Tyrone Guthrie	Owen Jones
Eliot Makeham	The Clerk
Dollie Mollinger	Lia
D. A. Ward	The Chieftain
J. Solomon	The Sergeant

RELEASE DATE: March 4, 1938

Too Many Husbands (*My Two Husbands* in the UK) (Columbia Pictures)

DIRECTOR: Wesley Ruggles
SCREENPLAY: Claude Binyon
MUSIC: Friedrich Hollaender

CAST: Jean Arthur	Vicky Lowndes
Fred MacMurray	Bill Cardew
Melvyn Douglas	Henry Lowndes
Harry Davenport	George
Dorothy Peterson	Gertrude Houlihan
Melville Cooper	Peter, the Butler
Edgar Buchanan	Adolph McDermott
Tom Dugan	Lieutenant Sullivan

RELEASE DATE: March 21, 1940

The Letter (Warner Bros.)

DIRECTOR: William Wyler
SCREENPLAY: Howard E. Koch
MUSIC: Max Steiner

CAST: Bette Davis	Leslie Crosbie
Herbert Marshall	Robert Crosbie
James Stephenson	Howard Joyce
Frieda Inescort	Dorothy Joyce
Gale Sondergaard	Mrs. Hammond
Bruce Lester	John Withers
Elizabeth Earl	Adele Ainsworth
Cecil Kellaway	Prescott
Sen Yung	Ong Chi Seng
Doris Lloyd	Mrs. Cooper
Willie Fung	Chung Hi
Tetsu Komai	Head Boy

RELEASE DATE: November 22, 1940

The Moon and Sixpence (United Artists)

DIRECTOR: Albert Lewin
SCREENPLAY: Albert Lewin

MUSIC: Dimitri Tiomkin

CAST: George Sanders   Charles Strickland
       Herbert Marshall   Geoffrey Wolfe
       Doris Dudley   Blanche Stroeve
       Eric Blore   Captain Nichols
       Albert Bassermann   Dr. Coutras
       Florence Bates   Tiara Johnson
       Steve Geray   Dirk Stroeve
       Elena Verdugo   Ata
       Molly Lamont   Mrs. Strickland

RELEASE DATE: October 27, 1942

The Hour Before the Dawn (Paramount Pictures)

DIRECTOR: Frank Tuttle

SCREENPLAY: Michael Hogan
   Lesser Samuels

MUSIC: Miklós Rózsa

CAST: Franchot Tone   Jim Hetherton
       Veronica Lake   Dora Bruckman
       John Sutton   Roger Hetherton
       Binnie Barnes   May Hetherton
       Henry Stephenson   General Hetherton
       Philip Merivale   Sir Leslie Buchanan
       Nils Asther   Kurt van der Breughel
       Edmund Breon   Freddy Merritt
       David Leland   Tommy Hetherton
       Aminta Dyne   Mrs. Muller

RELEASE DATE: May 10, 1944

Christmas Holiday (Universal Pictures)

DIRECTOR: Robert Siodmak

SCREENPLAY: Herman J. Mankiewicz

MUSIC: Hans J. Salter

CAST: Deanna Durbin   Jackie Lamont
       Gene Kelly   Robert Manette
       Richard Whorf   Simon Fenimore

Dean Harens	Charlie Mason
Gladys George	Valerie de Merode
Gale Sondergaard	Mrs. Manette
David Bruce	Gerald Tyler

RELEASE DATE: July 31, 1944

Dirty Gertie from Harlem (Sack Amusement Enterprises)

DIRECTOR: Spencer Williams
SCREENPLAY: True T. Thompson

CAST:	
Francine Everett	Gertie LaRue
Don Wilson	Diamond Joe
Katherine Moore	Stella Van Johnson
Alfred Hawkins	Jonathan Christian
David Boykin	Ezra Crumm
L. E. Lewis	Papa Bridges
Inez Newell	Mama Bridges
Piano Frank	Larry
John King	Al
Shelly Ross	Big Boy
Hugh Watson	Tight Pants
Don Gilbert	Manager
Spencer Williams	Old Hager
July Jones	Specialty Dancer
Howard Galloway	Specialty Dancer

RELEASE DATE: 1946

Of Human Bondage (Warner Bros.)

DIRECTOR: Edmund Goulding
SCREENPLAY: Catherine Turney
MUSIC: Erich Wolfgang Korngold

CAST:	
Eleanor Parker	Mildred Rogers
Paul Henreid	Philip Carey
Edmund Gwenn	Thorpe Athelny
Janis Paige	Sally Athelny
Patric Knowles	Harry Griffiths
Isobel Elsom	Mrs. Athelny

Alexis Smith	Norah Nesbitt
Henry Stephenson	Dr. Tyrell
Una O'Connor	Mrs. Foreman
Matthew Boulton	Mr. Foreman
Doris Lloyd	Landlady

RELEASE DATE: July 5, 1946

The Razor's Edge (20th Century Fox)

DIRECTOR: Edmund Goulding
SCREENPLAY: Lamar Trotti
MUSIC: Alfred Newman

CAST:	
Tyrone Power	Larry Darrell
Gene Tierney	Isabel Bradley
John Payne	Gray Maturin
Anne Baxter	Sophie MacDonald
Clifton Webb	Elliott Templeton
Herbert Marshall	W. Somerset Maugham
Lucile Watson	Louisa Bradley
Frank Latimore	Bob MacDonald
Elsa Lanchester	Miss Keith
Cecil Humphreys	the Holy Man
Fritz Kortner	Kosti

RELEASE DATE: December 25, 1946

The Unfaithful (Warner Bros.)

DIRECTOR: Vincent Sherman
SCREENPLAY: David Goodis
   James Gunn
MUSIC: Max Steiner

CAST:	
Ann Sheridan	Chris Hunter
Lew Ayres	Larry Hannaford
Zachary Scott	Bob Hunter
Eve Arden	Paula
Jerome Cowan	Prosecuting Attorney
Steven Geray	Martin Barrow
John Hoyt	Det. Lt. Reynolds

Peggy Knudsen	Claire
Marta Mitrovich	Mrs. Tanner
Douglas Kennedy	Roger
Claire Meade	Martha
Frances Morris	Agnes
Jane Harker	Joan

RELEASE DATE: July 5, 1947

Quartet (Gainsborough Pictures)

DIRECTORS: Ken Annakin
   Arthur Crabtree
   Harold French
   Ralph Smart
SCREENPLAY: R. C. Sherriff

CAST: Angela Baddeley	Mrs. Garnet
Cecil Parker	Colonel George Peregrine
Dirk Bogarde	George Bland
Françoise Rosay	Lea Makart
Mervyn Johns	Samuel Sunbury
Basil Radford	Henry Garnet
George Cole	Herbert Sunbury
Naunton Wayne	Leslie
Susan Shaw	Betty
Hermione Baddeley	Beatrice Sunbury
Mai Zetterling	Jeanne
Linden Travers	Daphne

RELEASE DATE: October 26, 1948

Trio (Gainsborough Pictures)

DIRECTORS: Ken Annakin
   Harold French
SCREENWRITER: W. Somerset Maugham
   Noel Langley
   R. C. Sherriff
MUSIC: John Greenwood
   Muir Mathieson

CAST: Anne Crawford   Mrs. Ramsay
Naunton Wayne   Mr. Ramsay
Roland Culver   Mr. Ashenden
Kathleen Harrison   Emma Foreman
James Hayter   Albert Foreman
Nigel Patrick   Max Kelada
Michael Rennie   Major George Templeton
Jean Simmons   Evie Bishop
Wilfred Hyde-White   Mr. Gray
Michael Hordern   Vicar
Felix Aylmer   Bank Manager
Clive Morton   Ship's Captain
Bill Travers   Fellows
Finlay Currie   McLeod
John Laurie   Campbell
Raymond Huntley   Chester
Betty Ann Davies   Mrs. Chester
Marjorie Fielding   Mrs. Whitbread
Mary Merrall   Miss Atkin
Andre Morell   Dr. Lennox

RELEASE DATE: August 1, 1950

Encore (Two Cities Films)

DIRECTORS: Pat Jackson
Anthony Pelissier
Harold French
SCREENPLAY: T. E. B. Clarke
Arthur Macrae
Eric Ambler
MUSIC: Richard Addinsell
CAST: Glynis Johns   Stella Cotman
Terence Morgan   Syd Cotman
Kay Walsh   Molly Reid
Noel Purcell   Captain Tom
Nigel Patrick   Tom Ramsay
Roland Culver   George Ramsay

Alison Leggatt Freda Ramsay
Peter Graves Philip Cronshaw
Ronald Squire Ship's Doctor
Margaret Vyner Gertrude Wilmot
Michael Trubshawe Ascot Man
John Laurie Andrews
Jacques François Pierre
Mary Merrall Flora Penezzi
Martin Miller Carlo Penezzi

RELEASE DATE: November 14, 1951

Miss Sadie Thompson (Columbia Pictures)

DIRECTOR: Curtis Bernhardt
SCREENPLAY: Harry Kleiner
CAST: Rita Hayworth Sadie Thompson
José Ferrer Alfred Davidson
Aldo Ray Sergeant Phil O'Hara
Russell Collins Dr. Robert McPhail
Diosa Costello Ameena Horn
Harry Bellaver Joe Horn
Wilton Graff Governor
Peggy Converse Mrs. Davidson
Henry Slate Private Griggs
Rudy Bond Private Hodges
Charles Bronson Private Edwards
Frances Morri Mrs. McPhail

RELEASE DATE: December 23, 1953

The Beachcomber (London Independent Pictures)

DIRECTOR: Muriel Box
SCREENPLAY: Sydney Box
MUSIC: Francis Chagrin
CAST: Glynis Johns Martha Jones
Robert Newton Honorable Ted
Donald Sinden Ewart Gray
Paul Rogers Owen Jones

Donald Pleasence	Tromp
Walter Crisham	Vederala
Michael Hordern	Headman
Auric Lorand	Alfred
Tony Quinn	Ship Captain
Ah Chong Choy	Wang
Ronald Lewis	Headman's Son

RELEASE DATE: August 10, 1954

Three for the Show (Columbia Pictures)

DIRECTOR: H. C. Potter
SCREENPLAY: Edward Hope
　Leonard B. Stern
MUSIC: George Duning

CAST: Betty Grable	Julian Lowndes
Jack Lemmon	Martin Stewart
Gower Champion	Vernon Lowndes
Marge Champion	Gwen Howard
Myron McCormick	Mike Hudson
Paul Harvey	Col. Harold J. Wharton
Robert Bice	Sgt. Charlie O'Hallihan
Charlotte Lawrence	Miss Williams

RELEASE DATE: February 24, 1955

The Seventh Sin (Metro-Goldwyn-Mayer)

DIRECTOR: Ronald Neame
SCREENPLAY: Karl Tunberg
MUSIC: Miklós Rózsa

CAST: Eleanor Parker	Carol Carwin
Bill Travers	Walter Carwin
George Sanders	Tim Waddington
Jean-Pierre Aumont	Paul Duvelle
Françoise Rosay	Mother Superior
Ellen Corby	Sister Saint Joseph
Judy Dan	Mrs. Waddington
Phyllis Stanley	Dorothy Duvelle

Frank Tang   Dr. Lee
Kam Tong   Colonel Yu

RELEASE DATE: June 28, 1957

Adorable Julia (Wiener-Mundus-Film)

DIRECTOR: Alfred Weidenmann
SCREENPLAY: Eberhard Keindorff
  Johanna Sibelius
MUSIC: Rolf A. Wilhelm
CAST: Lilli Palmer   Julia Lambert
  Charles Boyer   Michael Gosselyn
  Jean Sorel   Tom Fennel
  Jeanne Valérie   Avice Crichton
  Ljuba Welitsch   Dolly de Fries
  Tilly Lauenstein   Evie
  Charles Régnier   Lord Charles Tamerly
  Thomas Fritsch   Roger
  Herbert Fux   Inspizient
  Hanna Ehrenstrasser   Ein langbeiniges Mädchen
  Gustaf Elger   Stevenson
  Sylvia Lydi   Philipps
  Friedrich Neubauer   Sir Edwin
  Fritz Puchstein   Edwards
  Herta Risawy   Margery
  Otto Schmöle   Albert
  Fritz Weiss   Mr. Robinson

RELEASE DATE: May 1962

Of Human Bondage (Seven Arts Productions)

DIRECTOR: Ken Hughes—additional scenes Henry Hathaway
SCREENPLAY: Bryan Forbes
MUSIC: Ron Goodwin
CAST: Kim Novak   Mildred Rogers
  Laurence Harvey   Philip Carey
  Robert Morley   Dr. Jacobs
  Siobhán McKenna   Nora Nesbitt

Roger Livesey   Thorpe Athelny
Jack Hedley   Griffiths
Nanette Newman   Sally Athelny
Ronald Lacey   Matty Matthews
RELEASE DATE: September 23, 1964

Overnight Sensation (Bloom)

DIRECTOR: Jon Bloom
SCREENPLAY: Craig Buck
MUSIC: William Goldstein
CAST: Louise Fletcher   Evie Peregrine
      Robert Loggia   George Peregrine
      Shari Belafonte-Harper   Daphne
      Parley Baer   Lawyer
      Eric Poppick   Critic
      Lee Garlington   Sales Girl
      Vincent Guastaferro   Assistant
RELEASE DATE: October 1984

The Razor's Edge (Columbia Pictures)

DIRECTOR: John Byrum
SCREENPLAY: John Byrum
   Bill Murray
MUSIC: Jack Nitzsche
CAST: Bill Murray   Larry Darrell
      Theresa Russell   Sophie MacDonald
      Catherine Hicks   Isabel Bradley
      Denholm Elliott   Elliott Templeton
      James Keach   Gray Maturin
      Peter Vaughan   Mackenzie
      Brian Doyle-Murray   Piedmont
      Faith Brook   Louisa Bradley
      Saeed Jaffrey   Raaz
      Richard Oldfield   Doug van Allen
      André Maranne   Joseph, the Butler
      Bruce Boa   Maturin
RELEASE DATE: October 19, 1984

Up at the Villa (USA Films, United International Pictures)

DIRECTOR: Philip Haas
SCREENPLAY: Belinda Haas
MUSIC: Pino Donaggio
CAST: Kristin Scott Thomas — Mary Panton
Sean Penn — Rowley Flint
Anne Bancroft — Princess San Ferdinando
James Fox — Sir Edgar Swift
Massimo Ghini — Beppino Leopardi
Jeremy Davies — Karl Richter
Derek Jacobi — Lucky Leadbetter
Dudley Sutton — Harold Atkinson
Roger Hammond — Colin MacKenzie
RELEASE DATE: May 5, 2000

Being Julia (Sony Pictures)

DIRECTOR: István Szabó
SCREENPLAY: Ronald Harwood
MUSIC: Mychael Danna
CAST: Annette Bening — Julia Lambert
Jeremy Irons — Michael Gosselyn
Shaun Evans — Tom Fennel
Lucy Punch — Avice Crichton
Juliet Stevenson — Evie
Miriam Margolyse — Dolly de Vries
Tom Sturridge — Roger Gosselyn
Bruce Greenwood — Lord Charles
Rosemary Harris — Julia's Mother
Rita Tushingham — Aunt Carrie
Michael Gambon — Jimmie Langton
RELEASE DATE: October 15, 2004

The Painted Veil (WIP, Stratus Films, Bob Yari Productions)

DIRECTOR: John Curran
SCREENPLAY: Ron Nyswaner

MUSIC: Alexandre Desplat

CAST: Edward Norton   Walter Fane
      Naomi Watts   Kitty Fane
      Toby Jones   Waddington
      Diana Rigg   Mother Superior
      Anthony Wong   Colonel Yu
      Live Schrieber   Charles Townsend
      Juliet Howland   Dorothy Townsend
      Alan David   Mr. Garstin
      Maggie Steed   Mrs. Garstin
      Cheng Sihan   Warlord Kwei
      Lucy Voller   Doris Garstin
      Marie-Laure Descoureaux   Sister St, Joseph
      Zoe Telford   Leona
      Lǚ Yan   Wu Lien
      Feng Li   Song Qing

RELEASE DATE: December 20, 2006

Notes

Introduction

1. Leslie Rees, "Remembrance of Things Past: A Meeting with Somerset Maugham," *Meanjin Quarterly* (Summer 1967): 493.

2. Frederic Raphael, preface to *Two for the Road* (London: Jonathan Cape, 1967), 14.

3. Margaret Kennedy, *The Mechanized Muse* (London: Allen and Unwin, 1942), 13.

4. George Bluestone, *Novels into Films* (Berkeley: University of California Press, 1966), viii.

5. Alvin H. Marill, *Samuel Goldwyn Presents* (South Brunswick, NJ: A. S. Barnes, 1976), 19.

6. Selina Hastings, *The Secret Lives of Somerset Maugham* (London: John Murray, 2009), 267.

7. Hastings, *The Secret Lives of Somerset Maugham*, 267.

8. Gore Vidal, "Maugham's Half and Half," *New York Review of Books*, February 1, 1990, 41.

9. Somerset Maugham, "On Writing for the Films," *North American Review* 213 (May 5, 1921): 675.

10. Maugham, "On Writing for the Films," 674.

11. Associated Talking Pictures Limited prospectus, *Evening Standard*, May 8, 1929, 28.

12. Jolo, "The Tenth Man," *Variety*, September 1936, 21.

13. Bette Davis, *The Lonely Life* (New York: Lancer, 1963), 123.

14. Frederic Raphael, "Fiction and the Medical Mode," *The Listener*, April 3, 1975, 452.

15. Anthony Curtis, *The Pattern of Maugham: A Critical Portrait* (London: Hamish Hamilton, 1974), 3.

16. Sewell Stokes, *Pilloried!* (New York: Appleton, 1929), 46.

17. "Maugham Comes Back with Autobiography," *New York Times*, November 9, 1935, 13.

18. Garson Kanin, *Remembering Mr. Maugham* (New York: Atheneum, 1966), 138.

19. Quoted in Brander Matthews, "Tragedies with Happy Endings," *North American Review* 211, no. 772 (March 1920): 356.

20. Laurence Brander, *Somerset Maugham: A Guide* (London: Oliver & Boyd, 1965), 135, 139.

21. Emanuel Levy, *George Cukor* (New York: Morrow, 1994), 310.

22. Raphael, preface to *Two for the Road*, 14.

23. Brian McFarlane, *Novel to Film: An Introduction to the Theory of Film Adaptation* (Oxford: Clarendon Press, 1996), 8.

24. Brian C. McFarlane, "It Wasn't Like That in the Book," in *The Literature/Film Reader: Issues of Adaptation*, ed. James M. Welsh and Peter Lev (Toronto: Scarecrow Press, 2007), 6.

25. Robert Stam, "The Dialogics of Adaptation," in *Film Adaptation*, ed. James Naremore (New Brunswick, NJ: Rutgers University Press, 2000), 62.

26. Thomas M. Leitch, "Where Are We Going, Where Have We Been?," in Welsh and Lev, *The Literature/Film Reader*, 332.

27. Vidal, "Maugham's Half and Half," 44.

Chapter 1. A New Industry Finds Gold in Somerset

1. Kitty Kelly, "Adventure Tale at Orchestra Hall," *Chicago Tribune*, September 21, 1915, 14.

2. Grace Kingsley, "At the Stage Door," *Los Angeles Times*, July 27, 1915, 24.

3. "At the Strand Theater," *Brooklyn Daily Eagle*, September 21, 1915, 8.

4. "Joseph Kaufman Does Good Work in Billie Burke Film," *Motion Picture News*, December 15, 1917, 4188.

5. Hastings, *The Secret Lives of Somerset Maugham*, 170.

6. Mae Tinée, "Lacks Balance; Fault Due to the Star System," *Chicago Tribune*, December 18, 1917, 18.

7. "Leading Man for Many Lovely Ladies," *Los Angeles Times*, March 31, 1918, 39.

8. "Mr. Maugham's *Land of Promise*," *Times*, April 21, 1958, 3.

9. "The Land of Promise," *Variety*, December 1917, 43.

10. Mae Tinée, "Mr Maugham Brings You a Christmas Gift," *Chicago Tribune*, December 21, 1926, 29.

11. "Thomas Meighan in 'The Canadian,'" *Film Daily*, December 5, 1926, 24.

12. Skig, "The Canadian," *Variety*, December 1, 1926, 33.

13. "The Canadian," *Photoplay*, March 1927, 8.

14. "Miss Barrymore in 'Lady Frederick,'" *New York Times*, November 10, 1908, 9.

15. "Miss Barrymore Sure Fine in Well Suited Vehicle," *Film Daily*, January 26, 1919, 17.

16. "'The Divorcee'—Metro," *Motion Picture News*, January 25, 1919, 600.

17. Edward Weitzel, "The Divorcee," *Moving Picture World*, February 8, 1919, 803.

18. "Drew at His Best in 'Jack Straw,'" *New York Times*, September 15, 1908, 9.

19. Herbert Howe, "A Forecast of Films," *Picture-Play Magazine*, June 1920, 77.

20. Laurence Reid, "Jack Straw," *Motion Picture News*, April 10, 1920, 3365.

21. Fred, "The Ordeal," *Variety*, June 2, 1922, 34.

22. "Somerset Maugham Writes Down to Us," *Los Angeles Times*, July 10, 1922, 28.

23. "Newspaper Opinions," *American Film Daily*, January 10, 1926, 4.

24. Martin E. Dickstein, "The Cinema Circuit," *Brooklyn Eagle*, January 4, 1926, 3.

25. Skig, "Infatuation," *Variety*, January 13, 1926, 43.

26. George Shaffer, "Kay Francis Stars in Film of Army Life," *Chicago Tribune*, October 20, 1936, 20.

27. Philip K. Scheuer, "Tropics Scene of Film Romance," *Los Angeles Times*, June 24, 1937, 10.

28. Sally, "The Dressy Side," *Variety*, January 7, 1925, 15.

29. C.S. Sewell, "East of Suez," *Moving Picture World*, January 17, 1925, 269.

30. Mae Tinae, "The Breath of Scandal," *Chicago Tribune*, January 18, 1925, 61.

31. W. Somerset Maugham, *The Collected Plays of W. Somerset Maugham*, vol. 2 (London: Heinemann, 1961), 87.

32. Maugham, *The Collected Plays*, 2:78.

33. Quoted in "Newspaper Opinions," *Film Daily*, September 25, 1925, 8.

34. Quoted in "Newspaper Opinions," *Film Daily*, September 25, 1925, 8.

35. Quoted in "Newspaper Opinions," *Film Daily*, September 25, 1925, 8.

36. "Strictly Unconventional," *Film Daily*, July 20, 1930, 15.

37. Martin Dickstein, "Slow Motion," *Brooklyn Daily Eagle*, May 18, 1930, E3.

38. Raymond Toole Stott, *A Bibliography of the Works of W. Somerset Maugham* (London: Kaye and Ward, 1973), 51.

39. Preface to W. Somerset Maugham, *Liza of Lambeth* (London: Heinemann, 1934), xxv.

40. W. Somerset Maugham, "A Fragment of Autobiography," in *The Magician* (London: Penguin, 1967), 9.

41. Andre Soares, *Beyond Paradise: The Life of Ramon Novarro* (New York: Macmillan, 2002), 27.

42. Michael Powell, *A Life in Movies: An Autobiography* (New York: Alfred A. Knopf, 1987), 154.

43. Powell, *A Life in Movies*, 154.

44. Powell, *A Life in Movies*, 158.

45. "Rex Ingram's 'The Magician,'" *Motion Picture News*, July 1926; "Parade of Hits," *Motion Picture News*, July, 1926.

46. Paul Rotha, *The Film Till Now: A Survey of World Cinema* (London: Spring Books, 1967), 197.

47. Stokes, *Pilloried!*, 111.

48. Liam O'Leary, *Rex Ingram: Master of the Silent Film* (New York: Harper & Row, 1980), 166.

Chapter 2. Swanson, Crawford, and Hayworth

1. W. Somerset Maugham, *A Writer's Notebook* (London: Heinemann, 1949), 105.

2. Maugham, *A Writer's Notebook*, 106. Remarkably, Maugham used the woman's real surname, both in *A Writer's Notebook* and in the published short story, a fact confirmed by the log of the SS *Sonoma*, on which they sailed.

3. Graham Greene, *Journey without Maps* (London: Heinemann, 1950), 203.

4. Gloria Swanson, *Swanson on Swanson: An Autobiography* (New York: Pocket Books, 1980), 308.

5. Alma Whitaker, "Gamin Soul Is Set Free," *Los Angeles Times*, February 26, 1928, 49.

6. Brendan Gill, "Making a Voice in the World," *The New Yorker*, October 7, 1972, 96.

7. As quoted by Sara Mayfield, *The Constant Circle* (New York: Putnam's, 1972), 104.

8. Swanson, *Swanson on Swanson*, 311–12.

9. Janet Staiger, "'Because I Am a Woman': Identity and Agency for Historiography," *Film History* 25, nos. 1–2 (2013): 208.

10. Stephen Michael Shearer, *Gloria Swanson: The Ultimate Star* (New York: St. Martin's, 2013), 167.

11. Axel Madsen, *Gloria and Joe* (New York: Berkley Books, 1989), 170.

12. Swanson, *Swanson on Swanson*, 322.

13. "No Preacher in 'Sadie Thompson,' Says Schenck," *Motion Picture News*, June 17, 1927, 2364.

14. Swanson, *Swanson on Swanson*, 335.

15. Janet Staiger, "'Because I Am a Woman': Identity and Agency for Historiography," *Film History* 25, nos. 1–2 (2013): 212.

16. Edwin Schallert, "You Can't Do That," *Picture Play*, September 1928, 16.

17. Paul Rotha, *The Film Till Now: A Survey of the Cinema* (London: Cape, 1930), 139.

18. Laurence Reid, "Sadie Thompson: At Last Gloria Has a Picture," *Motion Picture News*, February 11, 1928, 451.

19. Marilyn Ann Moss, *Raoul Walsh: The True Adventures of Hollywood's Legendary Director* (Lexington: University Press of Kentucky, 2011), 106.

20. Laurence Reid, "Sadie Thompson: At Last Gloria Has a Picture," *Motion Picture News*, February 11, 1928, 451.

21. Frank Scully, *Rogues Gallery* (Hollywood: Murray and Gee, 1943), 30.

22. W. Somerset Maugham, "Rain," in *The Complete Short Stories*, vol. 1 (New York: Doubleday and Company, 1952), 6.

23. Maugham, "Rain," in *Complete Short Stories*, 1:39.

24. Maugham, "Rain," in *Complete Short Stories*, 1:34.

25. Mordaunt Hall, "Miss Thompson's Shadow," *New York Times*, February 12, 1928, 7.

26. Welford Beaton, "Trying to Delouse Sadie Thompson," *Film Spectator*, December 10, 1927, 9.

27. Raoul Walsh, *Each Man in His Time: The Life Story of a Director* (New York: Farrar, Straus and Giroux, 1974), 211.

28. Madsen, *Gloria and Joe*, 324.

29. Donald Spoto, *Possessed: The Life of Joan Crawford* (New York: William Morrow, 2010), 97.

30. Bob Thomas, *Joan Crawford: A Biography* (New York: Bantam, 1979), 77.

31. David Russell, "Is Garbo Queen?," *Picture Play*, February 1933, 16.

32. Thomas, *Joan Crawford*, 76, 77.

33. "What the Fans Think," *Picture Play Magazine*, October 1932, 6.

34. Abel Green, "Rain," *Variety*, October 18, 1932, 14.

35. Abel Green, "Rain," *Variety*, October 18, 1932, 14.

36. Molly Haskell, *From Reverence to Rape: The Treatment of Women in the Movies* (Harmondsworth, UK: Penguin, 1974), 177.

37. Mordaunt Hall, "The Screen: Sadie Thompson Again," *New York Times*, October 13, 1932, 22.

38. Norbert Lusk, "The Screen in Review," *Picture Play*, January 1933, 46.

39. Mordaunt Hall, "Miss Thompson's Shadow," *New York Times*, February 12, 1928, 7.

40. Abel Green, "Rain," *Variety*, October 18, 1932, 14.

41. Abel Green, "Rain," *Variety*, October 18, 1932, 14.

42. BBC memo from Lance Sieveking, March 19, 1948, BBC Written Archives Center, Caversham Park, Reading, UK.

43. Malcolm Winton, "The Part I'd Have Gone to Timbuctoo to Do," BBC *Radio Times*, May 2, 1970, 8.

44. Val Adams, "Marilyn Monroe May Star on TV," *New York Times*, January 6, 1961, 53.

45. Lois Banner, ed., *MM–Personal: From the Private Archive of Marilyn Monroe* (New York: Abrams, 2011), 186.

46. Julien's Auctions, Catalogue 142, Lot 951, 2014.

Chapter 3. Eagels and Davis

1. Maugham, "The Letter," in *Complete Short Stories*, 1:188.

2. Maugham, "The Letter," in *Complete Short Stories*, 1:216.

3. V. S. Pritchett, "Current Literature: Books in General," *New Statesman* 19, no. 486 (June 15, 1940): 750.

4. "The Letter," ad in *Motion Picture News*, March 16, 1929, 5.

5. "The Letter," *Motion Picture News*, 5.

6. Ruth Morris, "Uncommon Chatter," *Variety*, March 13, 1929, 48.

7. "The Lady Lies and Lies," *Picture Play*, July 1929, 15.

8. Quoted in Andre Soares, "*The Letter* Movie: Murderess + Adulteress Jeanne Eagels' Sole Extant Talkie," *Alt Film Guide*, January 27, 2012, http://www.altfg .com/blog/movie/the-letter-1929-review-jeanne-eagels-academy-award.

9. Maugham, "The Letter," in *Complete Short Stories*, 1:277.

10. Bernard Rosenburg and Harry Silverstein, *The Real Tinsel* (New York: Macmillan, 1970), 97.

11. "The Letter," ad, in *Picture Play*, July, 1929, 5.

12. "The Letter," ad, in *Motion Picture News*, March 16, 1929, 4.

13. Norbert Lusk, "The Screen in Review," *Picture Play*, June 1929, 68.

14. Rudy Behlmer, *Inside Warner Bros.: 1935–1951* (New York: Viking, 1985), 118–19.

15. Dawn B. Sova, *Forbidden Films* (New York: Checkmark Books, 2001), 274.

16. Behlmer, *Inside Warner Bros.*, 118.

17. Behlmer, *Inside Warner Bros.*, 119.

18. Swanson, *Swanson on Swanson*, 451–52.

19. Swanson, *Swanson on Swanson*, 452–53.

20. Graham Greene, *Graham Greene on Film* (New York: Simon and Schuster, 1972), 124.

21. Michael A. Anderegg, *William Wyler* (Boston: Twayne, 1979), 103.

22. Scott O'Brien, *Herbert Marshall: A Biography* (Albany, GA: BearManor Media), 98.

23. John Thomas McGuire, "Rending the Veils of Illusion: W. Somerset Maugham's 'The Letter' and Its Two Definitive Film Versions," *Framework: The Journal of Cinema and Media* 53, no. 1 (Spring, 2012): 9.

24. Mae Tinée, "Stevenson's Acting Superb in 'The Letter,'" *Chicago Tribune*, December 8, 1940, 4.

25. Maugham, *Complete Short Stories*, 1:204.

26. Ed Sikov, *Dark Victory: The Life of Bette Davis* (New York: Henry Holt, 2007), 165.

27. Pauline Kael, *5001 Nights at the Movies: A Guide from A to Z* (New York: Holt, Rinehart and Winston, 1982), 324.

28. Whitney Stine, *Mother Goddam* (New York: Hawthorn Books, 1974), 140.

29. Davis, *The Lonely Life*, 179.

30. As quoted by Stine, *Mother Goddam*, 134.

31. John Kinlock, "Review," *California Eagle*, December 26, 1940, 2.

32. Herbert Cohn, "The Sound Track," *Brooklyn Daily Eagle*, December 8, 1940, 48.

33. Stine, *Mother Goddam*, 135.

34. Edwin Schallert, "Maugham Lauds Bette," *Los Angeles Times*, November 16, 1940, 25.

35. Herbert Cohn, "The Sound Track," *Brooklyn Daily Eagle*, December, 1940, 48.

36. Mae Tinée, "'The Unfaithful' Is Mostly Just Another Movie," *Chicago Tribune*, August 7, 1947, 28.

37. Roderick Mann, "Remick Shifts Scenes in a Tale of Two Cities," *Los Angeles Times*, April 13, 1982, 4.

Chapter 4. Rebellious Wives, Secret Agents, and Beach Bums

1. Maugham, *The Collected Plays*, 2:188.

2. Maugham, *The Collected Plays*, 2:160.

3. Maugham, *The Collected Plays*, 2:181.

4. Maugham, *The Collected Plays*, 2:188.

5. Whitney Williams, "Charming Sinners," *Los Angeles Times*, July 28, 1929, 147.

6. Martin Dickstein, "Slow Motion," *Brooklyn Daily Eagle*, July 14, 1929, 53.

7. Maugham, *The Collected Plays*, 3:317, 318.

8. W. Somerset Maugham, *The Summing Up* (New York: Doubleday, Doran, 1938), 158.

9. Philip K. Scheuer, "Screen Play Starts at Warners," *Los Angeles Times*, February 3, 1930, 23.

10. "The Shadow Stage," *Photoplay*, February 1930, 88.

11. Mordaunt Hall, "The Screen," *New York Times*, November 23, 1929, 18.

12. Mae Tinée, "Saxaphone Toot Adds Nothing to 'Sacred Flame,'" *Chicago Tribune*, February 1, 1930, 13.

13. "Famous Actress Replies to Bishop," *Evening Standard*, June 4, 1929, 11.

14. Alexander Woollcott, "Our Betters," *New York Times*, March 25, 1917, 5.

15. Maugham, *Collected Plays*, 2:78.

16. "John D. Williams Presents a Play," *Brooklyn Daily Eagle*, March 13, 1917, 8.

17. *Picture Play Magazine*, March 1933, 5.

18. Levy, *George Cukor*, 69.

19. Patrick McGilligan, *George Cukor, A Double Life: A Biography of the Gentleman Director* (New York: St. Martin's, 1991), 94.

20. Jeff Wise and Robert Smith, *George Cukor: Interviews* (Jackson: University Press of Mississippi, 2001), 86.

21. W. Somerset Maugham, *The Narrow Corner* (New York: Doubleday, Doran, 1932), 314.

22. Maugham, *The Narrow Corner*, 160.

23. Robin Maugham to Kevin Byrne, in an interview commissioned by Robert Calder for the Canadian Broadcasting Corporation "Ideas" program.

24. Maugham, *The Narrow Corner*, 303–4.

25. A.D.S., "The Screen," *New York Times*, July 14, 1933, 15.

26. Darwin Porter, *Humphrey Bogart: The Making of a Legend* (New York: Blood Moon Productions, 2010), 270.

27. Eric Ambler, *To Catch a Spy* (London: The Bodley Head, 1964), 19.

28. W. Somerset Maugham, *Ashenden, or: The British Agent* (New York: Doubleday, 1927), 98.

29. Raymond Mander and Joe Mitchenson, *Theatrical Companion to Maugham* (London: Rockcliff, 1955), 287.

30. Sheridan Morley, *John G.: The Authorized Biography of John Gielgud* (London: Hodder and Stoughton, 2001), 128.

31. Stephen D. Youngkin, *The Films of Peter Lorre* (Secaucus, NJ: Citadel Press, 1982), 95.

32. Youngkin, *The Films of Peter Lorre*, 95.

33. "The Mystery of the Secret Agent," *The Observer*, May 10, 1936, 16.

34. "The Mystery of the Secret Agent," *The Observer*, May 10, 1936, 16.

35. Greene, *Graham Greene on Film*, 75.

36. Edwin Schallert, "Pre-'Amber' Feature Now Looms for Peggy," *Los Angeles Times*, May 2, 1946, 13.

37. W. Somerset Maugham, *The Tenth Man* (London: Heinemann, 1913), 197.

38. Ian Coster, "Big Thrills in the London We All Know," *Evening Standard*, December 5, 1936, 8.

39. Greene, *Graham Greene on Film*, 123.

40. C. A. Lejeune, "Films of the Week," *The Observer*, December 6, 1936, 14.

41. Maugham, "The Vessel of Wrath," in *Complete Short Stories*, 2:816, 824.

42. Maugham, "The Vessel of Wrath," in *Complete Short Stories*, 2:817.

43. Maugham, "The Vessel of Wrath," in *Complete Short Stories*, 2:847.

44. Simon Callow, *Charles Laughton: A Difficult Actor* (London: Methuen, 1987), 125.

45. Callow, *Charles Laughton*, 123.

46. Charles Higham, *Charles Laughton: An Intimate Biography* (New York: Doubleday, 1976), 87.

47. Anthony Slide, *"Banned in the USA": British Films in the United States, 1933–1960* (London: I.B. Tauris, 1998), 143, 144.

48. Callow, *Charles Laughton*, 124–25.

49. A.W., "The Screen in Review," *New York Times*, January 17, 1955, 27.

50. Kael, *5001 Nights at the Movies*, 44.

51. Donald Sinden, *A Touch of the Memoirs* (London: Hodder & Stoughton, 1982), 203.

52. A. H. Weiler, "On the Local Screen Scene," *New York Times*, December 12, 1954, X7.

53. Bosley Crowther, "It's an Old Story," *New York Times*, January 23, 1955, X1.

Chapter 5. Bette Davis's Corrosive Mildred

1. Theodore Dreiser, "As a Realist Sees It," *New Republic*, December 25, 1915, 202–4.

2. Vidal, "Maugham's Half and Half," 41.

3. W. Somerset Maugham, *Of Human Bondage* (London: Penguin, 1992), 479–80.

4. Maugham, *Of Human Bondage*, 524–25.

5. Sova, *Forbidden Films*, 231.

6. Kanin, *Remembering Mr. Maugham*, 138.

7. Leonard J. Leff and Jerold L. Simmons, *The Dame in the Kimono: Hollywood Censorship and the Production Code from the 1920s to the 1960s* (New York: Grove Weidenfeld, 1980), 35.

8. Gregory D. Black, *Hollywood Censored: Morality Codes, Catholics, and the Movies* (Cambridge: Cambridge University Press, 1994), 179.

9. Black, *Hollywood Censored*, 185.

10. Sova, *Forbidden Films*, 232.

11. Davis, *The Lonely Life*, 127.

12. James Spada, *More Than a Woman: An Intimate Biography of Bette Davis* (New York: Bantam Books, 1994), 135–36.

13. Davis, *The Lonely Life*, 123.

14. Haskell, *From Reverence to Rape*, 216–17.

15. Haskell, *From Reverence to Rape*, 138–39.

16. Mae Tinée, "Shirley Temple Chief Interest in This Movie," *Chicago Tribune*, September 5, 1934, 15.

17. *Film Weekly*, March 29, 1935, as quoted by Hastings, *The Secret Lives of Somerset Maugham*, 460.

18. Hedda Hopper, "Master Film Maker Reveals His Secrets," *Los Angeles Times*, November 12, 1944, 28.

19. Herbert Cohn, "Screen," *Brooklyn Eagle*, July 6, 1946, 12.

20. Bosley Crowther, "The Screen," *New York Times*, July 6, 1946, 11.

21. Paul Henreid, *Ladies Man: An Autobiography* (New York: St. Martin's, 1984), 174.

22. Philip K. Scheuer, "Hollywood Tries Repeat with 'Of Human Bondage,'" *Los Angeles Times*, July 20, 1946, 13.

23. Quoted in Peter Harry Brown, *Kim Novak: Reluctant Goddess* (New York: St. Martin's, 1986), 208.

24. Banner, *MM–Personal*, 155.

25. Anne Sinai, *Reach For the Top: The Turbulent Life of Laurence Harvey* (Oxford: Scarecrow Press, 2003), 283.

26. Brown, *Kim Novak*, 213.

27. Brown, *Kim Novak*, 217.

28. Brown, *Kim Novak*, 208.

29. Paul Gardner, "The Screen's Perfect Cad," *New York Times*, November 27, 1973, 47.

30. A. H. Weiler, "'Of Human Bondage' Returns Again," *New York Times*, September 24, 1964, 46.

Chapter 6. Garbo Speaks Maugham

1. W. Somerset Maugham, *The Painted Veil* (London: Penguin, 1952), 166–67.

2. Maugham, *The Painted Veil*, 237–38.

3. Antoni Gronowicz, *Garbo* (New York: Simon and Schuster, 1990), 337.

4. "The Painted Veil," *Motion Picture Daily*, October 9, 1934, 7.

5. André Bazin, "In Defense of Mixed Cinema," in *What Is Cinema*, vol. 1, ed. and trans. Hugh Gray (Berkeley: University of California Press, 1967, 74.

6. Helen Brown Norden, "The Screen," *Vanity Fair*, January 1935, 46.

7. C. A. Lejeune, "Some New Films of the Week," *Observer*, December 30, 1934, 10.

8. "Greta Garbo in 'The Painted Veil,'" *Film Daily*, November 24, 1934, 3.

9. Mae Tinée, "Praises Garbo for Acting in 'Painted Veil.'" *Chicago Tribune*, December 19, 1934, 15.

10. Richard Schickel, "The Legend as Actress," in *Garbo*, by Antoni Gronowicz (New York: Simon and Schuster, 1990), 451.

11. Hastings, *The Secret Lives of Somerset Maugham*, 266.

12. "The Seventh Sin," *Sydney Morning Herald*, September 15, 1957, 66.

13. "The Seventh Sin," *Sydney Morning Herald*, September 15, 1957, 66.

14. Colin Bennett, "The Seventh Sin," in *The Age* (Melbourne), October 14, 1957, 2.

15. Charles McGrath, "Another Encore for the Most Adaptable of Authors," *New York Times*, December 10, 2006, II, 6.

16. Maugham, *The Painted Veil*, 128.

17. Lewis Beale, "A Good Average," *Newsday*, December 20, 2006, B10.

18. Charles McGrath, "Another Encore for the Most Adaptable of Authors," *New York Times*, December 10, 2006, II, 6.

19. Liam Lacey, "Not Enough Love in This Time of Cholera," *The Globe and Mail*, December 29, 2006, R1.

Chapter 7. Fascism, Bigamy, and the Creative Spirit

1. Maugham, *Collected Plays*, 2:ix.

2. Alexander Woollcott, "The Play," *New York Times*, October 9, 1919, 16.

3. Maugham, *Collected Plays*, 2:288.

4. Maugham, *Collected Plays*, 2:324.

5. American Film Institute Catalog of Feature Films, https://catalog.afi.com/Catalog/moviedetails/6688.

6. "Dance Numbers Bolster 'Three for the Show' Film," *Los Angeles Times*, March 31, 1955, Section 3, 11.

7. Don Widener, *Lemmon: A Biography* (New York: Macmillan, 1975), 120.

8. David Payne-Carter, *Gower Champion: Dance and American Musical Theatre* (Westport, CT: Greenwood Press, 1999), 59.

9. Van Wyck Brooks, "The Hero as Artist," in *Sketches in Criticism* (New York: Dutton, 1932), 94.

10. Maugham, *The Summing Up*, 51.

11. Maugham, *Of Human Bondage*, 244.

12. W. Somerset Maugham, *The Razor's Edge* (New York: Doubleday, Doran, 1944), 1–2.

13. Maugham, *Complete Short Stories*, 2:241.

14. "The 'Moon' Comes Over the Mountain," *New York Times*, October 25, 1942, X4.

15. "John Barrymore in 'The Moon and Sixpence,'" *Variety*, May 24, 1932, 41.

16. Rosenberg and Silverstein, *The Real Tinsel*, 119.

17. Rosenberg and Silverstein, *The Real Tinsel*, 119.

18. Rosenberg and Silverstein, *The Real Tinsel*, 118.

19. Raymond Rohauer, *A Tribute to Albert Lewin* (New York: Gallery of Modern Art, 1966), 5.

20. W. Somerset Maugham, *The Moon and Sixpence* (New York: Doubleday, Doran, 1935), 280.

21. "UA's Cape Cod Preem for 'Moon-Sixpence,'" *Variety*, September 2, 1942, 20.

22. "Long Awaited 'Moon-Sixpence' Set for Tonight," *Pittsburg Press*, October 30, 1959, 47.

23. John Crosby, "Olivier's Performance Makes Top Fare of Moon and Sixpence," *Sacramento Bee*, March 30, 1959, 11.

24. W. Somerset Maugham, *The Hour Before the Dawn* (New York: Doubleday, Doran, 1942), 302.

25. Hastings, *The Secret Lives of Somerset Maugham*, 462–63.

26. Christopher Isherwood, *Diaries* (New York: Vintage, 1997), 263.

27. Bosley Crowther, "The Screen," *New York Times*, May 11, 1944, 25.

28. Edwin Schallert, "'Navy Way' Vies Strongly with 'Hour before Dawn,'" *Los Angeles Times*, June 2, 1944, 10.

29. W. Somerset Maugham, *Christmas Holiday* (New York: Doubleday, Doran, 1939), 314.

30. Glenway Wescott, *Images of Truth* (New York: Harper and Row, 1963), 71–72.

31. "Christmas Holiday: Notes," TCM, http://www.tcm.com/tcmdb/title/70901/christmas-holiday#notes.

32. Arthur Pollock, "Theater," *Brooklyn Daily Eagle*, June 30, 1944, 8.

33. "Screen," *Brooklyn Daily Eagle*, June 29, 1944, 4.

Chapter 8. The Greatest Generation's Quest

1. Kanin, *Remembering Mr. Maugham*, 113.

2. Alec Waugh, *My Brother Evelyn and Other Profiles* (London: Cassell, 1967), 288.

3. Maugham, *The Razor's Edge*, 343.

4. Rudy Behlmer, *Memo from Darryl F. Zanuck: The Golden Years at Twentieth Century–Fox* (New York: Grove Press, 1993), 93.

5. Behlmer, *Memo from Darryl F. Zanuck*, 93.

6. Behlmer, *Memo from Darryl F. Zanuck*, xv.

7. Gavin Lambert, *On Cukor* (New York: Putnam's, 1972), 229.

8. Stott, *A Bibliography of the Works of W. Somerset Maugham*, 294.

9. Lambert, *On Cukor*, 229.

10. George F. Custen, *Twentieth Century's Fox: Darryl F. Zanuck and the Culture of Hollywood* (New York: Basic Books, 1997), 285.

11. Hedda Hopper, "Looking at Hollywood," *Chicago Tribune*, November 2, 1946, 14.

12. Tyrone Power, "This Is What I Believe," *Screenland*, August 1946, 29, 92.

13. Hedda Hopper, "Looking at Hollywood," *Los Angeles Times*, November 27, 1944, 9.

14. Bosley Crowther, "The Screen," *New York Times*, March 11, 1948, 35.

15. "Marshall Portrays Maugham Again," *Brooklyn Daily Eagle*, November 10, 1946, 32.

16. Bosley Crowther, "Producer's Dispute," *New York Times*, December 1, 1946, X1.

17. Roger Manvell, "Critical Survey," in *The Penguin Film Review 1946–1949*, vol. 1 (London: Scolar Press, 1977), 14.

18. Philip K. Scheuer, "Power Wrestles with Soul in Diffuse 'Razor's Edge,'" *Los Angeles Times*, December 26, 1946, 11.

19. Dale Pollock, "Murray Walks a Razor's Edge in Hollywood," *Los Angeles Times*, October 21, 1984, 3.

20. Dale Pollock, "Murray Walks a Razor's Edge in Hollywood," *Los Angeles Times*, October 21, 1984, 3.

21. Gavin Edwards, *The Tao of Bill Murray* (New York: Random House, 2016), 230.

22. Janet Maslin, "Movies: Bill Murray in 'Razor,'" *New York Times*, October 19, 1984, C14.

23. Stephen Hunter, "'Razor's Edge' Is Blunted by Star's Strength," *Baltimore Sun*, October 22, 1984, 13.

24. Gene Siskel, "Bill Murray Up to the Job in Serious Film," *Chicago Tribune*, October 19, 1984, 106.

Chapter 9. Life in Short, Sharp Strokes

1. Bosley Crowther, "Little by Little," *New York Times*, October 4, 1942, X3.

2. David Scott Diffrient, *Omnibus Films: Theorizing Transauthorial Cinema* (Edinburgh: Edinburgh University Press, 2014), 133.

3. Raymond Durgnat, *A Mirror for England: British Movies from Austerity to Affluence* (New York: Praeger, 1971), 202.

4. Diffrient, *Omnibus Films*, 136.

5. Kate Cameron, "'Trio' Film Pleases Author," *Daily News*, October 15, 1950, 55.

6. Kanin, *Remembering Mr. Maugham*, 55.

7. Ludwig Lewisohn, *Among the Nations: Three Tales and a Play about Jews* (New York: Farrar, Straus, 1948), xii–xiv.

8. "'The Alien Corn' on Television," *Times* (London), March 18, 1960, 4.

9. Diffrient, *Omnibus Films*, 141.

10. W. Somerset Maugham, *Quartet* (London: Heinemann, 1948), 212.

11. Diffrient, *Omnibus Films*, 97.

12. W. Somerset Maugham, *Trio* (London: Heinemann, 1950), 10.

13. Maugham, *Trio*, 39.

14. In Maugham's original story, the ship and the entire crew are German, sailing from Hamburg to Cartagena. The film's producers changed the nationality to English and the destination to Trinidad, an alteration likely reflecting the post–World War II attitude to Germany or perhaps simply making it easier to use an all-British cast.

15. W. Somerset Maugham, *Encore* (London: Heinemann, 1952), 51.

16. Maugham, *Encore*, 124.

17. Stephen Watts, "Screen Scene on the Thames," *New York Times*, December 23, 1951, X5.

18. Maugham, *Encore*, 165.

19. Joseph McBride, *Orson Wells: Actor and Director* (New York: Harvest/HBJ Books, 1977), 69.

20. L. R. Swainson, "Orson Welles Film Rejected," *Sydney Sun*, August 19, 1954, 55.

21. Diffrient, *Omnibus Films*, 131–32.

Chapter 10. Twenty-First-Century Perspectives

1. "A Cool Hand," *Nation* 152 (May 3, 1941): 534.

2. Ted Morgan, *Maugham: A Biography* (New York: Simon and Schuster, 1980), 457.

3. Jonathan Fryer, *Isherwood: A Biography* (New York: Doubleday, 1978), 215.

4. Nick Johnstone, *Sean Penn: A Biography* (London: Omnibus, 2000), 174.

5. Johnstone, *Sean Penn*, 174.

6. A. O. Scott, "By Jove, This Tuscan Sun, It's a Bit Dicey, Eh What?," *New York Times*, May 5, 2000, E16.

7. Johnstone, *Sean Penn*, 174.

8. Richard Kelly, *Sean Penn: His Life and Times* (Edinburgh: Canongate, 2004), 350.

9. Joe Baltake, "'Up at the Villa' Comfortable but Passionless," *Sacramento Bee*, May 19, 2000, 19.

10. Joe Baltake, "'Up at the Villa' Comfortable but Passionless," *Sacramento Bee*, May 19, 2000, 19.

11. Ann Hornaday, "'Villa' Pretty but That's All," *Baltimore Sun*, May 19, 2000, 3e.

12. W. Somerset Maugham, *Theatre* (New York: Doubleday, Doran, 1937), 1.

13. Maugham, *Theatre*, 141.

14. Maugham, *Theatre*, 132.

15. Maugham, *Theatre*, 260–61.

16. Maugham, *Theatre*, 292.

17. A. O. Scott, "An Actress in Love with Love and with Herself, of Course," *New York Times*, October 15, 2004, E14.

18. Bob Strauss, "Being Annette Bening," *Sacramento Bee*, November 14, 2004, 31.

19. Bob Strauss, "Being Annette Bening," *Sacramento Bee*, November 14, 2004, 31.

Conclusion

1. James M. Welsh and Peter Lev, eds., *The Literature/Film Reader: Issues of Adaptation* (Toronto: Scarecrow Press, 2007), xxv.

2. Philip Holden, *Orienting Masculinity, Orienting Nation: W. Somerset Maugham's Exotic Fiction* (London: Greenwood, 1996).

3. Douglas Heil, "The Construction of Racism through Narrative and Cinematography in 'The Letter,'" *Literature/Film Quarterly* 24, no. 1 (1996): 20.

4. Heil, "The Construction of Racism," 21.

5. Heil, "The Construction of Racism," 24.

6. Marjorie Rosen, *Popcorn Venus* (New York: Avon Books, 1973), 178.

7. Curtis, *The Pattern of Maugham*, 116.

8. William Shakespeare, *Twelfth Night*, act 2, scene 3.

Bibliography

Ambler, Eric. *To Catch a Spy*. London: The Bodley Head, 1964.

Anderegg, Michael A. *William Wyler*. Boston: Twayne, 1979.

Banner, Lois, ed. *MM—Personal: From the Private Archive of Marilyn Monroe*. New York: Abrams, 2011.

Bazin, André. "In Defense of Mixed Cinema." In *What Is Cinema*, vol. 1, edited and translated by Hugh Gray, 53–75. Berkeley: University of California Press, 1967.

Behlmer, Rudy, ed. *Inside Warner Bros.: 1935–1951*. New York: Viking, 1985.

Behlmer, Rudy, ed. *Memo from Darryl F. Zanuck: The Golden Years at Twentieth Century–Fox*. New York: Grove Press, 1993.

Black, Gregory D. *Hollywood Censored: Morality Codes, Catholics, and the Movies*. Cambridge: Cambridge University Press, 1994.

Bluestone, George. *Novels into Films*. Berkeley: University of California Press, 1966.

Brander, Laurence. *Somerset Maugham: A Guide*. London: Oliver & Boyd, 1965.

Brooks, Van Wyck. *Sketches in Criticism*. New York: Dutton, 1932.

Brown, Peter Harry. *Kim Novak: Reluctant Goddess*. New York: St. Martin's, 1986.

Callow, Simon. *Charles Laughton: A Difficult Actor*. London: Methuen, 1987.

Curtis, Anthony. *The Pattern of Maugham: A Critical Portrait*. London: Hamish Hamilton, 1974.

Custen, George F. *Twentieth Century's Fox: Darryl F. Zanuck and the Culture of Hollywood*. New York: Basic Books, 1997.

Davis, Bette. *The Lonely Life*. New York: Lancer, 1963.

Diffrient, David Scott. *Omnibus Films: Theorizing Transauthorial Cinema*. Edinburgh: Edinburgh University Press, 2014.

Durgnat, Raymond. *A Mirror for England: British Movies from Austerity to Affluence*. New York: Praeger, 1971

Edwards, Gavin. *The Tao of Bill Murray.* New York: Random House, 2016.

Fryer, Jonathan. *Isherwood: A Biography.* New York: Doubleday, 1978.

Greene, Graham. *Journey without Maps.* London: Heinemann, 1950.

Greene, Graham. *Graham Greene on Film.* New York: Simon and Schuster, 1972.

Gronowicz, Antoni. *Garbo.* New York: Simon and Schuster, 1990.

Haskell, Molly. *From Reverence to Rape: The Treatment of Women in the Movies.* Harmondsworth, UK: Penguin, 1974.

Hastings, Selina. *The Secret Lives of Somerset Maugham.* London: John Murray, 2009.

Henreid, Paul. *Ladies Man: An Autobiography.* New York: St. Martin's, 1984.

Higham, Charles. *Charles Laughton: An Intimate Biography.* New York: Doubleday, 1976.

Holden, Philip. *Orienting Masculinity, Orienting Nation: W. Somerset Maugham's Exotic Fiction.* London: Greenwood, 1996.

Isherwood, Christopher. *Diaries.* New York: Vintage, 1997.

Johnstone, Nick. *Sean Penn: A Biography.* London: Omnibus, 2000.

Kael, Pauline. *5001 Nights at the Movies: A Guide from A to Z.* New York: Holt, Rinehart and Winston, 1982.

Kanin. Garson. *Remembering Mr. Maugham.* New York: Atheneum, 1966.

Kelly, Richard. *Sean Penn: His Life and Times.* Edinburgh: Canongate, 2004.

Kennedy, Margaret. *The Mechanized Muse.* London: Allen and Unwin, 1942.

Lambert, Gavin. *On Cukor.* New York: Putnam's, 1972.

Leff, Leonard J., and Jerold L. Simmons. *The Dame in the Kimono: Hollywood Censorship and the Production Code from the 1920s to the 1960s.* New York: Grove Weidenfeld, 1980.

Levy, Emanuel. *George Cukor.* New York: Morrow, 1994.

Lewisohn, Ludwig. *Among the Nations: Three Tales and a Play about Jews.* New York: Farrar, Straus, 1948.

Madsen, Axel. *Gloria and Joe.* New York: Berkley Books, 1989.

Mander, Raymond, and Joe Mitchener. *Theatrical Companion to Maugham.* London: Rockcliff, 1955.

Manvell, Roger. "Critical Survey." In *The Penguin Film Review 1946–1949,* vol. 1, 12–16. London: Scolar Press, 1977.

Marill, Alvin H. *Samuel Goldwyn Presents.* South Brunswick, NJ: A. S. Barnes, 1976.

Maugham, W. Somerset. *Ashenden, or, The British Agent.* New York: Doubleday, 1927.

Maugham, W. Somerset. *Christmas Holiday.* New York: Doubleday, Doran, 1939.

Maugham, W. Somerset. *The Collected Plays of W. Somerset Maugham.* 3 vols. London: Heinemann, 1961.

Maugham, W. Somerset. *The Complete Short Stories.* 2 vols. New York: Doubleday, 1952.

Maugham, W. Somerset. *Encore.* London: Heinemann, 1952.

Maugham, W. Somerset. *The Hour Before the Dawn.* New York: Doubleday, Doran, 1942.

Maugham, W. Somerset. *Liza of Lambeth.* London: Heinemann, 1934.

Maugham, W. Somerset. *The Magician.* London: Penguin, 1967.

Maugham, W. Somerset. *The Moon and Sixpence.* New York: Doubleday, Doran, 1935.

Maugham, W. Somerset. *The Narrow Corner.* New York: Doubleday, Doran, 1932.

Maugham, W. Somerset. *Of Human Bondage.* London: Penguin, 1992.

Maugham, W. Somerset. *The Painted Veil.* London: Penguin, 1952.

Maugham, W. Somerset. *Quartet.* London: Heinemann, 1948.

Maugham, W. Somerset. *The Razor's Edge.* New York: Doubleday, Doran, 1944.

Maugham, W. Somerset. *Selected Plays.* London: Mandarin, 1991.

Maugham, W. Somerset. *The Summing Up.* New York: Doubleday, Doran, 1938.

Maugham, W. Somerset. *The Tenth Man.* London: Heinemann, 1913.

Maugham, W. Somerset. *Theatre.* New York: Doubleday, Doran, 1937.

Maugham, W. Somerset. *Trio.* London: Heinemann, 1950.

Maugham, W. Somerset. *A Writer's Notebook.* London: Heinemann, 1949.

Mayfield, Sara. *The Constant Circle.* New York: Putnam's, 1972.

McFarlane, Brian C. "It Wasn't Like That in the Book." In *The Literature/Film Reader: Issues of Adaptation,* edited by James M. Welsh and Peter Lev, 3–14. Toronto: Scarecrow Press, 2007.

McFarlane, Brian. *Novel to Film: An Introduction to the Theory of Film Adaptation.* Oxford: Clarendon Press, 1996.

McGilligan, Patrick. *George Cukor, A Double Life: A Biography of the Gentleman Director.* New York: St. Martin's, 1991.

Morgan, Ted. *Maugham: A Biography.* New York: Simon and Schuster, 1980.

Morley, Sheridan. *John G.: The Authorized Biography of John Gielgud.* London: Hodder and Stoughton, 2001.

Moss, Marilyn Ann. *Raoul Walsh: The True Adventures of Hollywood's Legendary Director.* Lexington: University Press of Kentucky, 2011.

Naremore, James, ed. *Film Adaptation.* New Brunswick, NJ: Rutgers University Press, 2000.

O'Brien, Scott. *Herbert Marshall: A Biography.* Albany, GA: BearManor Media, 2018.

O'Leary, Liam. *Rex Ingram: Master of the Silent Film.* New York: Harper & Row, 1980.

Payne-Carter, David. *Gower Champion: Dance and American Theatre.* Westport, CT: Greenwood Press, 1999.

Porter, Darwin. *Humphrey Bogart: The Making of a Legend.* New York: Blood Moon Productions, 2010.

Powell, Michael. *A Life in Movies: An Autobiography.* New York: Alfred A. Knopf, 1987.

Raphael, Frederic. Preface to *Two for the Road.* London: Jonathan Cape, 1967.

Rohauer, Raymond. *A Tribute to Albert Lewin.* New York: Gallery of Modern Art, 1966.

Rosen, Marjorie. *Popcorn Venus.* New York: Avon Books, 1973.

Rosenburg, Bernard, and Harry Silverstein. *The Real Tinsel.* New York: Macmillan, 1970.

Rotha, Paul. *The Film Till Now: A Survey of the Cinema.* London, Cape, 1930.

Rotha, Paul. *The Film Till Now: A Survey of World Cinema.* London: Spring Books, 1967.

Scully, Frank. *Rogues Gallery.* Hollywood: Murray & Gee, 1943.

Shearer, Stephen Michael. *Gloria Swanson: The Ultimate Star.* New York: St. Martin's, 2013.

Sikov, Ed. *Dark Victory: The Life of Bette Davis.* New York: Henry Holt, 2007.

Silver, Alain, and James Ursini. *Film Noir Reader.* New York: Limelight Editions, 1996.

Sinai, Anne. *Reach for the Top: The Turbulent Life of Laurence Harvey.* Oxford: Scarecrow Press, 2003.

Sinden, Donald. *A Touch of the Memoirs.* London: Hodder & Stoughton, 1982.

Slide, Anthony. *"Banned in the USA": British Films in the United States, 1933–1960.* London: I.B. Tauris, 1998.

Soares, Andre. *Beyond Paradise: The Life of Ramon Novarro.* New York: Macmillan, 2002.

Sova, Dawn B. *Forbidden Films.* New York: Checkmark Books, 2001.

Spada, James. *More than a Woman: An Intimate Biography of Bette Davis.* New York: Bantam Books, 1994.

Spoto, Donald. *Possessed: The Life of Joan Crawford.* New York: William Morrow, 2010.

Stam, Robert. "The Dialogics of Adaptation." In *Film Adaptation*, edited by James Naremore, 54–76. New Brunswick, NJ: Rutgers University Press, 2000.

Stine, Whitney. *Mother Goddam.* New York: Hawthorn Books, 1974.

Stokes, Sewell. *Pilloried!* New York: Appleton, 1929.

Stott, Raymond Toole. *A Bibliography of the Works of W. Somerset Maugham.* London: Kaye and Ward, 1973.

Swanson, Gloria. *Swanson on Swanson: An Autobiography.* New York: Pocket Books, 1980.

Thomas, Bob. *Joan Crawford: A Biography.* New York: Bantam, 1979.

Walsh, Raoul. *Each Man in His Time: The Life Story of a Director.* New York: Farrar, Straus and Giroux, 1974.

Waugh, Alec. *My Brother Evelyn and Other Profiles.* London: Cassell, 1967.

Welsh, James M., and Peter Lev, eds. *The Literature/Film Reader: Issues of Adaptation.* Toronto: Scarecrow Press, 2007.

Wescott, Glenway. *Images of Truth.* New York: Harper and Row, 1963.

Widener, Don. *Lemmon: A Biography.* New York: Macmillan, 1975.

Wise, Jeff, and Robert Smith. *George Cukor: Interviews.* Jackson: University Press of Mississippi, 2001.

Youngkin, Stephen. *The Films of Peter Lorre.* Secaucus, NJ: Citadel, 1982.

Index

Ackland, Joss, 103
Adler, Stella, 223
The African Queen (Forester), 110
Aldington, Richard, 179
"The Alien Corn" (Maugham), 189,
  203–5, 209
Allen, E. H., 43
All Quiet on the Western Front
  (Milestone), 52
All Quiet on the Western Front
  (Remarque), 100
Ambler, Eric, 6, 99, 210–12
Among the Nations (Lewisohn), 204
Anderegg, Michael, 71
Anderson, Doris, 85
Anderson, Judith, 175, 232
Anderson, Maxwell, 52–53
Andrews, Robert Hardy, 97
Annakin, Ken, 206–7
Another Dawn (Doyle), 27
"The Ant and the Grasshopper"
  (Clarke), 210
Arbuckle, Roscoe, 42
Arthur, Jean, 122, 162
Ashenden or: The British Agent
  (Maugham), 98–100, 103. See also
  Assigned to Syria (Buckner); *Secret
  Agent* (Hitchcock); *The Secret Agent*
  (Conrad)

Assigned to Syria (Buckner), 103.
  See also *Ashenden or: The British
  Agent* (Maugham)
Atkins, Eileen, 82
Atlas, Leopold, 28
Auden, W. H., 181
Aumont, Jean Pierre, 153
Aurelius, Marcus, 94
Ayres, Lew, 81

Baddeley, Angela, 202
Badel, Alan, 213
Baker, Carroll, 56
Baltake, Joe, 220
Bancroft, Anne, 217
Bankhead, Tallulah, 27, 42, 52, 56
Bannen, Ian, 103
Barrymore, Ethel, 23–24, 220
Barrymore, John, 169–70
Barrymore, Lionel, 47–48, 117
Bates, Florence, 232
Baxter, Anne, 194–95, 199
Bazin, André, 15, 149
The Beachcomber (Box), 110–11. See
  also *Vessel of Wrath* (Laughton)
the Beat Generation, 193
Beaton, Welford, 34, 51
Being Julia (Harwood), 129, 224–28,
  234. See also *Theatre* (Maugham)

Bell, Monta, 62
Bellamy, Ralph, 95–96, 119
Belushi, John, 197–98
Bening, Annette, 129, 224–28
Bennett, Alan, 103
Bennett, Arnold, 4, 7
Bennett, Constance, 92, 194
Bennett, Joan, 149
Benson, E. F., 35
Berman, Pandro, 135
Bey, Turhan, 185
bildungsroman, 4, 131–32
Binyon, Claude, 162–63
Blanke, Henry, 142–43
Block, Ralph, 88
Bloom, Jon, 207
Bluestone, George, 5, 15
Boardman, Eleanor, 32
Bogarde, Dirk, 203
Bogart, Humphrey, 97–98, 110, 219
Boleslawksi, Richard, 149–50, 152
Bolton, Guy, 223
Bondi, Beulah, 52
Borzage, Frank, 32
Box, Sydney, 201–2, 206–8
Boyer, Charles, 224
Brando, Marlon, 143
The Breadwinner (Maugham), 86
Breen, Joseph, 68–70, 80, 89, 135. *See also* Production Code Administration (PCA)
Brent, George, 70–71, 88–89, 150
The Bridges of Madison County, 26
Brief Encounter, 26
British Board of Film Censors, 102
British Broadcasting Corporation (BBC), 200
Brook, Clive, 85
Brooks, Van Wyck, 165
Brown, Rowland, 169
Browning, Kirk, 81
Bryant, Michael, 56
Buchan, John, 99–100

Buckner, Robert, 103
Burke, Billie, 19–22, 113
Burton, David, 34
Butler, Frank, 34
Byrum, John, 197

The Cabinet of Dr. Caligari (Wiene), 36–37
Caesar's Wife (Maugham), 26–28, 231. See also *Infatuation*
Caine, Hall, 34
Cakes and Ale (Maugham), 3, 13–14, 235
Campion, Jane, 159
The Canadian (Stringer), 22, 117. See also *The Land of Promise* (Maugham)
Carey, Philip, 143
Cargill, Patrick, 82
Carroll, Leo G., 88
Carroll, Madeleine, 101
Catalina (Maugham), 229
Catholic Legion of Decency, 11, 68, 135, 164, 173–75
Catlett, Walter, 54
censorship, 11–13, 21–23, 31–33, 51–52, 82, 88, 102, 203, 211–12, 217. *See also* Hollywood Production Code
Champion, Gower, 164
Champion, Marge, 164
Chanson de Roland, 168
Chaplin, Charlie, 40
Charming Sinners (Anderson), 84–85. See also *The Constant Wife* (Maugham)
Chatterton, Ruth, 84–85
Chayefsky, Paddy, 59
Childers, Erskine, 98
Christmas Holiday (Mankiewicz), 184–86
Christmas Holiday (Maugham), 181–84, 216
The Circle (Maugham), 31–33, 115, 235

Clarke, Kenneth B., 32
Clarke, T. E. B., 210
Clay, Thornton, 189
Clive, Colin, 88
Cobb, Lee J., 175, 200
Cohn, Harry, 163
Cohn, Herb, 140
Colbert, Claudette, 71, 88
Cole, George, 202
Colleton, Sara, 154
"The Colonel's Lady" (Maugham), 206–7, 235
colonialism, 79, 231–33
Colton, John, 41, 44
communism, 182
Conrad, Joseph, 99
The Constant Wife (Maugham), 83–84, 235. See also *Charming Sinners* (Anderson); *The Marriage Holiday*
"The Construction of Racism through Narrative and Cinematography" (Heil), 231
Cooke, Alistair, 202
Cooper, Gladys, 62, 220
Cormack, Bartlett, 107–8
Cornell, Katharine, 62
Coward, Noel, 7, 195
Cowen, Sada, 30
Crawford, Joan, 52–56, 118, 149
Crews, Laura Hope, 85
Cromwell, John, 135–36
Cronyn, Hume, 175
Crosby, John, 176
Crossman, Henrietta, 88
Crowley, Aleister, 35–37
Crowther, Bosley, 141, 195–96, 201
Cukor, George, 14, 91–93, 191–93
Culver, Roland, 82, 210
Curran, John, 157
Curtis, Anthony, 9, 234
Curtiz, Michael, 28
Cusack, Cyril, 175

Dardé, Paul, 37
Darnell, Linda, 58, 194
David, André, 191
Davidson, Alfred, 48
Davies, Betty Ann, 209
Davies, Jeremy, 220
Davies, Marion, 42
Davin, Guy, 182
Davis, Bette, 8–10, 27, 56, 71–80, 120–23, 131–46, 185, 193, 217, 233
Davis, Tyrell, 93, 119
Defoe, Daniel, 167
Deighton, Len, 99
Desplat, Alexandre, 158
Dickenson, Morris, 34
Dickstein, Martin, 85
Dieterle, William, 27
Dietrich, Marlene, 233
Dietz, Howard, 56
Diffrient, David Scott, 202, 214
Digges, Dudley, 96
Dirty Gertie from Harlem USA (Williams), 56–57. See also "Rain" (Maugham)
The Divorcée (Maugham), 23
Dix, Beulah Marie, 25
The Doctor's Dilemma (Shaw), 167
A Doll's House (Ibsen), 84, 235
Donat, Robert, 100
Douglas, Melvyn, 122, 162
Doyle, Laird, 27
Dragon Seed, 185
Dreiser, Theodore, 131, 165
The Dresser (Harwood), 224
Drew, John, 24
Dreyer, Carl Theodore, 136
Duke, Vernon, 56
Dunne, Philip, 191
Durbin, Deanna, 185–86
Durgnat, Raymond, 202
Durrance, Jerry, 141
Dvorak, Ann, 52

Eagels, Jeanne, 41–42, 51, 54, 58, 62–68, 74–76, 118
East of Suez (Maugham), 28–31, 114, 232
Eastwood, Clint, 235
Eldridge, Florence, 58
Elliott, Denholm, 175, 198
Ellis, Edith, 169
Ellis, Patricia, 96, 119
Elvey, Maurice, 23
Encore (Clarke), 202, 210–14
The English Patient, 157
"Enoch Arden" (Tennyson), 160, 164
espionage literature, 99–100
Ethics (Spinoza), 132
euthanasia, 86–89
Evans, Shaun, 226
Everett, Francine, 57
The Explorer (Maugham), 5, 17–19

Fairbanks, Douglas, 8, 40, 95–96, 119
"The Fall of Edward Barnard" (Maugham), 187–89
feminist theory, 231–33
Ferrer, Jose, 58
fidelity criticism, 15
film adaptation, 15–16
Fitzgerald, Edith, 149
Fitzgerald, Geraldine, 28, 175
Fleming, Ian, 99
Fletcher, Louise, 207
Flynn, Errol, 27–28
Fontaine, Joan, 217
"Footprints in the Jungle" (Maugham), 203
Forbes, Bryan, 143–45
"Force of Circumstance" (Maugham), 203
Forester, C. S., 110
"The Formula," 11, 42. *See also* Hays, William; Motion Picture Production Code

For Services Rendered (Maugham), 86, 182
Fort, Garrett, 63
Fowler, Gene, 169
Fox, James, 217, 220
France, Anatole, 40
Francis, Kay, 27, 96
freedom, 3–4, 36, 132, 167, 221–22
French, Harold, 210
Frohman, Charles, 19

Galsworthy, John, 7
Gambon, Michael, 225
Garbo, Greta, 121, 141, 149–53, 156, 235
Gardner, Ava, 152
Gardner, Paul, 145
Garfield, John, 219
Gargan, William, 52
Garland, Judy, 194
Gaudio, Tony, 76, 80
Gauguin, Paul, 165–66, 173, 176
Gaynor, Janet, 51
"the gaze," 233
The Genius (Dreiser), 165
Geray, Steven, 171
German Expressionism, 76–77
Gershwin, George, 164, 195
Ghostbusters, 197
Gielgud, John, 100–102, 121
"Gigolo and Gigolette" (Ambler), 210
"Gigolo and Gigolette" (Maugham), 211–12
Gill, Brendan, 42
Gissing, George, 165
Gloria Swanson Productions, 43–44
Gogh, Vincent van, 165
"the Golden Age of Hollywood Cinema," 229
"the Golden Age of Television," 200
Goldwyn, Samuel, 5–6
The Golem (Wegener), 36
Goossens, Eugene, 29

Goulding, Edmund, 69, 140–42, 192, 195
Grable, Betty, 163–64
The Graduate, 207
Grant, Cary, 28
The Great God Pan and the Inmost Light (Machen), 35
Green, Abel, 54–55
Green, Alfred E., 96
Greene, Graham, 6, 40, 71, 99, 103–5, 183
Greenwood, Bruce, 226
Gribble, Henry Wagstaff, 91
Grierson, John, 109
Griffith, Corinne, 26–27
Griffith, D. W., 5
Griffith, E. H., 169
Guitry, Sacha, 171
Guthrie, Tyrone, 107

Haas, Belinda, 217–19
Haas, Philip, 217–19
Haines, William, 54
Hall, Mordaunt, 51, 55, 87
Harlow, Jean, 52
Harvey, Forrest, 151
Harvey, Laurence, 127, 143–45
Harwood, Ronald, 224–25
Haskell, Molly, 55
Hathaway, Henry, 143–44
Havilland, Olivia de, 193
Havoc, June, 56
Haxton, Gerald, 91
Hays, William, 11–13, 31–34, 42–56, 80–81, 102–9, 161–64, 173–74, 203–17, 235. *See also* "The Formula"; Motion Picture Producers and Distributors of America (MPPDA); Motion Picture Production Code
Hays Office, 11–13, 31–34, 42–44, 51–56, 67–68, 80–81, 102–9, 161–64, 173–74, 203–17. *See also* Hollywood Production Code

Hayter, James, 202
Hayworth, Rita, 57, 163
Heard, Gerald, 4, 189
Hearst, William Randolph, 42
Hedley, Jack, 143
Heggie, O. P., 62–63
Heil, Douglas, 231–32
Heinemann, William, 12, 34
Henreid, Paul, 125, 140–43
Hepburn, Katherine, 110, 193
Hicks, Catherine, 198
Higham, Charles, 109
Hilton, James, 28, 103
Hitchcock, Alfred, 13, 100–103
Hitler, Adolf, 205
Hogan, Michael, 179–80
Hohl, Hans, 96
Holden, Philip, 231
Hollywood Production Code, 68, 88–89, 135, 161. *See also* censorship; Hays Office
Home and Beauty (Maugham), 160–64. See also *My Two Husbands* (Ruggles)
homosexuality, 95, 231
Hopper, Hedda, 194
Hordern, Michael, 111
Horn, Barnard, 52
Hornaday, Ann, 220
The Hour Before the Dawn (Maugham), 6, 177–81, 191, 215
Howard, Leslie, 135–38, 141–43
Howells, William Dean, 10
"How to Write a Novel! After Somerset Maugham" (Crowley), 36
Hughes, Ken, 143–44
Hume, Benita, 136
Hunter, Ian, 97
Hunter, Stephen, 199
Huntley, Raymond, 209
Hurst, Brian Desmond, 105
Huston, Walter, 52, 55, 118
Hutchinson, Josephine, 88

Huxley, Aldous, 4, 189
Huysmans, Joris-Karl, 34
Hyde-White, Wilfrid, 82

The Image in the Sand (Benson), 35
"In Defense of Mixed Cinema"
    (Bazin), 15
Infatuation, 26–27, 232. See also
    Caesar's Wife (Maugham)
Ingram, Rex, 36–39, 169
Irons, Jeremy, 225
Irving, Ethel, 23
Isherwood, Christopher, 4, 14, 95, 179,
    189, 217, 231
The Island of Dr. Moreau (Wells), 35
Isle of Fury (Andrews), 97–98. See also
    The Narrow Corner (Maugham)

Jackson, Felix, 185
Jackson, Pat, 210
Jack Straw (Maugham), 24
Jacobi, Derek, 218–20
James, Henry, 91
Jennings, Alec, 103
Jewishness, 204–5
Johansson, Scarlett, 236
Johnson, Celia, 82
Johnson, Nunnaly, 103
Jones, Jennifer, 193
Jones, Toby, 157
Joyce, James, 4, 12, 165

Kael, Pauline, 75, 110
Kamijama, Sojin, 31
Kanin, Garson, 187, 203
Kavanaugh, Katherine, 24
Keach, James, 198
Keighley, William, 88
Kelly, Gene, 185–86, 200
Kemble-Cooper, Violet, 92–93, 119
Kennedy, Margaret, 5
Kibbee, Guy, 52
Kilgallen, Dorothy, 143

Kinlock, John, 78
Kipling, Rudyard, 61, 230
Knoblock, Edward, 6
Koch, Howard, 69, 76–77, 232
Koltai, Lajos, 225
Kramer, Stanley, 170
kunstlerroman, 164–65

Là-bas (*Down There*) (Huysmans),
    34
Lacey, Liam, 159
Lake, Veronica, 180
Lanchester, Elsa, 107
Landis, Jessie Royce, 223
The Land of Promise (Maugham),
    18–22, 113. See also *The Canadian*
    (Stringer)
Lansbury, Angela, 194
Lantos, Robert, 224
Lasky, Jesse, 5, 17–23, 41, 169
Laszlo, Victor, 141
Laughton, Charles, 106–11, 122, 169–
    72. See also Mayflower Pictures
    Corporation
Laurence, Jacqueline, 54
Laurie, John, 202
Lawrence, D. H., 4, 12, 165
Lean, David, 157
LeBaron, William, 68
Le Carré, John, 99
Leitch, Thomas M., 15
Lejeune, C. A., 71, 102, 105
Lemmon, Jack, 163–64
Le Queux, William, 98
"The Letter" (Maugham), 3, 7–9,
    60–61, 73, 81–82, 106, 147–48, 201,
    215, 231
The Letter (Maugham), 60–62, 65–71,
    74–78, 81–82, 118, 123, 151, 186,
    231–33
The Letter (Wyler), 79–80
Lewin, Albert, 170–75
Lewis, Ronald, 111

Lewis, Sinclair, 9
Lewis, Wyndham, 9
Lewisohn, Ludwig, 204
The Life of the Bee (Maeterlinck), 6
Limur, Jean de, 62–63
Lindsay, Margaret, 98
Litvak, Anatole, 217
Livesey, Roger, 143
Liza of Lambeth (Maugham), 3–4, 17, 34
Loew, David, 170–75
Loew, Marcus, 45
Loggia, Robert, 207
Löhr, Marie, 25
Lord, Daniel, 135
Lord, Robert, 69
"Lord Mountdrago" (Maugham), 213
Lorre, Peter, 101–3, 121
Lost in Translation (Coppola), 198
Louise, Anita, 92
Love, Montagu, 85
Love in a Cottage (Maugham), 25
Lupino, Ida, 140, 185
Lusk, Norbert, 55, 67

Machen, Arthur, 35
Mackenzie, Alex, 18
MacLaine, Shirley, 14
MacMurray, Fred, 122, 162
Macrae, Arthur, 210
Maeterlinck, Maurice, 6
The Magician (Maugham), 17, 34–39, 116
Mamoulian, Rouben, 56
Manette, Robert, 185
Mankiewicz, Herman, 184–85
Marbury, Elizabeth, 41
March, Frederic, 58, 151
Marcus, Lawrence B., 82
Margolyes, Miriam, 226
Marlowe, Ann, 58–59
The Marriage Holiday, 85. See also
    The Constant Wife (Maugham)

Marsh, Jean, 175, 232
Marshall, Herbert, 62–64, 70–73, 81–82, 118, 125, 151, 155, 170–71, 180, 195
The Mask and the Face (Maugham), 97
Maslin, Janet, 199
Massey, Raymond, 70
Mathis, June, 24, 169
Maugham, Robin, 231
Maupassant, Guy de, 9, 48
Maurier, George du, 35
Maxwell, Elsa, 92
Mayer, Louis B., 38, 169, 194
Mayflower Pictures Corporation, 106–7. *See also* Laughton, Charles; Pommer, Erich
Mayo, Archie, 88
McDonald, Frank, 97
McFarlane, Brian, 15
McGuire, John Thomas, 71
McKenna, Siobhan, 81, 143
McShane, Ian, 82
Meehan, John, 149
Meighan, Thomas, 20–22, 117
Merman, Ethel, 56
The Merry-Go-Round (Maugham), 4
Metro-Goldwyn-Mayer (MGM), 149–50
Milestone, Lewis, 51, 55
Milland, Ray, 180
Miller, Stanley, 217
Million Dollar Baby (Eastwood), 235
Mills, John, 81
Miss Sadie Thompson (Wald), 57–58, 233
Miss Thompson (Swanson), 52–56
"Miss Thompson" (Maugham), 40, 44–45, 49
Mitchell, Grant, 92
Mitchum, Robert, 219
Molina, Alfred, 103
Monroe, Marilyn, 58–59, 143–44

The Moon and Sixpence (Maugham), 3–13, 124, 164–77, 189, 195, 201, 221, 232
Moore, Matt, 52
Morell, André, 213
Morley, Robert, 143
Moskowitz, Joe, 143
Moss, Marilyn Ann, 46
Motion Picture Producers and Distributors of America (MPPDA), 11. *See also* Hays, William
Motion Picture Production Code, 11–12. *See also* "The Formula"; Hays, William
motion pictures. *See* moving pictures
Mountbatten, Edwina, 28
moving pictures, 4–5
Moy, Josephine, 65
"Mr. Know-All" (Maugham), 208
Mrs. Craddock (Maugham), 12, 147
Mulligan, Robert, 176–77
Murfin, Jane, 91
Murray, Bill, 128, 196–99
mysticism, 4, 148, 189, 193, 196
My Two Husbands (Ruggles), 162. *See also Home and Beauty* (Maugham)

Nagel, Conrad, 88
The Narrow Corner (Maugham), 4, 8, 93–97, 119, 196, 231. *See also Isle of Fury* (Andrews)
Negri, Pola, 30–31, 114, 232
Nehru, Jawaharlal, 28
Newton, Robert, 107, 110–11
Nielson, Claire, 217
"A Night in June" (Maugham), 215
Nolan, Mary, 85
Norden, Helen Brown, 149–50
Normand, Mabel, 11
Norton, Edward, 130, 154–59
Nosferatu (Murnau), 36–37
Novak, Kim, 127, 143–45, 226
the novel (medium of), 5

Novels into Film (Bluestone), 15
Nyswaner, Ron, 154–57

Oberon, Merle, 217
O'Brien, Pat, 97
O'Ferrall, George More, 213
Of Human Bondage (Maugham), 3–17, 36, 94, 120–46, 165–68, 190, 196, 233–36
O'Hara, John, 9
O'Hara, Maureen, 193–94
Oland, Warner, 232
Olivier, Laurence, Sir, 176–77
Omnibus Films (Diffrient), 202
the omnibus films, 200–214
On a Chinese Screen (Maugham), 29
Oppenheimer, Edward Philips, 98
The Ordeal (Maugham), 11, 25
Orienting Masculinity, Orienting Nation (Holden), 231
Our Betters (Maugham), 90–93, 119, 189–91, 216
Out of Africa (Lean), 157
"The Outpost" (Maugham), 28
Owen, Reginald, 62, 66, 96

The Painted Veil (Maugham), 4–7, 37, 94, 107–9, 121, 130, 141–59, 196, 232–34. *See also The Seventh Sin*
Palma, Mona, 22
Palmer, Julia, 224
Parker, Cecil, 202, 207
Parker, Eleanor, 125, 140–41, 152
La Passion de Jeanne d'Arc (Dreyer), 136
Patrick, Nigel, 202, 209–10
Pearl Harbor, 179
Pelissier, Anthony, 210
Penn, Sean, 217–19
Peterson, Dorothy, 163
Petrovic, Ivan, 36
Pickford, Mary, 40, 56, 62
Pickup, Ronald, 82

The Picture of Dorian Gray (Wilde), 34

Pinker, J. B., 34

Pirie, David, 103

Pleasence, Donald, 111

Pogostin, S. Lee, 176–77

political/financial dramas, 105

Pollock, Arthur, 185

Pommer, Erich, 106–7. *See also* Mayflower Pictures Corporation

Popcorn Venus (Rosen), 233

Pope, Alexander, 177

Porter, Cole, 195

A Portrait of the Artist as a Young Man (Joyce), 165

Powell, Michael, 36–38

Powell, Paul, 25

Powell, William, 85

Power, Tyrone, 125, 192–93

Prabhavananda, Swami, 191–92

Presnell, Robert, 95–96

Pressburger, Arnold, 13

Printzlau, Olga, 24

Pritchett, V. S., 61

The Private Papers of Henry Ryecroft (Gissing), 165

Production Code Administration (PCA), 68–69, 89. *See also* Breen, Joseph

Proudlock, Ethel, 60

Quartet (Sherriff), 202–5, 208–10, 214

Quinn, Anthony, 200

Quintet (Box), 201

Rabenstein, Ferdy, 189

Rain (Anderson), 52–57, 62

Rain (Maugham), 12, 42–46, 50–51, 58–59, 118, 232–33

"Rain" (Colton), 41

"Rain" (Maugham), 3, 7, 82, 106, 201, 215. *See also* *Dirty Gertie from Harlem USA* (Williams)

Rank, J. Arthur, 213

Raphael, Frederic, 5, 9

The Razor's Edge (Byrum and Murray), 197–99, 229

The Razor's Edge (Maugham), 3–9, 36, 94–95, 125, 128, 170, 187–99, 201–2

realism, 8, 87

Remarque, Erich Maria, 100

Rembrandt, 169, 172–73

Remick, Lee, 82

Rennie, Michael, 81, 203

Richardson, Miranda, 226

Rigg, Diana, 157

The Right to Live (Bloch), 89. *See also* *The Sacred Flame* (Maugham)

Rimbaud, Arthur, 165

Risdon, Elizabeth, 23

Robbie, Margo, 236

Roberts, Henry Chalmers, 91

Robinson, Edward G., 170

Robinson Crusoe, 167

Rogers, Ginger, 56

Rogers, Paul, 111

Roland, Gilbert, 92

Le Roman d'un Tricheur (Guitry), 171

Rosay, Françoise, 154, 202

Rosen, Marjorie, 233

Rotha, Paul, 39, 46

"The Round Dozen" (Maugham), 203

Rouvier, Suzanne, 194

Ruggles, Wesley, 162–63

Rumsey, John W., 169

Russell, Theresa, 199

The Sacred Flame (Maugham), 86–89, 235. *See also* *The Right to Live* (Bloch)

Sadie Thompson (Walsh), 45–52, 68, 117

Saemundson, Nina, 173

Saint Joan (Shaw), 40

Salter, Hans. J., 186

Samuels, Lesser, 179–80

"Sanatorium" (Maugham), 208–9

Sanders, George, 124, 153, 171
Sarris, Andrew, 63
Schallert, Edwin, 181
Schenk, Joseph, 44–45, 51–52, 169
Scheuer, Philip K., 87, 143, 196
Schickel, Richard, 152
Schreiber, Liev, 155
Scofield, Paul, 143
Scott, A. O., 219, 226
Scott, John L., 164
Scott, Zachary, 81
Scott Thomas, Kristin, 217–19
screenwriter (profession of), 5–6
Scully, Frank, 47
Searle, Alan, 230
Secret Agent (Hitchcock), 100–103, 121.
    See also *Ashenden or: The British
    Agent* (Maugham)
The Secret Agent (Conrad), 99. See also
    Ashenden or: The British Agent
    (Maugham)
Selfridge, Gordon, 90
Selznick, David, 177–80
Sen Yung, Victor, 79
Serling, Rod, 59
Seven Arts Production, 143
The Seventh Sin, 152–53. See also *The
    Painted Veil* (Maugham)
Shaw, George Bernard, 40, 167, 230
Shaw, Mary, 232
Shearer, Norma, 70
Sheppey (Maugham), 86, 220
Sheridan, Ann, 81
Sherriff, R. C., 201–8
Sherwood, Robert, 67
Sikov, Ed, 75
Simenon, Georges, 7, 200
Simmons, Jean, 203
Sinclair, Hugh, 92
Sinden, Donald, 110–11
Siodmak, Robert, 185–86
Sistrom, Joseph, 103
Skinner, Cornelia Otis, 223

Smith (Elvey), 23
Smith, C. Aubrey, 26, 88
"The Somerset Maugham TV
    Theatre" (CBS), 200, 212
Sondergaard, Gale, 79, 186
Sons and Lovers (Lawrence), 165
Sorel, Jean, 224
Sothern, Ann, 56
sound pictures, 7, 87–88, 171
spy fiction, 99
Staiger, Janet, 43–46
Stam, Robert, 15
Stanislavski, Konstantin, 223
Starrett, Charles, 92
Steiner, Max, 76–80
Stephenson, James, 73–74, 80–81
Sternberg, Josef von, 233
Stevenson, Juliet, 226
Stevenson, Robert Louis, 34, 68
Stewart, James, 192
Stowitts, Hubert, 37, 150
*The Strange Case of Dr. Jekyll and Mr.
    Hyde* (Stevenson), 34
Strasberg, Lee, 59, 143, 223
Strickland, Charles, 165
Strictly Unconventional (Thalberg &
    Butler), 33–34. See also *The Circle*
    (Maugham)
Stringer, Arthur, 22
Sturridge, Tom, 226
Sullivan, C. Gardner, 68
The Summing Up (Maugham), 3, 87,
    187
Susskind, David, 175, 177
Sutton, John, 180
Swanson, Gloria, 42–55, 58, 62, 68–70,
    117, 194
Swinburne, Nora, 202, 207
Szabó, István, 224, 227

The Taming of the Shrew (Shakespeare),
    19
Tandy, Jessica, 175, 200

Taylor, Elizabeth, 143–44
Taylor, William Desmond, 11, 25, 42
television, 200–201
Tellegen, Lou, 18
Tempest, Marie, 220
Tennyson, Alfred Lord, 160
The Tenth Man (Maugham), 104–5
Terry, Alice, 36
Thäis (France), 40
Thalberg, Irving, 42
Thalberg, Sylvia, 34
Theatre (Maugham), 147, 221–23,
   226, 234. See also *Being Julia*
   (Harwood)
"The Kite" (Maugham), 205
Then and Now (Maugham), 13, 229
The Thirty-Nine Steps (Buchan), 100
"This Is What I Believe" (Power), 193
Thompson, Jack, 82
Thompson, True T., 57
Three Cases of Murder (Maugham),
   212–13
Tierney, Gene, 194–95
Tinée, Mae, 21, 87, 138, 152
Tone, Franchot, 180
Too Many Husbands (Binyon), 122,
   160, 162–63
Travers, Bill, 152–55
The Trembling of a Leaf (Maugham),
   41, 52
Trilby (du Maurier), 35
Trio (Maugham), 126, 202, 208–10,
   214
Trotti, Lamar, 6, 191–92, 195
Tsen Mei, Lady, 65, 79
Tunberg, Karl, 153
Turney, Catherine, 140–42
Twelfth Night (Shakespeare), 235
Two Arabian Knights (Milestone), 52

The Unknown (Maugham), 12
Up at the Villa (Maugham), 13,
   215–20

Vanbrugh, Irene, 20, 220
Van Druten, John, 81
Van Dyke, W. S., 150
Verdugo, Elena, 232
"The Verger" (Maugham), 208
Verlaine, Paul, 165
Vessel of Wrath (Laughton), 108–11, 122.
   See also *The Beachcomber* (Box)
"The Vessel of Wrath" (Maugham),
   106–7
Vidal, Gore, 7, 16, 131, 229
Vidor, King, 93
Viertel, Salka, 149
voice-over narration, 171

Wagner, Richard, 165
Wald, Jerry, 57
Wallis, Hal, 27, 69, 95
Walsh, Kay, 202
Walsh, Raoul, 31, 46–47, 52
Walter, Harriet, 103
Wanger, Walter, 67, 184
Warner, Jack, 98, 140
Watson, Minor, 92
Watts, Naomi, 130, 155–56
Waugh, Alec, 188
Webb, Clifton, 125, 194–95, 198
Wegener, Paul, 36–37, 48
Weiler, A. H., 145
Wellcome, Syrie Barnardo, 90
Welles, Orson, 213
Wells, H. G., 35, 230
Welsh, James M., 230
Wescott, Glenway, 182–83
West, Mae, 233
"Where Do We Come From? What
   Are We? Where Are We Going?"
   (Gauguin), 173
Wilde, Oscar, 34, 195
Williams, Spencer, 56–57
Williams, Warren, 88
"Winter Cruise" (Macrae), 210–11
Wong, Anna May, 81

Wood, Natalie, 143
Wood, Peggy, 88
Wooland, Norman, 82
Woolf, Virginia, 9
Woollcott, Alexander, 90, 160, 162
Wurtzel, Sol, 42–43
Wyler, William, 70–81

Yoshiwara, Tamaki, 65
Young, Robert, 101

Zabel, Morton Dauwen, 215
Zanuck, Darryl, 6, 190–95
Ziegfeld, Florenz, 20
Zinneman, Fred, 95
Zola, Émile, 9
Zorina, Vera, 180

WISCONSIN FILM STUDIES

The Film Music of John Williams: Reviving Hollywood's Classical Style,
second edition
EMILIO AUDISSINO

The Foreign Film Renaissance on American Screens, 1946–1973
TINO BALIO

Somerset Maugham and the Cinema
ROBERT CALDER

Marked Women: Prostitutes and Prostitution in the Cinema
RUSSELL CAMPBELL

Depth of Field: Stanley Kubrick, Film, and the Uses of History
EDITED BY GEOFFREY COCKS, JAMES DIEDRICK,
AND GLENN PERUSEK

Tough as Nails: The Life and Films of Richard Brooks
DOUGLASS K. DANIEL

Making Hollywood Happen: The Story of Film Finances
CHARLES DRAZIN

Dark Laughter: Spanish Film, Comedy, and the Nation
JUAN F. EGEA

Glenn Ford: A Life
PETER FORD

Luis Buñuel: The Red Years, 1929–1939
ROMÁN GUBERN AND PAUL HAMMOND

Screen Nazis: Cinema, History, and Democracy
SABINE HAKE

A Cinema of Obsession: The Life and Work of Mai Zetterling
MARIAH LARSSON

Continental Films: French Cinema under German Control
CHRISTINE LETEUX

Escape Artist: The Life and Films of John Sturges
GLENN LOVELL

*Colonial Tactics and Everyday Life: Workers of the
Manchuria Film Association*
YUXIN MA

I Thought We Were Making Movies, Not History
WALTER MIRISCH

Giant: George Stevens, a Life on Film
MARILYN ANN MOSS

French Film History, 1895–1946
RICHARD NEUPERT

The Many Lives of Cy Endfield: Film Noir, the Blacklist, and "Zulu"
BRIAN NEVE

Six Turkish Filmmakers
LAURENCE RAW

Jean-Luc Godard: The Permanent Revolutionary
BERT REBHANDL, TRANSLATED BY EDWARD MALTBY

The Cinema of Sergei Parajanov
JAMES STEFFEN